Confucian China and Its Modern Fate

Joseph R. Levenson

CONFUCIAN CHINA AND ITS MODERN FATE

The Problem of
Intellectual Continuity

University of California Press

BERKELEY AND LOS ANGELES 1958

FOR
ROSEMARY MONTEFIORE LEVENSON

Preface

ALTHOUGH its themes may seem separate and miscellaneous at first and the chronological line irregular, this book deals with one continuous process of change—this change: during much of Chinese history, ideas had to face tests of compatibility with received tradition; in more recent times Chinese tradition has had to face tests of compatibility with independently persuasive ideas. Chinese values have continued to be prized, but by minds that seem more 'traditionalistic' than traditional—modern minds with nostalgia for the past, not minds with the past's authentic intellectual colour. And other minds, of course, have abandoned many of the older Chinese values.

The intellectual history that all these minds have made has sweep and depth, a sweep of change from major point to point, and a depth of change beneath the points themselves. That is why, when we seem to be sailing nicely from nineteenth to twentieth century, describing a transition from *t'i-yung* to *chin-wen* emphasis or from early nationalism to communism, we may take sudden dips of a few centuries or so; for the account of a modern transformation of an old idea adds an important dimension to the account of its modern abandonment. Politically nationalistic criticism of traditional Chinese culture, for example, is a story of recent decades. Change in connotations of the Chinese terms traditionally used to correlate political and cultural questions is a story of many centuries. But the stories point to the same conclusion and they ought to be put together, at whatever cost to the narrative ideals of smooth progression and never looking back.

Any writer of intellectual history has to face a challenge from sceptical 'populists': do the literary remains of an educated fringe really relate to the history of a total society? A recent critic has brushed off a collection of studies of formal Chinese thought as essentially relevant only to a 'mandarin sub-culture'. But just because 'Boxer' masses in 1900 show a peasant hostility to western innovations, shall we conclude that intellectual Confucian 'self-strengtheners' and 'reformers', with their various commitments to one or another degree of western innovation, were playing a fancy philosophical game, quite removed from the basic stuff of Chinese history? On the contrary—'mandarin' intellectual currents are as relevant as can be to the fate of Chinese society, right down to its most illiterate and least-recorded strata. And the intellectual historian believes this, not because he assumes, as a simple article of faith, that the spirit of the literary documents naturally permeates the whole society, even to minds incompetent to express it, but (to limit the case to China) because the Chinese intelligentsia has had a traditional role as exemplar in Chinese society. In their growing iconoclasm, literati cannot abandon that role and open a gulf in sentiment between themselves and apparently motionless masses (who traditionally had expected literati to embody their own conventional aspirations), without radically changing not only a 'sub-culture' but the map of the Chinese world.

The plan of the book and a good deal of the content were hammered out for the First and Second Conferences on Chinese Thought in 1952 and 1954. I am especially grateful to Arthur Wright and John Fairbank (the directors, respectively, of the Conferences), to all the participants, to Mary Wright, and to H. F. Schurmann for their criticisms and suggestions. But there is plenty of room for disagreement about the matter of the book, and one should by no means assume that my conclusions must be acceptable to the friends who have helped me.

Parts of the book in different form have been published in *Studies in Chinese Thought*, ed. Arthur F. Wright (University of Chicago Press: Chicago, copyright 1953 by the University of Chicago), *Chinese Thought and Institutions*, ed. John K. Fairbank (University of Chicago Press: Chicago, copyright 1957 by the University of Chicago), *The Far Eastern Quarterly*, *Pacific Affairs*, *Sinologica*, and *Asiatische Studien*. I wish to thank the publishers and editors for permission to use this material here.

Contents

CONTENTS

Part Two: Chinese Culture in Its Modern Metamorphoses: The Tensions of Intellectual Choice

CONTENTS

CONTENTS

Introduction:
The Special and General
Historical Quests

A traveller, who has lost his way, should not ask,
'Where am I?' What he really wants to know is, Where
are the other places? He has got his own body, but he
has lost them.

Alfred North Whitehead, *Process and Reality*

WITH the passing of time, ideas change. This statement
is ambiguous, and less banal than it seems. It refers
to thinkers in a given society, and it refers to thought.
With the former shade of meaning, it seems almost a truism:
men may change their minds or, at the very least, make a
change from the mind of their fathers. Ideas at last lose
currency, and new ideas achieve it. If we see an iconoclastic
Chinese rejection, in the nineteenth and twentieth centuries, of traditional Chinese beliefs, we say that we see ideas
changing.

But an idea changes not only when some thinkers believe
it to be outworn but when other thinkers continue to hold it.
An idea changes in its persistence as well as in its rejection,
changes 'in itself' and not merely in its appeal to the mind.
While iconoclasts relegate traditional ideas to the past,
traditionalists, at the same time, transform traditional ideas
in the present.

This apparently paradoxical transformation-with-pre-
servation of a traditional idea arises from a change in its
world, a change in the thinker's alternatives. For (in a Taoist
manner of speaking) a thought includes what its thinker
eliminates; an idea has its particular quality from the fact

xiii

that other ideas, expressed in other quarters, are demonstrably alternatives. An idea is always grasped in relative association, never in absolute isolation, and no idea, in history, keeps a changeless self-identity. An audience which appreciates that Mozart is not Wagner will never hear the eighteenth-century *Don Giovanni*. The mind of a nostalgic European medievalist, though it may follow its model in the most intimate, accurate detail, is scarcely the mirror of a medieval mind; there is sophisticated protest where simple affirmation is meant to be. And a harried Chinese Confucianist among modern Chinese iconoclasts, however scrupulously he respects the past and conforms to the letter of tradition, has left his complacent Confucian ancestors hopelessly far behind him.[1]

Vocabulary and syntax, then, may remain the same, late and soon, but the statement changes in meaning as its world changes. Is there another postulate, besides the postulate of the changing world, which confirms this change in meaning, as time passes, in the statement whose literal content remains unchanged?

There is such a postulate, the logical principle which states that 'a body of knowledge consists not of "propositions", "statements", or "judgments" . . . but of these together with the questions they are meant to answer.'[2] By this token, a proposition's meaning is relative to the question it answers.[3] A change, then, in the question behind an idea, like a change in the alternatives beside it, imposes change on the persisting positive content of the idea itself.

Let us consider, for example, European acknowledgment of the worth of Asian civilizations. In both the eighteenth and nineteenth centuries, there were Europeans who denied the doctrine of western superiority to China. But this denial, this freedom from parochialism, was quite a different idea in the eighteenth century than in the next one; for in the first case it was essentially an expression of rationalism, while in the second, it was anti-rationalistic.

Voltaire's admiration of China derived from his deism, a universalist disbelief in particular revelation. His denial of European pretensions was a negative answer to the question,

'Is possession of Christianity the criterion of cultural excellence?' But nineteenth-century opponents of Europocentrism derived not from Voltaire but from Herder, with his romantic principle that every age and every people has its own particular genius. Rationalism, with Turgot and Condorcet, had developed a theory of stages of progress of civilization and had turned from uncritical admiration of the non-European world to uncritical condemnation; Condorcet lowered China in the scale of nations to the level of the primitive agricultural state of society. 'Civilization', to the rationalists, now meant exclusively European civilization. The romantics, therefore, in their denial of European pretensions, meant to answer, negatively, the question, 'Is "secular progress" the criterion of cultural excellence?' Thus, successive 'same' ideas, western expressions of cosmopolitan sympathies, change as the questions behind them change.[4]

An idea, then, is a denial of alternatives and an answer to a question.[5] What a man really means cannot be gathered solely from what he asserts; what he asks and what other men assert invest his ideas with meaning. In no idea does meaning simply inhere, governed only by its degree of correspondence with some unchanging objective reality, without regard to the problems of its thinker.

In nineteenth-century China, the problems of thinkers imposed changes on earlier Chinese ideas. Most thinkers, with a strongly Chinese (if not generally human) predisposition towards the offerings of their own particular culture, continued to ascribe to them a universal validity. But some thinkers did not, and more and more of them failed to do so as the decades passed, and western society proved socially subversive in China, and western ideas alluring. In these circumstances of material change and iconoclastic challenge, tenacious traditionalists seem to have become not simply men believing in intellectually compelling ideas, which by chance were the products of Chinese history, but Chinese having a will to believe, an emotional need to feel the intellectual compulsion, just because the ideas in question came down from a Chinese past. When Confucian traditionalism comes to be accepted not from a confidence in its universal validity but from a *traditionalistic* compulsion to profess that confidence, Confucianism is transformed from a primary, philosophical commitment to a secondary, romantic one, and traditionalism from a philosophical principle to a psychological device. [6]

And then this inner change in a persisting idea, this change which works through the thinker's loyalty, furthers the trend to the other type of intellectual change in time—alienation.

Modern Chinese intellectual history, the period of western influence, may be summed up as two reciprocal processes, the progressive abandonment of tradition by iconoclasts and the petrifaction of tradition by traditionalists. But both of these processes—not only the traditionalistic, but the iconoclastic as well—show a Chinese concern to establish the equivalence of China and the West. Many different intellectual choices have been made in modern China, but the choosers' considerations were not, nor could they have been, entirely intellectual; always, along with the search for right answers, or ideas acceptable to anyone, there continued a search for ideas that *Chinese* could accept. Commitment to the general, commitment to the special, and a sequence of intellectual expedients to make these commitments seem to coincide—these appear to me to characterize the thought of modern China.

In pre-modern China, respect for precedent was one of the prime Confucian attitudes that pervaded intellectual life. In modern China—perhaps as one of the signs of the western intrusion on Chinese culture—precedent began to be treated not exclusively as a Confucian issue, but as an issue familiar enough in a western context: to what degree, if any, should precedent preclude man's free exercise of reason? May the products of one history be judged by reference to the products of any other? The issue is a real one for would-be cultural innovators. That is why eighteenth-century European rationalists, intending to criticize, by purely objective standards, anomalies and flaws in western culture, felt they must burst the confines of their own special history and invented a host of literary visitors—Turks, Persians, Moroccans, Hurons, Iroquois, Peruvians, Siamese, Chinese—to do the job.[7] Uninvolved in western history, they could presumably evaluate its fruits, they could deal abstractly, unhistorically, in universals.

An opposing view sees history as organic, not to be modified at will. A man makes choices not as a member of a bloodless, universal humanity ('The constitution of 1795 is ... made for men. But there is on earth no man as such ...'), but as a member of his proudly particular, vibrant people, with its own national spirit ('I have seen in my life Frenchmen, Italians, Russians ... but I declare that never in my life have I seen a man ...').[8] 'Those who have only the world's outlook without the requisite Burmese outlook,' says a premier of Burma, 'are like those who long for distant aunts over the heads of their own mother.'[9] For a people (Hegel, for one, especially stresses this point) is, in this relativistic view, an organization which pre-exists its members.[10] Montaigne, hating dogmatism, expressed this aversion in his sense of cultural relativism or historical contingency, the concrete refutation, as he felt, of reason's pretensions to create an order outside history, ideal states of philosophy in neither time nor place.[11] Though Montaigne characteristically did not push this idea too far, its implications were fully historicist; more reasonable than the mystagogic Hegel but no more rationalistic, he left history, in effect, to be autonomous, engulfing man, since human efforts to divert the stream towards freely chosen ends were so discountenanced.

If an intellectual choice which contravenes 'the spirit of the people' is impious or impossible (and, depending on its thoroughness, historicism makes it one or both), then the individual thinker, his scope determined for him in a world he never made, can have no standards which make him free to judge what his people's history offers him. Yet, in fact, history is made of his judgments, for a completely binding traditionalism would keep a people forever at the post, never moving into history. Some tempering of traditionalism by judgment must occur, or histories would be frozen by the law that nothing can be added to a way of life, if it seems a departure from what has gone before. Absolute traditionalism is a completely hypothetical, self-destructive concept; a sense of the past can never develop if an original unmitigated reverence for 'what is' precludes its ever becoming past.

Traditionalism, that is, can take its subjective tone only in a world in which alternatives to the worship of the 'eternal yesterday' have been sharply presented. A traditionalist may insist that 'mine or yours?', my history or your history, is the only relevant question which a man may ask before making a choice among cultural elements. But the conscious will to narrow the vision (and this will, not the blind plodding in the footsteps of the past, is the essence of traditionalism) can never exist apart from the realization that another question is always being asked: 'true or false?'

The modern Chinese commitment to the general, of which I have spoken, is the commitment to seek the answers that are 'true'; these thinkers' commitment to the special is their need of answers that are somehow 'theirs'. The first commitment brings many men to intellectual alienation from Chinese tradition, while the second leaves them with an emotional tie to it. And intellectual alienation and emotional tie intensify each other. As the former proceeds, the continued attribution of general validity to special inheritances stems more and more from the thinker's emotional need to harmonize his commitments, less and less from a genuine intellectual conviction that he has the best of both worlds. Finally the tie is snapped. No idea commended solely by the special imperative that it must be true and not at all by an unclouded general confidence that it *is* true can persist.

The reverse of that situation, however, is equally impossible. Values depend, in the last analysis, on their natural sources in particular places and times.[12] A man may be ready to reject the institutions, science, morality, or aesthetics which his history offers him, but he knows that whatever he does accept has its place in someone's history. And no one is so ethereal, so cleanly delivered from native soil and the limited culture which formed him, that he can see its relative disqualification with perfect equanimity. Man is not a neutral machine, calmly recording right answers; if a foreign answer is to be intellectually accepted as right, the native culture's emotional claims must somehow be squared.

I believe that an understanding of this principle makes the chronological sequence in modern Chinese history logically comprehensible. As traditional ideas change in losing their unquestioned intellectual acceptability, and traditionalists fail thereby to maintain the harmony of special and general, 'mine' and 'true', iconoclasm thrives. But iconoclasts, of the mildest or the deepest hue, face the danger of the same failure, and their ideas change—in a series of acceptance, rejection, and acceptance of something new—as they seek a formula which will keep the psychological peace. The quest for this formula has been the common ground of all the new currents of Chinese thought since the Opium War. How can the thinker scrap Chinese ideas which the western impact has made to seem inadequate, while he preserves his confidence of Chinese equivalence with the West? How shall he see himself as modern man and modern Chinese together?[13]

Was the posing of this question in modern China really inescapable? Such would be the case only if there was a marked distinction between earlier and recent values held in China, and if western influence could account for the transition while indigenous trends in Chinese history could not. Before one may suggest, then, that the great problem for Chinese thinkers in the last century has been the problem of reconciliation of their general intellectual avowals and their special Chinese sentiments, he must reflect on the history of early-modern, 'pre-western' Chinese thought. For if that history was a history of burgeoning modern values (a growing spirit of science, for example—such a major strain in modern thought), then a later nagging doubt about Chinese continuity was unnecessary; if, on the other hand, the modern values cannot be traced to pre-western roots in Chinese history, such a doubt was unavoidable.

Let us put the question.

Part One

THE TONE OF
EARLY-MODERN CHINESE
INTELLECTUAL CULTURE

CHAPTER I

The Abortiveness of Empiricism in Early Ch'ing Thought

IN Sung and Ming intellectual life, idealist philosophies came to the fore. Later, in the seventeenth and eighteenth centuries, to a number of Chinese thinkers, that predominance of idealism seemed a disaster, and they formally disavowed it. Is there an indication, perhaps, in the early existence of this group of materialists, that the seemingly stable, traditionalistic Chinese society had the capacity to develop under its own power, without a catalytic intrusion of Western industrialism, into a society with a scientific temper?

1. THE CRITIQUE OF IDEALISM

In the natural world described in the neo-Confucian philosophy of Chu Hsi (1130–1200), a thing exists as a complex of *li* and *ch'i*, ideal form and mutable matter. To *ch'i*, which is perceptible, *li* is the regulative principle; to *li*, which is intelligible, *ch'i* is the medium in which it manifests itself. *Li* is the universal which the intellect apprehends and the senses never reach, and the metaphysical order is from universal to particular, from Being to individual things.

Already in the Sung and Ming periods, there were thinkers who saw grave limitations in Chu Hsi's *li-hsüeh*. But the criticism came from the far side of idealism, from the subjective-idealist *hsin-hsüeh* of Lu Hsiang-shan (1139–93) and

3

Wang Yang-ming (1472–1529). Chu Hsi was an idealist in his search for an unmoving reality behind phenomena, but in his view, at least, reality had an objective existence, outside the mind which sought to apprehend it. For the Lu-Wang school, however, mind itself was the world of truth, and intuition the key to it. According to *li-hsüeh* neo-Confucianism, man's error was his failure to press on to absolutes (and finally to the Absolute, the *li* of *li*, the *t'ai-chi*) through phantasms of sense-experience. According to *hsin-hsüeh* neo-Confucianism, man's error was his very consciousness of these phantasms, or of the illusory distinction between sub-ject and object which is the first condition of any sense-experience at all.[1]

In the seventeenth century, voices began to be raised against both these speculative tendencies to disparage the sensible as compared to a hypothetical transcendent. 'Be-tween heaven and earth', wrote Huang Tsung-hsi (1610–95), 'there is only *ch'i* (matter), there is not *li* (form, idea, "law"). The names *li* and *ch'i* are devised by man. . . . One really existing thing (*wu*) has two names, not two really existing things one essence.' Thus, Huang considers *li* to be merely *ming*, or name, not *shih*, or actual fact.[2] Huang's contem-porary, Wang Fu-chih (1619–92), also emphasized the primacy of the tangible, concrete fact over the abstract, generic classification. *Ming* derives from *shih*, he said,[3] name from fact, i.e. the general formal term from particular cognizable examples. And Li Kung (1659–1733), similarly, in a move to vindicate the earthy, observable particular thing against the idealists' attitude of rarefied concern with higher, invisible realms, declared, 'It is said in the *Shih-[ching]*: "there are things, and there are rules for them"; apart from things, where is *li*?' And he charged the *li-hsüeh* philosophers with the error of seeking *li* apart from actual things.[4]

It was in such a fashion that Ch'ing critics of Sung idealism defended the metaphysical priority of the world of sense-perception. They shored up their materialistic position by asserting also that *ch'i* was not morally second to *li*, as their Sung adversaries would have it. Desire, the subjective correlative of *ch'i*, or matter, is good, said Wang Fu-chih, and Yen Yüan (1635–1704), and Tai Chen (1724–77). Only Buddhism, said Wang, not genuine Confucianism, separates Heaven's Law from human desire.[5] It is Buddhist or Taoist (and therefore wrong), said Yen, to teach that man is endowed with evil *ch'i*, as the allegedly Confucian Sung philosophers taught; that was what Buddha meant when he called the ears and eyes and mouth and nose 'six villains'.[6] And Tai agreed, condemning as Buddhist or Taoist the neo-Confucianist Chou Tun-i (1017–73), for preaching the need to annihilate physical desire.[7]

If there were men like these who attacked the *li-hsüeh* from a materialistic standpoint, it must, of course, follow that the *hsin-hsüeh*, an even more uncompromising idealism than the other neo-Confucianism, should also be attacked. Dualistic philosophers who emphasized the importance of objective matter—either explicitly, by denying the reality of forms, or implicitly, by defending subjective desire (whose object is something sensible)—naturally put under their ban Wang Yang-ming's monistic emphasis on mind and intuition. According to Wang Fu-chih, the subjective-idealist *hsin-hsüeh* was 'outside, Confucian; inside, Taoist',[8] or '*yang*, Confucian; *yin*, Buddhist'.[9] Huang Tsung-hsi, the foe of mysticism and 'airy vagueness', found the fatal stain of Zen on Lu and Wang.[10] Ku Yen-wu (1613–82) concurred,[11] and besides, in order to cite an example of one man's changing the course of history, he arraigned Wang Yang-ming for causing, almost single-handed, the decline and fall of the Ming empire.[12]

What was the prescription of these opponents of idealism for stopping the rot? *Tao* and *te*, the Way and Virtue, are inseparable from practicality, said Huang Tsung-hsi.[13] Recording empty words is not the equivalent of observing action, said Ku Yen-wu,[14] and he said, too, that the superior man studies in order to 'assist the world'.[15] The learning of the ancients was in practical matters, said Tai Chen.[16] Chinese thinkers, they all meant, should abandon world-denying quietism, and get away from abstractions and down to things.

5

2. SCIENCE AND CH'ING EMPIRICISM: THEIR DEGREE OF COINCIDENCE

How relevant to science are these injunctions to look without and not within, and to dwell on things and not on essences? They are relevant, we may say, in the sense that they are *compatible* with the development of modern science as the issue of a struggle against an anti-empirical, or rationalistic, metaphysics. The scientist must assume, like the Ch'ing denouncers of the *hsin-hsüeh*, that the material world is not a state of mind. And the scientist also assumes, like the Ch'ing critics of Chu Hsi's *li-hsüeh*, that the way to begin to acquire useful knowledge is to characterize material instances instead of groping for ethereal Ideas. For the question as to the essence of things (in neo-Confucian terms, the question of *li*) can produce nothing but tautological answers; 'Burrow down and still further down,' it has been said, 'and God will still be only godly, man only human, and the world only worldly.'[17] But a scientific statement has a true predicate. It begins, as the anti-*li-hsüeh* Ch'ing materialists would begin, with the thing, and then predicates something as a quality, a property, or an attribute of the thing.

Science, it is true, does not end with this predication of qualities to individual things. Indeed, it deals as seriously as philosophical idealism with the *type*, and the predicate which it considers meaningful, as a contribution to logical understanding, is the one which affirms of the single instance what is true of all its kind. But the scientist's type is his own construction, a generalization which he makes from a detailed experience of the behaviour of individual things; as a scientist, an inductive empiricist, he cannot explain that behaviour by the generalization. As Locke put it, species and genera are the 'workmanship of the understanding', not the mind's discovery.[18]

Kant, in his *Critique of Judgment*, has made perhaps the clearest distinction between Platonic or neo-Confucian idealism and the empirical theory of their respective early modern opponents. The *intellectus archetypus*, he says, is a form of reason 'which being, not like ours, discursive, but intuitive, proceeds from the synthetic universal (the intuition of the whole as such) to the particular, that is, from the whole to the parts'. Such a reason, according to Kant, lies outside human possibilities. The reason peculiar to man is the *intellectus ectypus*, which is restricted to taking in through the senses the single details of the world as such and constructing pictures of their totalities, but these pictures have only a hypothetical character and claim no reality for themselves. 'Our understanding has this peculiarity as concerns the judgment, that in cognitive understanding the particular is not determined by the universal and therefore cannot be derived from it.' [19]

By Kant's criterion, then, of a reason possible to man, a reason that can win for man some knowledge of nature, Huang Tsung-hsi's statement that *li* is 'name, not fact', Li Kung's sceptical question, 'apart from things, where is *li*?' —taken utterly seriously—are subsumed in any genuine expression of the scientific spirit.

3. SCIENCE AND CH'ING EMPIRICISM: THEIR NON-IDENTITY

But that is the most we can say. The empirical attitudes of these early Ch'ing thinkers, while in harmony with the scientific critique of idealism, are neither scientific themselves nor necessarily conducive to the birth of science. In European history, divergence from idealism could take the form of the pre-scientific nominalism of Peter Abelard (1079–1142) as well as the form of Francis Bacon's (1561–1626) inductive empirical science; our Chinese thinkers seem, on the whole, more like Abelard than like Bacon.

Abelard's nominalism (or rather, his so-called 'conceptualism', a somewhat disguised version of his teacher's, Roscelin's, nominalism) denied the objective existence of universals. Rejecting the extreme Augustinian 'realism', which regarded the individual material thing as simply the shadow of an eternal idea, he held that universals were created by the mind by means of abstraction, and that the true reality was the object and not the idea, not the 'name'.[20] Wang Fu-chih and his Chinese colleagues said as much.

7

Bacon, however, said more. He went beyond simply ascribing ultimate reality to the world of phenomena instead of to a hypothetical realm of pure Being. He meant not merely to define the real world but to encroach upon it. It was not enough for him to banish abstractions, which can only be contemplated, in favour of tangibles, which can be observed, for observation was not enough. One had to observe with a method and a purpose. Bacon's method was induction from experimentally verified 'irreducible and stubborn facts', his purpose the eliciting of general laws for the organization of facts into science.[21]

It has already been suggested that the Ch'ing empiricists were not so ambitious. Let there be practical action in the real phenomenal world—that was the sum of their challenge to contemplative idealists, and their practical ethic implied for them a simple epistemology, a common-sense opinion that knowledge comes to the mind when the mind is put in compresence with facts. But according to Bacon (and also, Descartes), what makes a natural scientist is not his knowledge of facts about nature but his ability to ask questions about nature; knowledge comes only by answering questions, and these must be the right questions, asked in the right order.[22]

Our Chinese critics of idealism could agree with Bacon that 'the wit and mind of man, if it work upon matter . . . worketh according to the stuff and is limited thereby; but if it work upon itself, as the spider worketh his web, then it is endless and brings forth indeed cobwebs of learning . . . of no substance or profit'. They might say, too, with Bacon, that their method was 'to dwell among things soberly. . . .' But although they might pride themselves, like Ku Yen-wu, on looking around them and 'testing books with facts', they rarely asked questions systematically which might make them see the essential relevance of some orders of facts to others, they never aspired, as Bacon did, 'to establish for ever a true and legitimate union between the experimental and rational faculty'.[23] Though he might go as far as the Renaissance scientist in deprecating search for the universal, eternal form of particular things, the empirically-minded Ch'ing

Confucianist had a temper predominantly nominalist, unembarrassing to scientific spirit, but by no means its equivalent nor its guaranteed precursor.[24]

4. PROTEST AND STABILITY: THE REMINISCENCE OF AN EARLIER AFFIRMATION

It appears, then, that the early Ch'ing empiricists need not be seen as budding scientists. This conclusion—that their thought was not necessarily a sign of any indigenous Chinese trend towards the establishment of science in its modern intellectual pre-eminence—suggests a positive corollary. We must acknowledge that these philosophers were genuinely critical of their prestige-laden Sung and Ming predecessors, critical enough so that some historians have delighted to call them scientific. But was the dissidence perhaps *within* the world of Chinese tradition, and witness to its stability, not a sign of its transformation irrespective of the West?

Bacon expressed his distrust of traditional authority and his faith in science in these words: 'He that would begin in certainties shall end in doubts; but if he be content to begin with doubts and have patience a while he shall end in certainties.'[25] The Ch'ing empiricists expressed doubts of a sort, but they began in certainty, the traditional Chinese certainty that modern opinion, if legitimate, conforms to the truths in the classics of Confucian antiquity. There is more than rhetoric, there is serious acceptance of Confucian authority, in the reams of Ch'ing denunciation of the earlier *li-hsüeh* and *hsin-hsüeh* Confucianists (the latter especially) for their alleged Buddhist and Taoist deviations. Tai Chen was particularly keen against Taoists and Buddhists in Confucianists' clothing,[26] and even with Tai, the latest and most independent of the thinkers we consider, there is no question, I think, of subterfuge, no reasonable suspicion that he may be making an oblique attack on Confucian authority itself. Before he would come to conclusions about contemporary needs and expedients, he demanded contemporary evidence; but always, he said, to be finally certain of his conclusions, he required corroboration from antiquity.[27]

9

Tai was a traditionalist, then, in accepting a traditional check on his own researches. And the outer, social end of his studies made them traditional, too. He and the other empiricists were taking a time-honoured stand, for a matter-of-fact approach, in the running, traditional Chinese conflict between practical and mystical intellectual tendencies.

The obvious, historic Confucian alternative to anti-intellectual mysticism was textual scholarship. Some of the Ch'ing scholars, notably Yen Yüan and Li Kung, had such an antipathy to mysticism that they were unequivocal in their commitment to empiricism, and they disparaged inordinate textual study as another deterrent to practical observation. Two of the three grave flaws which Yen Yüan saw in contemporary scholars were 'absorption in phraseology' and 'fascination with commentaries' (the other was 'carelessness about false doctrines', the Buddhist and Taoist miasmas).[28] He pointed with alarm to the scholars of the Han and Chin periods, busying themselves with 'sentences and phrases' while society went to ruin.[29] Li Kung distinguished between 'paper' and 'affairs of the world', and deplored the fatal triumph during the Sung and Ming periods of 'pen and ink' over the spirit of 'capacity to govern'.[30]

But the school of the 'Han Learning' (of which Ku Yen-wu was a leading member), not the Yen-Li school, was the really prominent foe of the Sung Learning. And for the Han Learning, empiricism, practical observation, seems to have been less a positive philosophy than a symbol of opposition to mystical introspection; the true emphasis of the Han Learning was on another classic alternative to introspection—on that most fundamental of Confucian practices, the study of texts. The Han Learning could attack *mind* (where truth exists for subjective idealism)—in the name of *nature* (where truth exists, though perhaps unattainably, for science) —in the interests, really, of *books* (where truth exists for Confucian literati).

Now, was this a sign of disruption, a fresh challenge to the Sung Learning *in toto*, or was it a sign of stability, in effect a restatement of an old challenge from one of the wings of the Sung Learning to the other? Chu Hsi himself, after all, in distinguishing his objective-idealist *li-hsüeh* from the contemplative *hsin-hsüeh*, had urged *ko-wu*, 'investigation of things'; and this quasi-empiricist appeal, which, like the later one, denied the *hsin-hsüeh* philosophy in one manner, only swept the field clear for Chu Hsi's fixing of a textual orthodoxy, which denied the *hsin-hsüeh* in another way. Chu Hsi, we know, was no hero to the scholars of the Han Learning. Yet, though they rejected his *li-hsüeh* metaphysics, it is hard to see from its consequences how their 'practicality' was more of a challenge to bibliolatry than Chu Hsi's *ko-wu* had been. Ku Yen-wu's avowed purpose in 'investigating things' was not the neo-Confucian purpose of divining their *li*, but he came to a neo-Confucian end, a traditional Chinese celebration of the Confucian classics. From the standpoint of the development of science, it was as dead an end as any.

It is sometimes suggested that Ch'ing philological scholarship (e.g. the efforts of Ku Yen-wu and others to find out the ancient pronunciations of Chinese characters) is evidence of an indigenous Chinese commitment to scientific method. Nevertheless, however favourably Ch'ing philology may compare with the eighteenth- and nineteenth-century 'scientific philology' of Sir William Jones, Max Müller, and other Europeans, it can hardly be seen as subversive of Confucian anti-scientism. Strictly speaking, scientific method is in fact as applicable to the study of language as to the study of stars. But in general usage, where there is perhaps a proper feeling for the historical priorities, the adjective *scientific*, used in connection with such studies as philology, is essentially metaphorical, and the metaphor is drawn from natural science; natural science is the point of reference which gives meaning to the adjective when it is applied in other fields. One might proceed, as European scholars did, from contemplating natural science to thinking 'scientifically' about philological problems, but we have no grounds for turning the metaphor inside-out, and expecting that the Chinese would have necessarily proceeded from sound philology to the point of thinking 'philologically' about the basic fields of natural science. If the most successful intellectual explorations of the early Ch'ing period—so successful that they have earned our modern accolade, 'scientific'—were, indeed, in the field of philology, which is so near to Confucian concern with texts and history, this very fact shows how far early Ch'ing thinkers were from any deep concern with the riddle of nature.

However, when an appreciation of science did at last begin to make headway in China, there was a role of a sort for the Han Learning. But it was not the role which one might expect if he read too much into Ku Yen-wu's empiricism. The Han Learning was exploited by the so-called *chin-wen* reformers of the later nineteenth century (of whom more will be said below), who admired modern science but were troubled by its foreign origins, and who had to tamper with the orthodox classical canon—the Sung canon of Chu Hsi—since it failed to lend itself to a modernistic interpretation. Thus, it was not its crusade against idealism but its concern with textual authenticity which linked the Han Learning, through the Reform Movement, with the coming of science to China. And the link existed not because the early-Ch'ing anti-Sung critical scholarship pointed the way itself, but because it seemed possible to wring from this scholarship the sanction of Confucius for the scientific convictions which men arrived at by submitting to other authority.

A number of historians in modern China have tried to find an impressive Chinese pedigree for modern science; their efforts seem, paradoxically, a subjective response to the fact that none exists. In so far as science, whose prestige and progressive development came from the West, has been intellectually forced on Chinese minds in the last century, an emotional need has developed, a need to defend the intellectual history of China against any suggestion of failure. Liang Ch'i-ch'ao (1873–1929), Hsiao I-shan (1902–), and others, over-interpreting Ch'ing empiricism, occasionally imply that a modern Chinese scientific consciousness is a natural product of Chinese history, and that western example and western disruption of traditional China were never indispensable.[31] But these protestations arise, perhaps, from the situation whose existence they contest, a Chinese cultural situation of fractured continuity.

5. CONCLUSION

There was important scientific achievement in China before the modern period; recent research has begun to show us just how extensive it was.[32] But on the whole the Confucian literati were consistently uninterested, and the intellectual affinities of science were mainly Taoist and unorthodox. As Needham says, science had no social prestige, and it would never have occurred to traditional Chinese scholars that kudos were to be gained from claiming discoveries or inventions.[33]

When this did occur to modern Chinese scholars, it was the steady advance of a western tradition of science that furnished criteria for reappraisal of the Chinese intellectual past. Chu Hsi's philosophy, from the vantage point of twentieth-century science, may well be seen not as the idealism which the Ch'ing empiricists disputed but as an organic philosophy of nature, closely resembling the point of view which scientists have reached in the West after three centuries of mechanical materialism.[34] And yet, it is the three centuries of mechanical materialism which endow the organic philosophy with its content, everything implied in the upsetting of those centuries' conclusions. This was the tradition of cumulative inquiry which could not be found in China, and therefore had to be sought. In its universal persuasiveness it impelled the search for a Chinese parallel; it provided the touchstones for identification; and, in being set against the subsequent Chinese findings, it distinguished these as a brilliant cluster of scientific *aperçus*, but not a coherent tradition of science flowing into the universal stream.

What is at issue here, of course, is not ability but taste. If Chinese in modern times have been forced to wonder where science belongs in their heritage, it is not because their forbears were constitutionally unable to nurture a growing tradition of science, but because they did not care to; early Ch'ing empiricists were not aiming at science and falling short, but living out the values of their culture. There can be no presumptuous western question of 'failure' in Chinese civilization—only recognition of a Chinese taste for a style of culture not the style of the modern West, nor of modern China.

This pre-western Chinese style had other ingredients besides a tepid concern for science. A whole pattern of cultural preferences hung together, all appropriate to one another and to a specific social order, which was to fall into jeopardy soon. Many apparently narrow avenues could lead us into that whole coherent, precarious intellectual world. We shall try the road of inquiry into Chinese painting.

CHAPTER II

The Amateur Ideal in Ming and Early Ch'ing Society: Evidence from Painting

The master said, 'The accomplished scholar is not a utensil.'

Lun-yü II, xii

Another common and important feature of these functions is their *political* character; they do not demand particular, special knowledge, but a *savoir-vivre* and a *savoir-faire*. . . .

Etienne Balázs, 'Les aspects significatifs de la société chinoise', *Asiatische Studien* 6 (1952), 83

WHILE the alien Mongols ruled in China (Yüan dynasty, 1279–1368), Confucian literati were at one of their relatively low points of social importance. The Ming dynasty raised them high again, and as a ruling intelligentsia they naturally cherished an ideal of social stability.[1] As a corollary, in matters of taste they deprecated the idea of change and the quest for originality.[2] By and large, the literati were classicists, like Jonathan Swift in England, and in Swift's defence of the ancients against the moderns, in his vast preference for the humanities over the natural sciences, and in his patrician uneasiness with material utility as the touchstone of value, we see the pattern of literati culture with significant clarity.[3]

Swift died in savage indignation and derangement. The

15

moderns were taking his world and he knew it. Science, progress, business, and utility, the combination he deplored, would soon be leading themes in modern western culture. But in Ming and early Ch'ing China, the China of the four or five centuries before westerners came in force, science was slighted, progress denied, business disparaged and (with possibly increasing difficulty) confined; and with these three went the fourth of Swift's desiderata, an anti-vocational retrospective humanism in learning. Artistic style and a cultivated knowledge of the approved canon of ancient works, the 'sweetness and light' of a classical love of letters—these, not specialized, 'useful' technical training, were the tools of intellectual expression and the keys to social power.[4] These were the qualities mainly tested in the state examinations, which qualified the winners for prestige and opportunities.[5]

The *élite*, in short, were not permitted (as Balázs puts it) to 'impoverish their personalities in specialization'.[6] The Ming style was the amateur style; Ming culture was the apotheosis of the amateur.

I. THE MING STYLE, IN SOCIETY AND ART

i. In Society

Probably more in the Ming period than ever before, as the extreme aestheticism of the Ming eight-legged essay suggests, Chinese officials were amateurs in office. They were trained academically and (for the most part) tested by written examinations, but they were not trained directly for tasks to be undertaken; whatever the case among aides in official yamens, mere hirelings without the proper Confucianist's claim to leadership, the higher degree-holding members of the bureaucracy—the ruling class *par excellence*—were not identified with expertise.[7] The prestige of office depended on that fact. The scholar's belle-lettristic cultivation, a type of learning divorced from the official tasks for which it qualified him, was essential—not to performance of official functions with technical efficiency (there it was rather inhibiting), but to the cultural celebration of those functions.

If the knowledge characteristic of officials had been a vocational, technical, 'useful' knowledge, then it would have been only a professional means, with no intrinsic quality to dignify the bureaucratic end. But when office could be taken to symbolize high culture, knowledge for its own sake, the terminal values of civilization, then office-holding was clearly superior to any other social role. No other sort of success (commercial, military, technological, or the like), which might be assumed to depend on a body of professional knowledge devised as a logical means to produce it, could compete in prestige with success in winning office; for the peculiar preparation for the latter success, by its aesthetic independence, its very irrelevance, logically, to the bureaucratic end —at least in a specialized, technical sense, if not in a broadly moral one—made of that end the end of life.[8] A course in classical letters might train the official ideally to rule by virtuous example—to be himself, as it were, the finest product of art and thought, radiating harmony to society—but it was far from a training in special techniques for effecting social harmony, not by magical sympathy, but by logical consequence.

In China, of course, because of the nature of its institutions, this aesthetic brand of knowledge really was for the sake of something: office. But it was a symbolic, not a logical qualification. To see the genuine significance of this distinction, let us compare the Ming situation with the modern English one, for in England, too, classical training has frequently given entrée to civil office. A recent tribute to a British civil servant, after praising his classical scholarship, attempted, rather defensively, it seems, to make an ordinary logical reference of his classical training to his official role:

He read classics at Malvern and became a humanist. . . . Then in 1932, like many a classical scholar before him, he entered the Home Civil Service. . . . He is certainly a great civil servant, and I have no doubt whatever that he owes his quality to his humanism. It is that which gentles his will and disciplines his mind to the delicacies of human relationships.[9]

Living, as he does, in a highly specialized society, in which the amateur yields to the expert almost all along the line, a society in which 'amateur' as a term, in fact, has developed rather its connotation of imperfect skill than of disinterested love, the writer here must strike us as quasi-apologetic (which no Ming classicist, in a similar case, would ever have been) in making such a 'professional' plea for the classical curriculum: he writes as though he feels that his public—a practical, vocationally-minded public with a common-sense indifference to educational frills—must be doubting the genuine relevance of antique studies to modern professional tasks. He cannot simply assume a general public acceptance of an obvious affinity between classical education and a managerial office. The prestige of letters, it is true, has lent a greater prestige to the higher bureaucracy in England than it has to its western counterparts. But in England—and here it has differed from China—the bureaucracy, though thus enhanced, has not been able to reflect its glory back to the source. For while the social facts of Chinese history made bureaucracy the central point of power, the social facts of English history have relegated bureaucracy to a role of service to other powers in the English state. Socially, the rise of 'business' (which Swift had seen with such distress), with its anti-traditional, anti-humanist bias, put bureaucracy in the shade, while intellectually it forced the classics from their solitary eminence. To be sure, the nineteenth-century Oxford and Cambridge ideal, like the Confucian, was the educated gentleman, prepared for the world of affairs and his place in the governing class by a course in humane letters, with nothing crudely purposive about it; but this ideal in the Victorian age has been called 'almost the sole barrier against an all-encroaching materialism and professionalism'.[10] In England, instead of the splendid, symbolic Ming alignment of the highest cultural values with the highest social power, we finally find bureaucracy rather more just a useful employment, while the classics, in so far as they preserve vestigial links with power, tend to be justified as a logically useful means to an end which is only a means itself.

Culture, 'the best that has been thought and known' (as Matthew Arnold paraphrased 'sweetness and light'),[11] has a bad time in a world of utilitarians. When the 'yahoos' and 'philistines' of Swift and Arnold dominate society, the defence of culture may tend to lean on philistine criteria. An amateur's love of the liberal arts, his belief that they justify themselves, may be complicated by society's insistence that he find a professional point in their cultivation. But in China, the men of social consequence in the Ming and early Ch'ing periods were hardly cultural philistines; the professional point in their humanistic studies was in their failing to have any specialized professional point. They were amateurs in the fullest sense of the word, genteel initiates in a humane culture, without interest in progress, leanings to science, sympathy for commerce, nor prejudice in favour of utility. Amateurs in government because their training was in art, they had an amateur bias in art itself, for their profession was government.

Long before, in the Sung dynasty, Wang An-shih (1021–86) had tried, among other things, to make the civil-service examinations more practical than aesthetic. Although Wang was unquestionably a dedicated Confucianist, trying to revive in Confucianism its primal concern with political science, his finest official and scholarly contemporaries, who began by largely sharing his convictions, finally turned away, and ordinary Confucianists never forgave him. Was it only impracticability they saw in his sweeping programme, or disputable points in his classical exegesis, or an immediate material challenge to their perquisites; or did they also sense that a Confucian landed bureaucracy would rule as intellectual amateurs, or not at all? Had Wang struck a false note, a possible knell for the omnicompetent, socially superior sophisticates, who were no mere scribes in a feudal state, nor professional civil servants in a business one?

Su Tung-p'o (1036–1101), one of the foremost serious opponents of Wang An-shih, seems to have been the first painter to speak of *shih-ta-fu hua*, the 'officials' style' in painting, a term which became in the Ming era one of the several interchangeable terms for the 'amateur style'.[12]

ii. In Painting

By the end of the Ming dynasty, one rule had been firmly established in the world of painting: officials themselves were painters, and they liked their painting best. Painters *by profession* were disparaged. The Ming emperors had revived the court academy of painting (*Hua-yüan*), associated mainly with the names of Hui-tsung (*regn.* 1101–26, the last real emperor of the Northern Sung) and his Southern Sung successors.[13] But the Ming academy differed from the Sung in that the latter had merely honoured painters with official titles, while their Ming counterparts were genuinely court-painters, working to specifications.[14] Accordingly, the Ming academy, unlike Hui-tsung's, was never put on an equal footing with the *Han-lin yüan*, the highest circle of literary scholars, and Ming *Hua-yüan* painters by no means had the rank or prestige of *Han-lin* literati.[15] There were court painters in the Imperial Guard—a surprising place for them, on the face of it, but not so surprising when one reflects that the Imperial Guard was a catch-all for non-bureaucratic types, and that it represented the emperor and his personal corps of eunuchs in their character as rivals to the civil-official interest.[16]

Wen Cheng-ming (1470–1567), a scholar who had the *Han-lin* rank, and a famous painter as well, clearly expressed the amateur's creed. 'The cultivated man,' he said, 'in retirement from office, frequently takes pleasure in playing with the brush and producing landscapes for his own gratification.'[17] Or for the gratification of his cultivated friends—like the gentleman-painter Shen Shih-t'ien (1427–1509), a model of leisurely, exquisite taste; he identified a stray ink-landscape in his hall as the calling-card of one of his fellow-spirits, who had splashed it playfully on a bit of silk that was lying at hand, and whom Shen recaptured and kept as his guest for a casual matter of three months.[18] Mo Shih-lung, a very important late-Ming critic, highly approved of some earlier artists for looking at painting as a joy in itself, not as their profession.[19] His friend, Tung Ch'i-ch'ang (1555–1636), echoed Mo in praising one of the fourteenth-century Yüan masters as the first to make the painter's pleasure as well as expression the end of his art.[20] Tung himself, painter and calligrapher as well as the foremost critic of his time, was perfectly careless about what became of his own productions. It was said of him that if a person of station asked directly for some of his work, the petitioner might be fobbed off with anything—Tung's signature, perhaps, or a poem from his brush, on a painting by somebody else. If people wanted a Tung original, they learned to seek it from the women of his household, for whom he would frequently, idly, paint or write.[21]

Tung had, quite simply, a contempt for professionalism. One of its connotations, he felt, was narrowness of culture. The true wen-jen, the 'literary man', the amateur, had a feeling for nature and a flair for both painting and poetry.[22] It was a familiar thing for painters to deprecate their special talents by offering themselves as rounded personalities; the sixteenth-century painter Hsü Wei, for example, said of himself (though critics disagreed) that his calligraphy came first, poetry second, prose composition next, and painting last.[23] The Ch'ing scholar Shen Tsung-ch'ien (fl. ca. 1780?) summed up the persisting amateur's bias against narrow specialization: 'Painting and poetry are both things with which scholars divert their minds. Generally, therefore, those who can participate in the writing of poetry can all take part in painting.'[24]

The amateur's scorn of professionals had an aspect, too, of patrician contempt for the grasping climbers who were not the gentry's sort. There were overtones of anti-commercial feeling in the scholar's insistence that the proper artist is financially disinterested. Mi Fu (1051–1107), the famous intuitive Sung artist who was a classical hero to the Ming amateur school, had written, 'In matters of calligraphy and painting, one is not to discuss price. The gentleman is hard to capture by money.'[25] That was the finding of the hapless nobleman who came to Lu Chih (1496–1576) with a letter from one of Lu's friends, secured a picture on the strength of it, and then committed the horrible gaffe of offering sums of money; there is something almost mythic in the account of Lu's passionate act of rejection, as though a vital nerve of a culture had been touched.[26] Much later, the 'Mustard-seed Garden' manual (*Chieh-tzu yüan hua chuan*), an encyclopedic instruction book for painters, appearing in several parts between 1679 and 1818 (though its earliest stratum was late Ming), made the same equation between professionalism and a falling short of literati standards of gentility. 'When one has the venal manner,' it loftily proclaimed, 'one's painting is very vulgar.'[27] And the Ch'ing painter Tsou I-kuei (1686–1772) laid down the rule that the *shih-ta-fu* painter, the amateur painter-official, 'is not acquisitive in the world, nor does he distract his heart with considerations of admiration or detraction'.[28]

In short, in the amateur's culture of the Ming and early Ch'ing, officials as critics commended officials as painters to officials as connoisseurs. 'Wang Yü, tzu Jih-ch'u, hao Tung-chuang Lao-jen painted landscapes and grasped in them the very marrow of the Vice President of the Board of Revenue's art.'[29] A remark like this, ordinary enough in its own day, will joyously strike the modern reader as comically incongruous; he could hardly sense more vividly the individual quality of the culture which knew it as commonplace.

2. THE PARADOX OF AN ACADEMIC ANTI-ACADEMICISM

i. *The 'Northern' and the 'Southern' Schools of Painting*

Since they were intellectual leaders and social leaders at the same time, the painting *élite* formed a school of thought as well as a league of amateurs. By the end of the Ming dynasty an aesthetically expressive term, *nan-hua*, 'southern painting', had become assimilated to *wen-jen hua* and *shih-ta-fu hua*, sociologically expressive, equivalent terms for the painting of the 'gentleman'. Not its inventor, but the scholar who made the distinction between northern and southern styles a canon of connoisseurship, was the anti-professional Tung Ch'i-ch'ang, the acknowledged doyen of calligraphers, painters, and critics in late Ming times, 'master of a hundred generations in the forest of art', whose reputation as the arbiter of elegance had spread as far as Liu-ch'iu and Korea.[30]

He traced the northern and southern schools through various masters, from the T'ang dynasty's Li Ssu-hsün (651–716 or 720) and Wang Wei (698–759), respectively, down to his own day. The names 'northern' and 'southern' referred, not to a geographical distribution of painters, but to two T'ang dynasty schools of Ch'an (or Zen) Buddhism, whose philosophical principles were said to colour the two aesthetics.[31] However, the term *Ch'an-hua*, Ch'an painting, came to be reserved for the southern style, as a term contrasting with *yüan-hua*, academic painting of the northern school.[32] The idealist landscape of the southern school was inspired by the artist's 'sudden awakening' (a concept usually called in the West *satori*, from the Japanese Buddhist terminology), the shock of intuition of the nature of reality; and Tung considered that paintings in this style were superior to those of the northern school, which was intellectual rather than intuitive, more meticulous in detail, and interested rather in the formal relations of objects than in their spirit. 'True classic elegance', he said, 'does not lie in exact and punctilious execution.'[33]

This sort of caveat against painstaking, conscious workmanship was the first commandment in the southern aesthetic. According to theory, the literati-painter, without design, hurled his inner conception of landscape on the silk.[34] Spontaneity was all, and the elliptical phrase *ch'i-yün*, 'spirit-consonance', from the first of the famous 'six laws' of painting of Hsieh Ho (*fl. ca.* 500), was taken over as the southern concept of intuitive communion of the painter with his subject; intellectual apprehension was 'academic', and despised. ' . . . *ch'i-yün* is the result of something that is inborn; the more skill is applied, the further *ch'i-yün* recedes,' said Tung Ch'i-ch'ang,[35] and while Mo Shih-lung would allow that the academic style was *ching-miao*, refined and subtle, he found it correspondingly deficient in *tzu-jan*, the priceless spontaneity.[36] 'There are painters', he said, 'who take the old masters as teachers. But whoever wants to make forward strides himself must choose Heaven and Earth as teachers.'[37]

Hsiung-chung i-ch'i, 'spirit flashing into the mind', was the motto professed in the *wen-jen hua*[38]—not cool knowledge, but searing insight.

ii. The Confucianist Choice of a Buddhist Aesthetic

A question now arises of momentous importance for the understanding of Ming culture: how could Ming Confucian intellectuals, the most academic of men in their literary practice, committed to the preservation of recorded wisdom —and a wisdom, at that, which referred in the main to human relations in civilization—how could such a group reject a theory of painting which they associated with learning, and prize instead an anti-intellectual theory of mystical abstraction from civilized concerns? One might expect that Confucian traditionalists, who looked for the gradual education of man in society, would feel an affinity with the academic northern aesthetic and oppose the southern Ch'an; for the latter, after all, in its original emphasis on the sudden enlightenment of man in nature, challenged the whole Confucian view of life and culture. A purely aesthetic explanation of the literati-school's disparagement of the Academy, like the partisan suggestion that the Ming and Ch'ing authorities just failed to grasp the spirit and value of *Hua-yüan* art,[39] raises more questions than it answers. For, even entertaining the hypothesis of simple lapse in taste, how shall we account for this *wen-jen* blind spot?

Yet, what is logically curious is sociologically comprehensible. An idea's meaning, we have observed, depends not only on what a thinker affirms but on what he denies, and for Ming Confucianists, with their amateur leanings, the intuitive Ch'an need not mean—as it could not mean to such bookish custodians of an intellectual tradition—anti-intellectualism;[40] *anti-professionalism* would fill the bill. A flash of intuitive insight is nothing if not 'natural', and how could a professional painter, who worked to order, be natural? How could the academic be natural, planning his strokes and carefully painting them in?[41] The very idea of a special vocation of 'fine arts' was equally distasteful to Ch'an mystics and Confucian literati; 'natural' is opposed to 'artistic', and the latter word has a queasy, professional sound.[42]

The southern aesthetic, then, took hold in literati circles not because they were *philosophically* committed, committed to inspiration over tradition, but because they were *socially* committed, committed to genteel amateurism over professionalism. More than one writer has suggested that it was practical compulsion, especially in early Ch'ing times, which made the officials such southern enthusiasts; deep literary culture was obligatory, painting could only come second, as an amateur's pastime, and the scholars made a virtue of necessity, opting for intuition since a really rigorous painter's training was impossible.[43] Such a view is doubtless inadequate—many literati-painters, after all, were exquisitely accomplished virtuosi—but nevertheless, though for reasons less practical than symbolic (and not philosophical at all), an anti-academic aesthetic was the popular choice of the amateur. The Ch'an of the Ming Confucianists was not serious.

Buddhism in general had ceased to be serious for Confucian literati as long ago as the Sung period. The intellectual synthesis of Chu Hsi was a Confucian raid on Buddhism and a blunting of its point as an intellectual rival; and organized Buddhism—ecclesiastical, iconological, and always repellent socially to the gentry-official class—was relegated to the peasant masses and finally lost its one-time intellectual lure. Ch'an ideas, which were anti-ecclesiastical, anti-iconological, and thereby divorced from an anti-Confucian social organization, remained in the gentry's world and animated its landscape painting (Buddhist figure painting, once an important branch of Chinese art, languished almost completely in the Ming phase of the church's decline and the amateur-painter's rise).[44] But this last shred of Buddhism was not a foreign body in the gentry's Confucian environment. The Ch'an intuitive nature-cult of the Ming painters was not an antithesis to Confucian humanism, but a tame, learned element in the Confucian humane culture—not a bold challenge to didacticism, but a cultural possession of didactically educated men.

iii. *The Routinization of Intuition*

An ostensibly Buddhist doctrine, once embraced in that Confucian spirit, must be changed in itself. The real paradox of the Ming aesthetic was not in the harmonizing of two warring creeds, but in the self-contradiction of one of them. Peace was easy to arrange when one of the pair of rivals denied itself. In the last analysis, the conventionally learned *shih-ta-fu* painter felt quite at ease in the southern school of individual inspiration—because the southern school had conventional rules for manufacturing inspiration. An anti-academicism which was socially vital to the amateur gentry-officials, but intellectually alien, was safely academicized.

Ambivalence was built into the Ming intuitive southern theory, for it was a theory not intuited but learned. Sung literati, predecessors of the Ming in the Confucian taming of Buddhism, had already made the basic statements of the credo which the Ming called southern. The academic use-lessness of the imitation of outward form, the indispensable oneness of immediate perception and immediate execution, the impossibility of learning *ch'i-yün*, that 'spirit-consonance' which man derives solely from innate knowledge—all these were Sung lessons to Tung Ch'i-ch'ang and his fellow-critics of the Ming and Ch'ing.[45]

And behind the Sung was Hsieh Ho, whose six principles were handed down (especially the first: 'spirit-consonance, life-movement') as prescriptions for the unprescribable, bind-ing rules for untrammelled intuitive genius. 'In painting there are six canons . . .', a Ming treatise flatly began.[46] That was the law—all the rest was commentary. Wang Yü (*fl. ca.* 1680–1724), whose painting was said to betray him as 'a parasite on others', solemnly preached about quite unconscious creative activity.[47] His aesthetic, opposed to stereotype, was a stereotype as an aesthetic; his painting, failing to follow it, was consistent with it.

There was no getting around it. The free, natural southern souls of literati-amateurs were pervaded with traditional-ism. It was said of Tung Ch'i-ch'ang (who may be found, incidentally, on a Ch'ing list of select Ming masters of the eight-legged essay)[48] that he copied the works of the old masters—especially those of his Sung namesake, the Ch'an artist, Tung Yüan—with such a zeal that he forgot to eat and sleep.[49] A late Ming source reported that a wonderful scroll by Shen Shih-t'ien had been executed, in the true amateur spirit, as a gift for a friend on his travels; that the scroll was modelled completely after Tung Yüan; and that it later became the outstanding treasure of a most famous connoisseur.[50] Obviously, with the anti-academic Ming and Ch'ing critics, no painting failed of an accolade just for its being patently derivative. It was right and proper to imitate the ancients—because the ancients were spontaneous.

This is why, in the Ming and early Ch'ing China of the gentry-scholar-official, who was anti-professional in his outlook but never anti-traditional, the implications of anti-academicism were so far from what they were in the West. By definition, anti-academicism anywhere depends on a common conception of genius: that genius, a general quality, is shared only by artists who spontaneously choose their individual ways to express it. 'A good work of art must be *mehr gefüllt als gemessen*[51] . . . he that imitates the divine *Iliad*, does not imitate Homer[52] . . . the men who have reduced locomotion to its simplest elements, in the trotting wagon and the yacht *America*, are nearer to Athens at this moment than they who would bend the Greek temple to every use. . . .'[53]

Pronouncements on genius like these seemed to be made in China as in the West. The warning against missing Homer by hitting the *Iliad* was paraphrased, in effect, by Wang K'en-t'ang, a *chin-shih* of 1589: 'If one paints water, mountains, trees, and stones and roams "only thus" with the brush, such is not the old method.'[54] Yün Shou-p'ing wrote in the seventeenth century about the intuitive southern technique of *hsieh-i*, the representation of the idea, the immanent form, of visible objects:

It was said in the Sung period: 'If one can reach the point where he creates unconsciously, like the ancients, this is called *hsieh-i*. . . . If the artist creates unintentionally, then he attains the unconscious creativity of the ancients.'[55]

And Ou-yang Hsiu (1007–72), perhaps the very Sung spokes-man to whom Yün referred, had begun a poem in the following way: 'In ancient painting, they painted *i*, the idea, not *hsing*, the (mere) outer appearance.'[56] Presumably then, by this token, only a spark of intuitive insight, not a copyist's talent, could bring an artist close to the works of ancient genius.

But in the West these reflections were arguments of an *avant-garde*; in China they were arguments of traditionalists. Given the social context in China of anti-academicism, its intellectual sequence was twisted around. Spontaneous crea-tivity was as much the prize in one society as in the other. Yet it became in China not the means of reaching the ancient end of genius, but the end reached through the ancient means of genius. The very words which acclaimed the Chinese ancients for their spontaneity were really acclaiming spontaneity for its ancient embodiment. In the poem of Ou-yang Hsiu, the 'mere-ness' of *hsing*, or outer appearance, in comparison with *i*, the idea, was conveyed by the linking of *ku-hua*, ancient painting, with *i*.

In western anti-academicism, then, fidelity to the inner voice of genius justified abandonment of ancient outer appearances. In Chinese anti-academicism, it was fidelity to the outer voice, the voice of antiquity, speaking through outer appearances, which justified fidelity to the inner voice. Small wonder that southern theory seemed to chase itself in circles, and that Tung Ch'i-ch'ang appealed to master-models, while he solemnly intoned that genius could not be taught.

How could anti-academicism in Ming China take the form it did in the West, where an *avant-garde* in the arts, straining against the conventional taste of an outside public, was part of a generally vaguely displaced intelligentsia, iconoclasti-cally restless in a world it could not dominate? In China, where the intelligentsia (artists among them) did dominate, as gentry-officials, disdain of the elders and contempt for the public were unlikely, to say the least. The easy western association of anti-academicism with youthful individualism was impossible there. No higher praise could be meted out, by Tung Ch'i-ch'ang or any other southern critic, than to say of a painter that he entered completely into the spirit of some old master.[57]

It was not that he should copy his master directly; that would be pedantic, academic, entirely unsuitable. Nevertheless, as a Ch'ing literati-painter significantly put it, he had to copy old examples in a certain fashion, as the student of literature must thoroughly examine the productions handed down from the past.[58] He was supposed to copy in a manner called *lin-mo*, which would divine the spirit of the master-work, not repeat the letter. One Ming critic mentioned four great painters who had studied a painting of Tung Yüan, copied it in the *lin-mo* way, and produced works quite dissimilar among themselves. If 'vulgar men' (i.e. academics, professionals, not literati) had been set this task, the critic said, their works would all have been quite the same as the original model.[59]

What has happened here? Unmistakably, the field for Buddhist artistic intuition has been subtly transferred by Confucian literati from nature to art itself. The academic is still condemned. Careful surface copying of visible phenomena is properly anathematized, in accordance with southern principles. But communion with masters in a great tradition (a congenial Confucian idea) has superseded the Buddhist communion with nature. It was not the persistence of the old landscape themes which compromised the amateurs' creed of anti-academicism. Chinese painters from Wang Wei on (at least those whom the *wen-jen* mainly honoured) had forsworn individualism in subject-matter in order to ignite and reveal their individuality of soul, their personal intuition of an already existing beauty.[60] But to the traditional subjects, Ming literati-painters come to adapt traditional insights. A painter's 'spirit-consonance' need not be with mountains, but with a classic painter of mountains. The southern artist's immersion in nature through landscape-painting is not a Ch'an rejection of cultural sophistication, but a Confucian extension of it.

Once art had been thrust between the artist and nature, the quest for intuitive knowledge was flatly compromised. Unless an act of cognition is a directly experienced *knowledge of . . .*, it is not intuitive; the only alternative form of cognition, relational *knowledge about . . .*, is intellectual, and it disrupts the single whole of experience which theoretically the southern aesthetic envisaged.[61] In the true artist of 'sudden enlightenment', art and contemplation are indistinguishable, what he sees is not external, he becomes what he represents.[62] The object of such enlightenment is a 'thing-in-itself', a super-sensible reality, beyond sensation; for thing-in-itself, the non-ephemeral ideal, is implied in intuitive understanding with absolute necessity, and can only be grasped, as Kant put it, by 'art's free conformity to rule'. The 'imposition of rules on art' is not intuitive, and Cézanne, who affirmed this completely, proclaimed a significant corollary: 'les causeries sur l'art sont presques inutiles.'[63]

But the Ming and early Ch'ing period was the great age of *causeries*, treatises which precisely did impose rules on art.[64] In the foreword to the last section (1818) of the *Mustard-seed Garden*, the painter's manual which epitomized the movement, the author made the fatal promise that genius could be taught, 'spirit-consonance' and 'life-movement' distilled in explanation. 'Thus can he [the reader] enter the "divine class" and the "skilled class", and follow in the steps of painters like Ku K'ai-chih and Wu Tao-tzu.'[65]

It was another passage in the same foreword, but from a different hand, which plainly exposed the intellectual corruption of the intuitive process. In a dialogue, a question was raised about portraiture. Why was there no manual for this most difficult form of art, when there seemed to be a manual for everything else? The answerer stated that everything else—mountains, rivers, grasses, trees, birds, beasts, fish, insects—had fixed forms. If one studied them assiduously, one could reach the point of reproducing them by rules. But the human face had most varied forms, not lending themselves to stereotyping, and it was hard to convey these forms in words.[66]

Fixed forms, then, were presumably easy to convey in verbal formulas. But fixed forms remind us of things-in-themselves, ideals beneath the sensible surface of phenomenal life. The very concept of the type-form is correlated essentially with the concept of intuitive apprehension. And this is the antithesis of intellectual apprehension, which is the fruit of didactic exposition, or just what artists were invited to find in the *Mustard-seed Garden*.

In itself, of course, the mere will to deal with technical problems of execution, and to study their resolutions, need not bar intuitive penetration. Every art has a technical language, upon which even the most personal of artists depends for communication, and even, perhaps, for seeing. Freed from concern with the hand when technique is automatic, the mind may be free for vision, and a codification of technical knowledge can assist in this liberation.

Accordingly, the role of technique in Chinese painting, intellectually formulated and transmitted, has occasionally been compared with the creative musician's standard equipment in harmony or fugue.[67] For the most part, however, Ming-Ch'ing painters' technical mystery tends to seem a larger part of their art than that, as another analogy drawn from music illustrates: 'When a Chinese artist reproduces a composition of an old master or paints in his style, it is no more plagiarism than when Horowitz plays a composition by Brahms.'[68] Such a statement quite properly reduces any 'moral' question about *lin-mo* representation to absurdity. But in the aesthetic realm of questions, if Ming is to Sung as pianist to composer, then Ming knowledge of technical rules, vocabulary of typeforms, and the like is not a simple pre-condition of creativity, but an interpreter's key to what was once created. The later landscapist's technical lore opened the way not directly from mind to nature, but to earlier sudden meetings of nature and mind. Insight into silence, for music which must be there, is not the same as insight into music.

The sum of the matter is this: Ming and early Ch'ing aesthetic anti-academicism was academically perpetuated. While thus inconsistent internally, it was appropriate to its exponents in their character as part of a dominant social class, traditionalistic, humanistic, and fundamentally opposed to specialization. No other society had an aesthetic ostensibly more favourable to genius, the foe of the academy; and no other society was less likely to practise what it preached—or even to preach what it said it did. This society, which had come to its anti-academicism naturally, not philosophically logically but socio-logically, was the home of authority, prescription, and routine, restraints on genius but spurs to conventional learning. Matthew Arnold, who took from Swift, the Ming scholar-gentleman *manqué*, his definition of culture as 'sweetness and light', said what the Ming scholar-gentleman-painters could never say, though in practice they proved it—that cultural continuity depends on intelligence, which is more transferable than genius, and which academies cause to thrive.[69]

iv. *Bureaucracy and the Stereotyped Aesthetic: a Negative Confirmation of the Link*

In the seventeenth century, three eccentric painters flourished whose devotion to Ch'an was much more freely given than that of the ordinary southern painter, and whose work was far less stereotyped than their contemporaries'. They were the Buddhist priests Shih-t'ao (Tao-chi), Shih-ch'i, and Pa-ta-shan-jen.

It was said of the two Shih, in awe, that they were *san-seng ju-sheng che*, beings for whom no space of time existed between their leaving the priesthood and entering sage-hood.[70] They were painters, that is, who had reached the heights not step by step, with progressive learning, but in a leap of sudden enlightenment. 'Only so might I paint landscapes,' Shih-ch'i wrote on a painting, 'so, as if I conversed with mountains.'[71] He was said to have been 'naturally intelligent' (*su-hui*, a Buddhist phrase) from early youth, and to have read no Confucian books.[72]

'Knowledge is secondary, natural gifts are primary, and acquired gifts are not gifts,'[73] Shih-t'ao wrote, and 'I am I, and in me there is only I!'[74] Schools and models were death to art. What he longed to establish was a method of painting so natural that it would prove to be no method.[75] 'Shih-t'ao loved a wild manner in painting bamboo,' wrote Cheng Pan-ch'iao (1693–1765), 'almost disordered, without rule;

but rule lay naturally prepared within it.'[76] ('... art's free conformity to rule'.)

He felt a real affinity with Pa-ta-shan-jen, and unconventionally praised him as unprecedented: 'In his manner of calligraphy and painting, he stands ahead of earlier men; and his eye has none in antiquity to compare with it, to a height of more than a hundred generations.'[77] Whenever Pa-ta-shan-jen had the passionate urge to paint (wrote another near-contemporary), he bared his arm and snatched his brush and scattered everything all around, while he uttered loud cries like a crazy man.[78] Pa-ta-shan-jen was of Ming royal lineage and became a priest after 1644. One day he wrote 'Dumb' on his door, and never spoke a word again to anyone. 'His brush was very free and did not adhere to rules.'[79]

It is surely no accident that these free spirits, whose southern aesthetic was straight and undistorted, should have led peculiar civil lives. They were not of the normal intelligentsia, conventional Confucian officials (like Tung Ch'i-ch'ang), or retired gentlemen (like Shen Shih-t'ien) who owed their cultured ease to their official affiliations and whose Apollonian temperaments were hardly attuned to frenzy. If their theory and practice of painting had an uncommon logical consistency, they themselves had an uncommon sociological status. As deviants in society and deviants in art, they confirm the correlation between the gentry-scholar's domination and an amateur, unadmitted academicism.

These early Ch'ing eccentrics, then, had no unsettling influence in the world of painting, for the Manchu conquest left the *shih-ta-fu*, *wen-jen* position socially unimpaired. Many scholars in the first generation of Manchu rule, it is true—the so-called 'Ming remnants' (*i-lao* or *i-ch'en*), who declined or were denied office—were disturbed and disaffected. Among them were some of the empiricists we have met, who, in their opposition to idealist introspection, skated close to the edge of literati anti-vocationalism and urged that practical, technical problems of agriculture and water-works and military tactics and weapons be subjects of serious study.

They called also for *applied* historical and classical research. And of all this welter of topics, only literary scholarship survived in the mainstream of education, once the conquest-situation had shaken down and the bureaucratic society, with its appropriate cultural ideals, had shown its persistent quality.[80] A few partisans of the Ming, disillusioned, like Pa-ta-shan-jen, might leave the great world and reflect their resignation in their painting. But the main body of the literati accepted the Ch'ing as the conventional type of dynasty it was, kept their careers with their sense of proportion, and maintained, with all its implications for their southern style of painting, their anti-professional, traditionalistic cultural continuity.

Indeed, the independence of even these painting rebels may be over-estimated. Shih-t'ao, for one, like quite the literatus, frequently used phrases of Li Po, Tu Fu, and other early writers in his own poetic inscriptions on his paintings.[81] And in any case, if he really did revive the pure southern spirit, his own and subsequent generations of undisturbed traditionalists failed to understand. His antipathy to 'rules', his intuitive sentiments about 'method', were echoed in the *Hua-hsüeh ch'ien-shuo* of Wang Kai, another seventeenth-century painter ('The summit of method is the return to no method'),[82] and Wang was none other than the teacher of elementary method in the *Mustard-seed Garden*, the queen of rulebooks. And, 'How could he [Shih-t'ao] have attained such deep merit and strength', asked an early nineteenth-century scholar, 'if he had not absorbed all the masters of T'ang and Sung in his heart and spirit . . . ?'[83]

3. ECLECTICISM AND CONNOISSEURSHIP

i. *The Softening of Partisan Lines*

Tung Ch'i-ch'ang's aesthetic distinction between south and north implied tension between intuition and intellect, nature and books. But since southern intuitive theory was compromised by the social commitments of its highly intellectual adherents, north–south tension was inevitably relaxed.[84] For

all his southern sympathies, Tung believed that a fusion of
northern and southern procedures was possible, that reality,
to some extent, could be not merely seized upon but learned
about. 'If one has studied ten thousand volumes, walked
ten thousand li, and freed one's mind from all dust and
dirt, beautiful landscapes will rise quite naturally in the
mind. . . .'[85]

Even Shih-ch'i, one of the intensely southern Buddhist
painters of the seventeenth century, injected a northern note
in an inscription on a painting: ' . . . In peace we discussed
the ideas of the Buddhists and the fine points of the six laws
[of Hsieh Ho]. Whoever wishes to say anything about them
must have absorbed a great deal from books and history, and
must climb mountains, to push on to the essence of the
sources.'[86] And Yün Shou-p'ing, his contemporary, also reflected on the need to harmonize intuition and intellect.
He repeated a saying of Ni Tsan (1301–74), one of the four
Yüan masters who were heroes of the southern school. Ni
had said, 'Making a picture is nothing other than drawing one's inner spontaneity.' Yün went on, 'This remark is
most subtle'—and, after this genuflection to the approved
concept of intuition—'and yet, one must speak with cog-
noscenti.'[87]

This flexibility in theory was matched by a certain catholicity in taste. Tung Ch'i-ch'ang found himself admiring a
scroll by the Emperor Hui-tsung, the arch-northern founder
of the Sung academy. Somewhat embarrassed at seeing his
preference outrun his principles, he questioned the attribution.[88] But Mo Shih-lung, professedly just as sternly dis-
criminating as Tung—and equally the architect of the system
of discrimination—sometimes frankly owned to his basically
eclectic taste. Theoretically he rejected the northern school;
in practice, when he was faced with actual productions of
great painters whom he called northern, like Li T'ang of the
Sung and Tai Chin of the Ming, he simply commended
them.[89]

But the low temperature of aesthetic controversy in the
Ming and early Ch'ing period was indicated not only by
relaxed discrimination but by confused discrimination. A

Ch'ing note on the Ming painter, Hu Chung-hou, reported both that he had great skill in *ch'ing-lu* (blue-green) landscape (an unequivocally academic province) and that his master in brush-method was Tung Yüan (one of the Sung masters whose southern credentials were most impeccable).[90] Lan Ying (*fl. ca.* 1660), always classified as a painter of the *Che* (Chekiang) school, a perpetuator of the northern traditions of the Sung academy, was said to resemble Shen Shih-t'ien, one of the great literati-painters of the *Wu* (Wu-hsien, modern Soochow—by extension, Kiangsu) school, which was considered safely southern. The fact of the matter was that Lan Ying, like hosts of others, eluded rigid classification. The north–south dichotomy, a formal abstraction imposed on the history of Chinese painting for extra-aesthetic reasons, could prove suggestive for identification of differing elements of style, but it could not be fitted to the body of work of individual artists. Lan Ying did, in fact, range in his painting all the way from Che to Wu. He and so many others, by abstract southern standards, were eclectics.[91]

More famous than Lan Ying were his predecessors, Ch'iu Ying (*fl.* 1522–60) and T'ang Yin (1470–1524). They, too, were usually numbered among the academics and sometimes among the angels of the southern school.[92] For they could be labelled as northern, southern, and syncretic in turns. Ch'iu Ying, in particular, was felt to have magnificent talents in *lin-mo* copying, which he exercised especially in reinterpreting the masterpieces of the renowned Yen collection. It was said that of the famous brushes of T'ang, Sung, and Yüan, there were none, whatever their tendencies, whose essence he could not grasp.[93] Essentially uncommitted stylistically, he produced, for example, a picture-book of sixteen paintings, illustrations of T'ang poems, in which he exhibited various methods. Both northern style and southern style, according to the canons of the later critics, were represented, and types of line both 'thick and turbid', as the experts called it, and 'pure and elegant'.[94] T'ang Yin, too, changed methods and models according to impulse.[95] And Wen Cheng-ming, universally considered a paladin of the Wu school, the southern stronghold, roamed like the others

36

through a wide variety of Sung and Yüan styles and was said to have mastered them all.[96]

Eclecticism, however, meant more than divided loyalties between the northern and southern styles; it meant the fusion of them in individual works. For instance, one of the Ch'iu Ying paintings in his album of T'ang illustrations shows an emperor's visit to a newly-built mansion. This is executed in the right foreground in a meticulous academic style, while in the background and on the left suggestively misty pale-wash mountains taper off towards southern infinity.[97] Such stylistic complexities were common. The late Ming painter, Sheng Mao-yeh (*fl. ca.* 1635), was described by connoisseurs as painting northern pines, detailed and stylized, among southern rocks and mountains.[98]

The movement towards the joining of the two styles culminated in Wang Hui (1632–1717), celebrated during his lifetime as the *hua-sheng*, the painter-sage, and later on as the greatest genius among the 'six great masters' of the early Ch'ing. All question of trends and schools aside, Wang Hui beyond a doubt was a superb painter, one of the most compelling figures in art history, but the grounds on which he was early appreciated were more truly expressive of his age than his own individual mastery was. An accepted proof of his merits, his claim to special appreciation, was this: 'In painting there were northern and southern schools; Wang Hui brought them together.'[99] He was avowedly an eclectic, drawing on legions of the old masters (Yüan for the use of brush and ink, he recommended, Sung for mountains and rivers, T'ang for expression of the spirit), and his favourite model, significantly enough, was the earlier many-sided eclectic, T'ang Yin.[100]

The eclecticism of T'ang Yin has been described as that of a transitional figure, standing midway in time between the domination of the Che school (which, led by Tai Chin [*fl. ca.* 1664], the 'modern Ma Yüan', had early Ming imperial favour for its revival of the style of the Southern Sung imperial academy) and the Wu school, citadel of the amateurs.[101] If this was so of T'ang Yin, Wang Hui's eclecticism was of a different order, with special implications. Whether or not T'ang Yin should really be seen as an unconscious figure, adrift in a process of qualitative change between one vogue and another, Wang Hui can only be seen as a deliberately syncretic figure, reintegrating the first vogue into the second, consciously striving for harmony and an end to conflict (however unspirited) which might have led to renewal of process, and change.

ii. Virtuosi and Connoisseurs

Syncretism is not by definition (and unquestionably not in Wang Hui) a source of artistic sterility. It is certainly possible to express a genuine aesthetic insight by combining techniques which were once exploited to different ends. But the late Ming, early Ch'ing syncretism came not from an arrival at a new insight to which earlier techniques were adapted, but from a virtuoso's fascination by techniques.

The techniques of painting which syncretists pieced together had each existed, in the first instance, because the painter had seen his subject in a certain way and had used the brush in a manner contrived to convey it. In the eclectic spirit which had come by the seventeenth century to dominate Chinese painting, however, interest in the brushwork itself transcended interest in the subject, the aesthetic vision which brushwork might presumably have been intended to realize. 'No brushwork method at all,' an eighteenth-century Chinese artist said of western painting, and he therefore dismissed it in the typical *wen-jen* manner: it was only *chiang*, or artisanship.[102] To the connoisseur, variety of brush-strokes became an important criterion of value, and critics were as ready to analyse single strokes as to contemplate a composition as a whole. They expressed their refined discriminations in vague and elusive language ('his brushwork manner was exceedingly elegant and smooth, fine and close, but it was slightly weak'), as if to imply the exquisite subtlety of their aesthetic appreciations.[103]

The spirit which invested this eclectic connoisseurship —whether one's principles were supposed to be southern, northern, or in between—was the traditional Chinese inclination to follow early models. We have observed how artists like Ch'iu Ying had diverted the painter's efforts from divining the spirit of nature to divining the spirit of previous paintings. It became a virtue, really, to have no stylistic commitment; all styles were simply like natural features, whose essence the genius captures. Tung Ch'i-ch'ang, with his practically canonical pronouncements, made this vogue of *ni-ku*, imitation of the ancients, all-prevailing, and he approved the methods of eclectics who sought to make masterpieces by synthesizing details from the works of different masters.[104] It was a virtuoso's task, and a connoisseur's delight.

Upon request the late Ming, early Ch'ing painter, Lan Ying, produced for his friend, the governor of Shansi, whose connoisseurship he admired, a painting combining the different manners of Tung Yüan, Huang Kung-wang, Wang Meng, and Wu Chen.[105] The manners were different, but all were southern; which meant that one needed a nice sense of discrimination to blend and yet distinguish them, and that such intellectual subtlety transcended intuition in importance (even the intuitions that the connoisseurs were subtle about), and that southern models could serve a northern painter— Lan Ying, it may be remembered, was supposed to follow the *Che* tradition—for a sophisticated amateur's pastiche.

When the painter's emphasis was on fidelity to models instead of on fidelity to vision—which is what animated the men who created the models—there was no stylistic, aesthetic reason why various techniques developed in the past could not be mixed. And so the modern painter could throw everything into the pot, all the technical elements devised by men who had been aesthetically serious, committed to some end behind their technical means. By late Ming times, the end of the approved painter was the demonstration of his mastery of means. Style became a counter in an artist's game of self-display, while gentry-literati-officials and their set were the self-appreciative happy few who recognized the rules and knew the esoterica.[106]

4. CONCLUSION: MODERNIZATION AS THE CORROSION OF THE AMATEUR IDEAL

i. The Relativity of Judgments of 'Decadence'

Historians of the arts have sometimes led their subjects out of the world of men into a world of their own, where the principles of change seem interior to the art rather than governed by decisions of the artist. Thus, we have been assured that seventeenth-century Dutch landscape bears no resemblance to Breughel because by the seventeenth century Breughel's tradition of mannerist landscape had been exhausted.[107] Or we are treated to tautologies, according to which art is 'doomed to become moribund' when it 'reaches the limit of its idiom', and in 'yielding its final flowers' shows that 'nothing more can be done with it'—hence the passing of the grand manner of the eighteenth century in Europe and the romantic movement of the nineteenth.[108]

How do aesthetic values really come to be superseded? This sort of thing, purporting to be a revelation of cause, an answer to the question, leaves the question still to be asked. For Chinese painting, well before the middle of the Ch'ing period, with its enshrinement of eclectic virtuosi and connoisseurs, had, by any 'internal' criteria, reached the limit of its idiom and yielded its final flowers. And yet the values of the past persisted for generations, and the fear of imitation, the feeling that creativity demanded freshness in the artist's purposes, remained unfamiliar to Chinese minds. Wang Hui was happy to write on a landscape he painted in 1692 that it was a copy of a copy of a Sung original;[109] while his colleague, Yün Shou-p'ing, the flower-painter, was described approvingly by a Ch'ing compiler as having gone back to the 'boneless' painting of Hsü Ch'ung-ssu, of the eleventh century, and made his work one with it.[110] (Yün had often, in fact, inscribed 'Hsü Ch'ung-ssu boneless flower picture' on his own productions).[111] And Tsou I-kuei, another flower-painter, committed to finding a traditional sanction for his art, began a treatise with the following apologia:

When the ancients discussed painting, they treated landscape in detail but slighted flowering plants. This does not imply a comparison of their merits. Flower painting flourished in the northern Sung, but Hsü [Hsi] and Huang [Ch'üan] could not express themselves theoretically, and therefore their methods were not transmitted.[112]

The lesson taught by this Chinese experience is that an artform is 'exhausted' when its practitioners think it is. And a circular explanation will not hold—they think so not when some hypothetically objective exhaustion occurs in the art itself, but when outer circumstance, beyond the realm of purely aesthetic content, has changed their subjective criteria; otherwise, how account for the varying lengths of time it takes for different publics to leave behind their worked-out forms? There were Ch'ing experiments in western-style perspective, but these remained exoticisms; suspicion of sterility in modern Chinese painting, embarrassment about the extent of traditional discipleship (instead of a happy acceptance of it) began in China only late in the nineteenth century, when Chinese society began to change under western pressure and along western lines, and when modern western value-judgments, accordingly—like praise of 'originality'—were bound to intrude their influence. We have seen how the amateur commitments of the literati-official class in early-modern China brought Chinese painting to its late Ming, early Ch'ing condition. A reassessment of that condition never came until a change in role was thrust on the official class, and a change in its education, and a change in the general currency of its amateur ideal.

ii. Nationalism: Culture-change and the Professionalization of Bureaucracy

The world of painting in early-modern, pre-western China issued from and reflected a broader world of social institutions. Behind the amateur painter and the southern critic was the anti-professional official, whose socially high estate was the mark of his deeply respected humanistic culture, not a technically specialized one. It was felt, of course, that Confucian moral learning was especially appropriate to government-service, since administration was supposed to be less by law than by example. Still, the official's education failed to make him professional, it was not vocational, for this important reason: his learning was not just valuable for office, but happened to be *the* body of learning, artistic as well as moral, which was valuable in itself, and which lent itself more easily, for examination purposes, to aesthetic exposition than to practical implementation. It was this intimate association of bureaucracy with the mastery of high culture which was cracked by modern western pressure and its concomitant, Chinese nationalism.

When the Chinese nation began to supersede Chinese culture as the focal point of loyalty,[113] sentiments grew for changing, and finally for abandoning, the examination system (this was done in 1905). An education sacrosanct in the old heyday of the amateurs when 'the accomplished scholar was not a utensil', came to be criticized more and more, towards the end of the nineteenth century, as being far too predominantly literary—as failing, that is, to equip officials with specialized, useful knowledge for the national defence.[114] The Chinese state was changing its identity, from that of a world, an environment in which the officials' culture flourished, to that of a nation, whose needs should colour its bureaucracy's educational purposes. It meant the end of the 'aesthetic value' and self-sufficiency of the bureaucratic Confucian 'princely man', which had been at opposite poles (as Weber saw it) from the Puritan—and capitalist—'vocation'.[115]

With the pressure, then, of modern western industrialism (and those attendant concepts—science, progress, business, and utility—unhonoured, we have noticed, in the Ming literati culture) on Chinese society and Chinese consciousness, the charge of formalism came to be levelled at the official examinations and at the intellectual ideals which the latter sustained. But objectively, at the time such censure began to be effective, the examinations were not essentially more formalistic than in Ming and early Ch'ing times, when the 'eight-legged essay', such a scandal to the moderns, was perfected and prescribed.[116]

Only then (almost, only now) was the scholar-official's emphasis on form, on the subtleties of style, in the literati-painting as in the literary essay, generally felt to be the symptom of a weak concern with content.[117] Earlier, the idea had occurred to a few individuals: in the seventeenth century Ku Yen-wu had called the eight-legged essay more harmful than the ancient burning of the books, since it led, in effect, by the prominence given to formal technique, to the destruction of books through their not being read.[118] To rationalistic, insufficiently historically-minded moderns, to whom such criticism appeared incontrovertible, the fact that Ku's views had not prevailed seemed a bad accident or a Manchu Machiavellian achievement. But a less desperate or question-begging explanation than these lies in one's awareness of the amateur ideal as a long-continued condition of Chinese thought. Only when the modern West impinged on China and undermined the position of the gentry-literati-officials, who had set the styles in art and expression as they set the rates in taxes and rents—only then did the concept of 'amateur' slide into its modern sense of something less than 'specialist', and what had once been precious to tradition-alists and classicists seem mainly preciosity to a new youth in a new world of science and revolution.

Interlude: Confucianism and the End of the Taoist Connection

WHERE are the Taoists of yesteryear in modern Chinese history? As the amateur ideal and the world that made it faded, Confucian institutions and loyalties still persisted. But Confucianism changed in its persistence, and one of the signs of its transformation was the fact that men who abandoned it appraised it by novel western standards, not by Taoist ones. When, arising from affirmations about science, progress, business, and utility, doubts were voiced about official careerism and its typical intellectual background, these were allegations against one form of action and education, not (in the Taoist vein) against action itself and education in the abstract.

In earlier times, as the old saw has it, a man might be 'a Confucianist in office and a Taoist out'—indulge with part of his being a Confucian passion for the ordering of social life, and with the other part seek, or affect to seek, the Taoist harmony of man immersed in nature, as distinct from the Confucian harmony of men among masses of men. Together, Confucianism and Taoism made the whole man, the one implying a testimonial to civilization and the values and goals of social life, the other, release from society and social concerns. The common thread of harmony tied them together, and a Taoist intuitive aesthetics made a precedent for Ch'an in the high art of Confucian ruling circles (as the Taoist spirit of detachment favoured the Confucianist-amateur's coolness to professional commitment). But the opposing emphases on nature and society made Taoism potentially, especially at times of crack-up in the society's

44

bureaucratic structure, more of an alternative to Confucianism than a complement. As popular Taoism, it could mean peasant rebellion, like the late Han revolt of the Yellow Turbans against landlord-Confucianist-officialdom. As sophisticated Taoism, it could mean literati withdrawal from social action into third-century A.D. 'pure-talk' (*ch'ing-t'an*), or the euphoria of the 'Seven Sages of the Bamboo Grove', or the T'ang poet's nostalgia for men

> . . . whose hearts are without guile.
> Gay like children. . . .[1]

That is how, traditionally, the Confucian-official role would be disparaged.

But rebels tended to reconstitute the Confucian state, and the sophisticated critics implicitly, in the escapist form of their censure, rendered to Confucianism, Confucianism alone, the real world of social life and action. How different the modern censure has been—neither Taoist blind protest nor Taoist world-denying quietism, but conscious revolution, and rejections of Confucianism in the nineteenth and twentieth centuries which were not at all rejections of the great world, but a choosing of other ideals for action in society. The tone of Chinese culture was changed; intellectual life was newly strained. For the new choices were not easy to make, and the new defence of the old was difficult, too.

Part Two

CHINESE CULTURE IN ITS MODERN METAMORPHOSES: THE TENSIONS OF INTELLECTUAL CHOICE

CHAPTER III

Eclecticism in the Area of Native Chinese Choices

I. CONSIDERATIONS OF TIME BECOME CONSIDERATIONS OF SPACE

IN intellectual controversies within the Confucian tradition, each school tried to score a point by claiming for itself a sort of apostolic succession from the sages. Opponents would almost invariably be accused of deviation from a right path laid down in antiquity. The old was prized over the new, and seventeenth- and eighteenth-century critics of Sung and Ming thought charged primarily not that it failed to meet needs of the present, but that it strayed from truths of the past.

Ku Yen-wu, for example, criticizing the Ming-Ch'ing school of Wang Yang-ming, charged that this school was really a revival of the ill-famed fourth-century *ch'ing-t'an* (pure talk) school, but that, whereas the original *ch'ing-t'an* was frankly Taoist, their modern descendants masqueraded as Confucianists. In truth, said Ku, they were far from the thought of Confucius and Mencius. They 'dwelt upon the surface (lit. "coarseness") without reaching the essence (lit. "fineness") [of the sages]'. They 'never asked about the great principles of the master's sayings on learning and government'.[1] Lu Shih-i (1611–72) also stated that many of his contemporaries in the intellectual world were really like the *ch'ing-t'an* school, which had been so injurious in the Chin period. As empty speculators, he charged, they were guilty of straying from the path of Confucius, in whose *Lun-yü* (Analects) Lu discerned a call to practical action.[2] Prominent Ch'ing critics of the neo-Confucian 'Sung Learning', we may recall, were known as the school of the 'Han Learning', not as the school of the 'Ch'ing Learning'. Such was the zeal of Chinese thinkers to sally forth under ancient colours.

The pedigree, then, of an intellectual position was one of the main criteria of its value or truth. This was true for traditional thought before the western intrusion, and it was true after it. But in the nineteenth century, with antiquity still a Chinese criterion of value, the West forced revision of Chinese judgments on the older contending philosophies. Petty distinctions and conflicts between Chinese schools paled into insignificance before the glaring contrast of western culture to everything Chinese. Grounds for discrimination between Chinese schools were blurred when a new western alternative existed for them all, a more genuine alternative than they afforded one another. Chinese thought was shocked into a semblance of unity; when the West was a serious rival, Chinese rivals closed their ranks. The question 'new or old?' as a test of value continued to be asked, but the question was removed from a Chinese world to the larger world of the West and China. As a first effect of their comprehending that western culture had to be taken seriously, the Chinese schools became less contentious about which of them was old. They all were old (having existed before the West came) and the West was new.

Why was it the nineteenth-century West that first offered a sufficiently strong alternative to press the Chinese schools together? Why did the seventeenth-century West, revealed to China by the scholarly Jesuit missionaries, miss having this effect? For one thing, of course, the Jesuits were far fewer than their modern successors as representative westerners, and the earlier exposition of western culture was bound to seem less strident. However, difference simply in the weight of western numbers is probably not the whole story behind the difference, during these two encounters, in relative Chinese awareness of intellectual challenge. To some extent, to be sure (as we shall consider at a later stage of the book), the Jesuits used their western learning as a calculated irritant, but on the whole they used it to establish themselves as educated gentlemen, qualified to mingle with Confucian literati. The Jesuits largely satisfied Confucian expectations as to the likely course of intelligent foreigners in Chinese society: they gave their actions a Chinese cast and tried, in great measure, to accommodate their own ideas to Chinese civilization. But Europeans in the nineteenth-century treaty-ports, after the Opium War (1839–42), were independent spirits, unconcerned with Chinese susceptibilities. Where the early Jesuits extended to China a graceful invitation to embellish and enrich its existing civilization, which was universally respected, later Europeans exposed to China an uncompromisingly foreign alternative.

The Jesuits were culturally conciliatory because Chinese society, in their day, was stable, and they would receive a hearing more or less as candidates for membership or not at all. But the Chinese who heard them were only casually interested in such frankly western knowledge as the Jesuits offered. For, since seventeenth-century Europe was unable to jeopardize the stability of Chinese society, western knowledge was superfluous to the Chinese literati; it had no relevance to power or success. A mastery of traditional Chinese learn-ing was not only necessary but sufficient—at least, to the extent that intellectual factors counted—to enable a Chinese to get the most out of Chinese life and the Chinese state.

Traditional Chinese learning, that is, was the intellectual substance of the state examinations; the examinations were the conventional and the only really approved path to the mandarin-bureaucracy; and the bureaucracy was the radi-ating centre of the highest social and economic power. The Jesuits, bringing only European ideas, with no European military or economic force behind them, made no dent at all in the prevailing bureaucratic system of power, so that the examination-road remained the usual road of ambition, and classical literary culture remained the core of education. For, whatever its intrinsic validity or its piquant surface attractive-ness, the Jesuits' intellectual offering was mainly scientific and technological (even in art, it was the geometrical illusionism of Renaissance perspective which gave the Jesuits' oil paintings their degree of interest in Chinese eyes). And nothing had happened socially to make the Chinese literati either unable or unzealous to guard their amateur standing. They were of the type of humanistic gentleman, whose characteristic quest is the mastery of an already ordered culture, an inheritance in the liberal arts; on the face of it, science was uncongenial to them, and in its heart as well—for the scientific spirit could only be subversive of traditionalism, which came so naturally to them in their social personalities and was so explicit intellectually in their formal Confucian code.

Thus western science, which ideally, potentially, was a threat to Confucian letters in the seventeenth and eighteenth centuries, was not yet actually a threat, and this was because the social position of Confucian officials, while ideally, potentially threatened by business power (whose growth in the West had paralleled the growth in the fields of science),[3] was not yet actually threatened. Business values, like scientific values, were still overshadowed. The Confucian official, his moralistic bias militating against a system of impersonal abstract legal relationships, without which commerce is never secure, still ruled the roost, without western interference, in a rent and tax economy. He was still able, by a combination of threat (bureaucratic squeeze) and lure (the somewhat imperfectly open examination system, highway for social mobility), to render abortive any revolutionary impulse in proto-capitalist elements. In this society of bureaucratic dominance, Confucian learning was, not utilitarian, but supremely useful—and utterly demanding.

After the Opium War, however, European industrialism and commercial enterprise began to act as a catalyst in traditional Chinese society. Before the establishment of treaty-ports in 1842, with their provision for the operation of western law on Chinese soil, there had already arisen a Chinese group of commercial intermediaries, the 'compradores', who were associated with western business firms. They became the nucleus of a new Chinese business community, déclassé from the point of view of the older Chinese society, but relatively protected from the consequences, political and economic, of the mandarin's disapproval. The treaty-ports became havens of personal and commercial security, where funds could be safe from the depredations of powerful officials, and where the commercial climate and the legal code encouraged reinvestment of business profits in business, instead of perpetuating the traditional flight of capital into land, the traditional hunger of business families for bureaucratic gentility. At the very moment that the western powers, by their physical assault, were contributing to the demoralization of the Ch'ing regime and therefore making problematic the advantages of an official career in its service, western political penetration was pointing the way to unorthodox alternatives.

It was a small beginning in the middle of the nineteenth century, small in numbers and small in noise. Confucianism, the examinations, the civil service, and the imperial state still had a reasonable life to run and kept prestige in the ports, and it would be wrong to suggest that even today the Confucian mentality has been finally superseded. But the conditions for corrosion were established with the treaties. In the eighteen-sixties, after the T'ai-p'ing Rebellion (1850–64) had been put down, when the classical examinations were reinstituted in the Shanghai region, troubled Chinese observers noted that candidates were inordinately few.[4] And Shanghai was the centre of the western business network.

Thus, new roads to power for Chinese, roads smoothed by western knowledge, had come to be dimly seen. A challenge was offered to the usefulness of Chinese thought, and when the question of its usefulness could be raised, the question of its truth came alive. Chinese thought, all schools of it, had a genuine, serious western rival.

2. THE ECLECTICISM OF TSENG KUO-FAN

The tendency to turn away from purely Chinese intellectual disputes was characteristic of those who were really aware of the western intrusion. But facts, of course, may run well ahead of awareness, and in the nineteenth century, particularly in its earlier decades, there were many parochial minds which persisted in treating China as the world and in analysing Chinese thought according to its traditional refinements. T'ang Ching-hai (1778–1861), for example, in his *Ch'ing Ju hsüeh-an hsiao-shih* (Short history of the intellectual situation of Ch'ing Confucianism), published in 1845, made a systematic and thoroughly partisan classification of Ch'ing philosophers. He exalted the *li-hsüeh* of the Sung neo-Confucianists Ch'eng I and Chu Hsi and disparaged the *hsin-hsüeh* of Lu Hsiang-shan and Wang Yang-ming, of the Sung and Ming dynasties, respectively.[5]

Tseng Kuo-fan (1811–72), however, the most powerful governor-general during the T'ai-p'ing Rebellion and the T'ung-chih reign (1860–74), was implicated in dealings with the West and exposed to western ideas as few of his contemporaries among the Chinese literati could be. He remained certain of the universality of Chinese spiritual values; nevertheless, his Chinese ethnocentrism was not that of a man whose complacency had never been challenged, but of one who has known a rival claim and disposed of it. And though Tseng flatly rejected the rival western claim (and condemned the anti-Confucian, pseudo-Christian T'ai-p'ing rebels of mid-century for seemingly accepting it), Tseng's very facing it affected his view of the heritage he defended.

He came to admire the practical techniques of the West and to feel, correspondingly, that the peculiar excellence of China (which he always affirmed) need not be assumed to characterize traditional Chinese practice in that sphere of practical techniques. And in the sphere of ultimate values of civilization—the sphere which was left to Tseng for the indulgence of his pride in being Chinese—he became more of a composite Chinese, an antithesis to westerners, and less of a partisan sectarian, an adherent of one pre-western Chinese school against another. As a loyal Chinese, but a Chinese among westerners, he seemed to lose the will to dwell on intramural distinctions. An eclectic in the larger sense, ready to infuse something of western civilization into Chinese civilization, he was comprehensive, too, in the field of native Chinese choices, and sought to impose a peace on traditional Chinese enemies.

He would synthesize the best points of all systems of thought, he asserted. The various philosophers of the late Chou period were not as great as Confucius because they were biased or one-sided. But if the biases could be rectified and the deficits made up, if these philosophers could lend themselves to a composite—with Lao-tzu's and Chuang-tzu's doctrine of emptiness and tranquillity for relaxing the mind, and Mo-tzu's doctrine of industry and frugality for regulating the self, and Kuan-tzu's and Shang Yang's doctrine of severity and orderliness for unifying the people— then all of them would be worth following and indispensable.[6]

To combine the industry and frugality of Emperor Yü and Mo-tzu with the tranquillity and emptiness of Lao-tzu and Chuang-tzu—is not this the art of simultaneously accomplishing self-cultivation and group-regulation?[7]

By gratifying oneself with the way of Chuang-tzu and restricting oneself with the way of Hsün-tzu, may not one be a princely man attaining the Way?[8]

Coming to classical Chinese conflicts in this conciliatory spirit, Tseng had similar views about more recent intellectual controversies. (And so, indeed, had his properly filial son, Tseng Chi-tse, 1839–90, who scorned the fashionable Ch'ing criticism of Lu-Wang idealism, and intimated, in his father's vein, that modern writers liked to dwell on comparisons between Chu Hsi and Lu Hsiang-shan just for the joy of sectarianism.)[9] The elder Tseng wrote approvingly of both the Sung Learning and of its later rival, the Han Learning, which dismissed the tradition of the 'five Sung philosophers' as 'loosely fanciful'. The scholars of the Han Learning had been attacked in turn, as 'renegade', and accused of 'splitting the classical tradition into fragments and causing the true path such harm as would never come to an end'. Yet, according to Tseng Kuo-fan, the peace-maker, there was little distinction between them, and he urged their adherents not to be inflexible. Their differences could be easily adjusted and the schools could fit together. Why should the two denounce each other?[10] For himself, Tseng subscribed to the catholic motto of Yao Nai (1731–1815), founder of the so-called *T'ung-ch'eng p'ai*, a moribund school of thinkers (named after a place in Anhui province) whose intellectual influence Tseng revived: '*I li* (the Sung learning's ethics and metaphysics), *k'ao-chü* (the Han learning's textual study), *tz'u-chang* (their literary expression)—these three equally important.' [11]

It was his philosophy of *li-hsüeh* (the classic *li* of 'rites', not the neo-Confucian *li* of archetypical 'forms'),[12] Tseng maintained, which would bring about the unification of the Han and Sung schools and put an end to intellectual warfare.[13] The *li-hsüeh* was indeed a philosophy of wholeness, drawing together complementary pairs of classical concepts, all of them ancient expressions of a working dichotomy of 'inner' and 'outer'. There are *t'i* and *yung*, substance and function, what one is and what one does; and there are *sheng* and *wang*, the sage in spirit and the king in action, whose *t'i* is evinced in *hsiu-chi*, his inner cultivation of the self, and whose *yung* is evinced in *chih-jen*, the governing of men in the outer world. *Li* is the common noumenon underlying the self-nurturing, world-pacifying sage-king's being and activity; without *li*, from the standpoint of the inner there is no *tao* or *te*, metaphysical truth or rightness, and from the standpoint of the outer there is no *cheng-shih*, no governing.[14]

In the eyes of Tseng Kuo-fan, Chinese philosophical factions stood, at worst, for parts of the whole Confucian conception. But the *li-hsüeh* embraced them all, for the *li-hsüeh* recaptured the whole.

When Tseng referred to this whole in contrasting it with western principles (whether these were being expressed by Europeans or by Chinese peasant T'ai-p'ing rebels), he called it *ming-chiao*, the teachings of the sages, a definition of civilization which was in the broadest sense Chinese. Hellmut Wilhelm has called it characteristic of Tseng that he did not use the term for Confucianism (*ju-chiao*) or for orthodoxy (*cheng-chiao*), by which usually Sung Confucianism was understood.[15] Another time, noting with some satisfaction the Protestant-Catholic schism in Christianity, Tseng oversimplified the history of Confucianism, making it, in comparison, a steadily standing monolith, with no cracks and no decay.[16]

When western conceptions were seen as alternative, the Chinese creed for a man like Tseng had to be close to all-inclusive.[17]

3. THE ENCROACHMENT OF 'CHINA' ON GENERAL JUDGMENTS OF VALUE

Why, with Tseng and others like him, was there a waning of discrimination between Chinese alternatives, while to their predecessors and their less worldly-wise contemporaries, such discrimination was both natural and important? The positive content of the Sung Learning and the Han Learning, for example, had not changed. But some change had occurred —a redefinition of the Chinese ideas in terms of new alternatives, and a consequent reordering of the psychology of Chinese thinkers. When Tseng, unlike some others, declared such Chinese controversy intellectually insignificant, perhaps he did so, in part, because for him, at least, it was emotionally undesirable.

For all his consistently serene Chinese self-confidence, he knew the West as a rival, a rival so formidable that he felt compelled to encourage an infusion of western material culture into Chinese civilization. This recommendation, this implied deference to the West as a centre of value, was wrapped in a saving rationalization, which preserved the claims of China to a basic superiority. If, then, in this broad eclecticism (which we shall shortly examine), we find Tseng unable to accept the western value simply, as a matter of intellectual persuasion, but find him concerned instead, out of considerations irrelevant to a general intellectual quest, to make it seem legitimate for a *Chinese* to accept, may not this same special commitment have a place in his narrower, indigenously Chinese eclecticism? It is easy to see how such eclecticism would indulge the will of Chinese traditionalists, of whatever stamp, to hold their own against western rivals who raise the spectre of doubt among them all. For agreement might seem to shore up defences of the Chinese intellectual world. Literati who could recognize, even dimly, the western onslaught for what it was, could have little stomach for civil war. It was more than unjustifiable—it was unwelcome. However freely they had indulged themselves in the luxury of dissension in the safe old days, now, when the West had challenged Confucius himself, all the bickering claimants of the mantle of Confucius were in real danger, and they were in it together.

Yet, in so far as acceptance of Chinese ideas was beginning to be more and more emotionally willed, it became less and less intellectually forced. When attachment to Chinese inheritances, with their latent emotional associations, had not been threatened (before Chinese society seemed in danger of being torn), the quest for intellectually acceptable answers had been undertaken freely, and Chinese philosophies had been worked out as distinct serious efforts to describe the way of the world. But when Chinese philosophers, defensively ranged against the West, came to be rather indiscriminate in their Chinese intellectual tastes and to sip at all the flowers, their eclecticism was an intellectually delicate thing; for the flowers would never have existed, had serious thinkers of earlier times not cultivated individual gardens and developed their own ideas by marking them off from the others.

Therefore, as considerations of special tie to China intrude on considerations of general judgment in the Chinese approach to Chinese ideas, western ideas, to some extent, are forced on reluctant Chinese minds. And Sino-western syncretisms, inspired by that force and that reluctance, pre-empt the field of Chinese intellectual history.

CHAPTER IV

T'i *and* Yung—
'Substance' *and* 'Function'

I. THE RATIONALIZATION

BEGINNING slowly in the eighteen-forties, after the British show of technical prowess in the Opium War, and picking up speed by the end of the century, numbers of faithful Confucianists spoke out in favour of change in Chinese culture. Paradoxically, they insisted on change because they had a traditionalistic bias against it. They parted company with unshakable traditionalists not over the question of ends—the ascription of value to Chinese civilization —but over the question of the means to preserve it. To admit innovation in certain areas of life, declared the bolder spirits, was the only means.

Uncompromising anti-westernizers had an attitude of radical simplicity: the way to stay Chinese was to stay Chinese in all the aspects of culture. But the cautious eclectics, protesting their perfect loyalty to the basic Chinese values, believed that immobility would be a self-defeating tactic and an impossible ideal. The only alternative to outright destruction of Chinese civilization by foreign conquerors was selective innovation by dedicated Chinese traditionalists. To justify their proposal in the special sense, to satisfy their will to believe that Chinese superiority was still unchallenged, they emphasized that these areas of innovation from the West were areas of only *practical* value, not of essential value. Western knowledge would be used only to defend the core of Chinese civilization, and it would not impinge upon it.

59

If there should be argument on this point, if some traditionalists should doubt that western ideas could be sterilized
just by Chinese rhetoric, or be turned into passive instru-
ments simply by decree, any one of this school of westernizers
would respond, in effect, like Li Hung-chang (1823–1901),
cutting off discussion with the blank, apodictic apologia: 'If
one knows oneself and knows one's opposite number, in a
hundred battles one will have a hundred victories.' [1]

This rationalization, whereby something of western culture
could have a place in China and yet be kept in its place, was
an article of faith for a whole school of Confucian-official
westernizers, the 'self-strengtheners', from Lin Tse-hsü (1785–
1850) to Chang Chih-tung (1837–1909). It was Chang, a
great advocate of railroads and heavy industry, who made
the most explicit philosophical statement of what they all
assumed—that since elements of western culture would be
introduced only for use, condescension could be heaped on
'practicality', and China could seem, not beggarly, but
even queenly in borrowing western methods. Taking his
terminology from Chu Hsi, he advocated Chinese learning
for *t'i* ('substance', 'essence') and western learning for *yung*
('function', 'utility'). In the general excellence of its cultural
product, China could still seem more than equivalent to the
West. Special Chinese ties need not be strained. [2]

2. THE FALLACY

Why should this rationalization not serve its purpose? Why
should the Chinese not be able to rest on this middle ground?
The *t'i-yung* dichotomy might well appear to fit the conditions of Chinese self-awareness, as a psychologically suitable
camouflage for the infiltration of foreign value—at least in
the field of science. In that field, considered apart from other
areas of civilization, the modern Chinese have had the least
hope of linking their special and general quests, of making an
emotional Chinese particularism respectable intellectually.
Valid conclusions of science, the sphere of the empirically
demonstrable, finally enforce their claims to acceptance, re-
gardless of their cultural origins. But scientific values are

distinguished from moral and aesthetic values not only by being empirically demonstrable but by being widely and obviously useful. Now, since the Chinese are forced to accept modern science, developed in the West, what could be more plausible than that they accept it in the spirit of Chang Chih-tung, emphasizing not that western science is more valuable than Chinese science but that western science is less valuable than Chinese morals and aesthetics, less valuable because of its usefulness? As something useful, it is a means, and a means is less than an end.

Yet, this rationalization, which was meant to compromise the differences between the *avant-garde* and the obscurantists, was attacked in both these quarters, and with considerable cogency. Both stubborn traditionalists and impatient inno-vators came to feel that the needs for special and general assurance, the *meum* and *verum*, were not really welded to-gether by the *t'i-yung* formula. Since that formula seemed to fail to justify innovation, traditionalists rejected innovation and innovators sought a new formula.

The failure of the *t'i-yung* rationalization to consolidate Chinese devotion to Chinese culture in the modern world of western techniques can be explained in its own terms: Chinese learning, which was to be the *t'i* in the new syncretic culture, was the learning of a society which had always used it for *yung*, as the necessary passport to the best of all careers. Western learning, when sought as *yung*, did not supplement Chinese learning—as the neat formula would have it do— but began to supplant it. For in reality, Chinese learning had come to be prized as substance because of its function, and when its function was usurped, the learning withered.[3] The more western learning came to be accepted as the prac-tical instrument of life and power, the more Confucianism ceased to be *t'i*, essence, the naturally believed-in value of a civilization without a rival, and became instead an his-torical inheritance, preserved, if at all, as a romantic token of no-surrender to a foreign rival which had changed the essence of Chinese life.

'Officials read Confucian writings now, but what they assiduously seek out is the foreign learning':[4] Yu Yüeh

(1821–1907) resentfully saw it, the coming eclipse of the Confucian *tao*, lingeringly preserved *pro forma* while another way took over the title of necessary knowledge.

T'i-yung westernization began in China, as one might expect, with emphasis on the bare means of military defence —ships and guns—'to drive away the crocodile and to get rid of the whales', to control the barbarians through their own superior techniques.[5] Soon the list of indispensable superior techniques lengthened, to cover industry, commerce, mining, railroads, telegraphs . . ., and essential traditional attitudes were almost casually dissipated by seekers after the useful techniques which were to shield the Chinese essence. Feng Kuei-fen (1809–74) was ready to trade the *chü-jen* and *chin-shih* literary degrees for artisanship at least equal to the foreign.[6] Hsüeh Fu-ch'eng (1838–94), one of those ostensibly only-material innovators whose ideal in matters of spirit was *wan ku pu i* (unchanged from time immemorial),[7] betrayed an enthusiasm for commerce, as a contributor to the national health and as an index of it, which ill accorded with the old Confucian bureaucratic, gentlemanly temper. In three essays celebrating the publication, during the T'ung-chih reign (1860–74), of Imperial Maritime Customs statistics—in itself, a western-sponsored procedure, since the Customs, firmly established by treaty in 1858, was a foreign bureaucracy in its higher strata—Hsüeh said that the figures on duties levied were a mirror reflecting the degree of seclusion or accessibility of the land, poverty or wealth of the people, flourishing or declining of material well-being, and swelling or shrinking of revenues.[8]

This infection of spirit by techniques, of *t'i* by *yung* (in the terms of those who thought the two could be sealed apart), was a consequence of the novelty, in Chinese experience, of the type of foreigner who brought these techniques to China. Chinese had learned from history to expect of their foreign conquerors (if the latter came to rule and not simply to raid) some effort, in varying degree, to become Chinese. The traditional Chinese attitude of self-defence against foreign invaders was a variation on a bit of homely popular wisdom

—'if you can't lick them, join them'—or, more precisely here, 'make them join you'. But the Chinese problem with nineteenth-century Europeans was not the same as with earlier Turks or Manchus; for western conquerors, who could not be beaten by the Chinese devices which lay at hand, were able, with their own industrial and commercial devices, to manipulate China to their own advantage *from a distance*. The bases of their power to perpetuate their power in China remained outside of China. They had no need to become Chinese in any degree whatever.

Hence the only recourse for a traditionally-minded Chinese, anxious to maintain Chinese autonomy by either conversion or dispersion of the foreigners, fitting them in or throwing them out, was to give up on the chances of the former,[9] and to try to develop safe new material devices to defend China by force—safe, that is, from implications of spiritual apostasy. With earlier recalcitrant foreign conquerors, like the Mongols of the thirteenth century, who were more unwilling than most to join the Chinese, the latter could not retaliate by trying to turn the secret of the Mongols' conquest against them; for their secret, the Mongols' successful technique, was nothing less than their tribal-nomadic militant way of life, and the spread of that culture at the expense of Chinese sedentary culture was just what the literati wished to preclude. (The Ming did try border horse-raising, but the ultimate Ch'ing tack was to change the *Mongol* culture, through religious and political policies aimed at pinning the Mongols down, in sedentary fashion, to permanent localities.) But while the source of Mongol military strength was thus quite obviously culturally taboo, western techniques—supposedly tame machines—could offer the illusion of exploitability. The very devices which made it unnecessary for conquerors to meet Chinese at least half-way and become a Chinese dynasty (one of the early Chinese recourses) gave Chinese the fatal vision of the other recourse, development of the means of self-defence, western learning for *yung*, a treacherous 'mere utility'.

Positivistic historians have been criticized for imagining a vain thing, that they can 'appease a new discovery by fitting it into an old world, not allowing it to transform the whole of that world'.[10] The *t'i-yung* dichotomists had just such a misconception. If a man read Mencius and an engineering manual, they felt, Mencius would speak to him just as he had to his father, who read Mencius and Tu Fu. But they were wrong, for the meaning of Mencius changed in his new context, the questions changed which Mencius was taken to answer, and the western ideas accepted as *yung* were not tame, nor dead, but dynamic. For,

Whatever we know, we know as a whole and in its place in our whole world of experience . . . The process of knowledge is not a process of mere accretion. To speak of 'adding to knowledge' is misleading. For a gain in knowledge is always the transformation and the recreation of an entire world of ideas. It is the creation of a new world by transforming a given world. If knowledge consisted in a mere series of ideas, an addition to it could touch only the raw end . . . But, since it is a system, each advance affects retrospectively the entire whole, and it is the creation of a new world.[11]

What was the 'new world' in China? Not the Confucian intellectual world with western technical interests pasted on, but the Confucian world transformed by the western interests, the Classics paling into fuctional insignificance. This is the intellectual side of what we have seen already in social terms—the rise of business (historically associated with the rise of '*yung*-ian' science), under western aegis, to a point of possible rivalry with Confucian-official status. Western *yung*, embraced by literati, corrupted the literati's way of thought, ultimately sapping the fullness of their conviction of the Confucian learning's indispensability; and western *yung*, wielded by westerners, put a challenge to the literati's way of life, by encouraging a social alternative, the commercial-industrial way of life, which likewise made the Confucian learning seem more and more irrelevant—and Confucian sanctions (like those behind the family-system) more and more impossible.[12]

3. THE PHILOSOPHICAL ATTENUATION OF THE *T'I-YUNG* CONCEPT

The *t'i-yung* argument for innovation, then, suggested that the heart of Chinese civilization, its spiritual values, would be defended, not jeopardized, by Chinese 'self-strengthening' in the merely practical spheres of life where westerners had their eminence. However, this psychologically appealing formula failed to produce what it promised. No clean line could mark off a material segment of culture from a spiritual segment, and the modern *t'i-yung* dichotomy, for all its traditional Confucian pedigree, was really a cover for essential change and the waning of tradition.

But it was not simply that traditionalists, with the best of Confucian wills, used *t'i-yung* to ease a catalyst, western industrialism, into their world and thereby prepared the way for iconoclasm; there was more to the paradox than that. For *t'i-yung*, in its nineteenth-century usage, not only had Confucian breakdown as an outer consequence but Confucian breakdown in its inner core. The Confucian formula which failed to contain industrialism also failed to express an authentic Confucianism. *T'i-yung*, as Chang Chih-tung invoked it, was a vulgarization of a Sung Confucian principle. The traditionalist tried to assure himself that western machines were tame, but when the terms he used for reassurance were so strangely warped from their orthodox meanings, the ravages of western intruders were exemplified, not belied.

In the Sung neo-Confucianism of Chu Hsi which Chang implied he was perpetuating, *yung* might be described as the functional correlative of *t'i*. Both an essence and a function inhered in the single object; *t'i* and *yung* were two modes of identification of being, while the existing object of identification was one. This *t'i-yung* correlation was a fairly ordinary proposition, and one can find the sense of the neo-Confucian usage in non-Chinese philosophies. With perhaps differing degrees of stress, Goethe's definition of function as 'existence conceived in activity',[13] Whitehead's concept of functional activity ('that every actual thing is something by reason of its activity')[14] seem suggestions of *yung* as Chu Hsi understood it. And Aristotle and the great Aristotelians in effect described *t'i* when they spoke of that which is present in an individual as the cause of its being and unity,[15] or of a name —that which is signified in a definition,[16] or of the object of intuition, the scientifically undemonstrable apprehension of the intellect alone.[17] A thing *is*, and it *does*. Essence, or substance—*t'i*—inexorably implies action, or function—*yung*; and Aquinas, perhaps, was close to Chu Hsi when he wrote that a thing has a disposition towards an operation proper to the thing. '. . . no thing is lacking in its proper operation.' [18]

Chu Hsi's similar sense of the correlation between the quiddity of a thing and its proper operation is apparent in his analyses of classical Confucian qualities. For example, interpreting in a dialogue with his disciples the *Lun-yü* phrases, '*Li chih yung ho wei kuei*',[19] he treated the *yung* of the passage as establishing the functional tie of *ho*, 'harmony' or Legge's 'natural ease', to *li*, the principle of ordered human relationships. He held that *li* became manifest in the production of *ho*. The existence of *ho* was the outer test of the existence of *li* (the inner core of *li* was *ching*, 'reverence'); if *li* was really in being, the operation of *ho* was naturally, necessarily implied.[20]

This absolute naturalness of the correlation between inner essence and outer manifestation was insisted upon by Chu Hsi. Where Mencius, in listing the attributes of the great man, used the phrases, 'to dwell in the wide house of the world', 'to stand in the correct seat of the world', and 'to walk in the great path of the world',[21] Chu Hsi gave as equivalents *jen* ('human-heartedness'), *li* ('propriety'), and *i* ('right conduct'), respectively, and continued:

In the case of the first and second phrases, 'dwelling in the wide house' is *t'i*, 'standing in the correct seat' is *yung*. In the case of the second and third phrases, then 'standing in the correct sea' is *t'i*, 'walking in the great path' is *yung*. If one knows how to dwell in the wide house of the world, he naturally can stand in the correct seat of the world and walk in the great path of the world.[22]

The 'naturally' (*tzu-jan*) in this passage underscores the necessity of the tie between *t'i* and *yung*, and in this case between *jen* and *li* and *i*, the first bringing the second two in its train, since a *yung* may be also a *t'i* and have its own *yung* inevitably as a correlative. In the Mencius passage, it would seem that these qualities were cumulating to make the great man, but in the *t'i-yung* thinking of Chu Hsi the qualities were considered unequivocally not as independent and added to one another, but as interdependent and expressive of one another, inconceivable without one another.[23] Thus, *ai* ('love'), as an emotion (*ch'ing*), is the necessary projection into action—the *yung*, in short—of a human being's innate nature or predisposition (*hsing*); the innate nature which points toward *ai* is *jen*. Or, *ai* is *yung* to *jen*, one of the functional correlatives which Chu Hsi saw as implicitly bound to this particular *t'i*.[24]

This authentically neo-Confucian interpretation of *t'i-yung* was still preserved in the thought of Tseng Kuo-fan. Tseng was a powerful advocate of western technical achievement for China, along the line of reasoning to which the *t'i-yung* dichotomy would soon be misapplied; but Tseng, still an early figure in the history of Chinese westernization, reserved this terminology for his *li-hsüeh*, an attempted synthesis of Chinese philosophies, and thus kept both concepts in the realm of 'spirit' instead of allotting one to the realm of 'matter'. Tseng's *li*, as we have seen, was supposed to pervade the linked worlds of 'inner' and 'outer' and symbolize their union. Sageliness and kingliness, virtue and statesmanship were knit together in the one fabric, substance-and-function.[25]

For Tseng Kuo-fan, then, *t'i-yung* was still an orthodox, neutrally equivalent substance-and-function, not a normatively differentiated end-and-means. The idea that *yung* was *merely yung*, as means are *merely* means in relation to a cherished end, was Chang Chih-tung's ominous note of departure from the neo-Confucian world in which Tseng had still lingered. Western technology, something useful for the material defence of the home of Chinese spiritual values, was the *yung* that Chang accepted for the sake of superior *t'i*. Chu Hsi would never have recognized it.

For Chu Hsi had a word for such an instrument, a means, not end—and the word was not *yung*, but *ch'i*. Commenting on *Lun-yü* II, xii ('The master said, "The accomplished scholar [*chün-tzu*] is not a utensil [*ch'i*]" ',[26] Chu Hsi said that a *chün-tzu* had *te* ('virtue') as his *t'i* and *ts'ai* ('talent') as his *yung*. Man fell short of being a *chün-tzu* and hence remained a mere utensil (*ch'i*), when the *t'i* appropriate to a *chün-tzu* (i.e. *te*) was only approached, so that its *yung*, or manifestation in action, was incomplete.[27] With Chu Hsi, then, in this example, it was not the existence of *yung* but the *incompleteness* of *yung* that made an object, seen under these categories of *t'i* and *yung*, a utensil, means, or instrument. *Yung* here was clearly a different concept from what Chang Chih-tung made of it; it was not an equivalent of 'instrument' but a necessary antidote to instrumentalization.

Chang Chih-tung, seeking a material shield for spiritual values, told Confucians more conservative than he that *t'i* and *yung* belonged together. To that extent, he sounded like Chu Hsi, who had once condemned the Buddhists for allegedly defending 'empty stillness' (*k'ung-chi*) or '*t'i* without *yung*', i.e. complete abstraction.[28] Chang might see himself as deriving from Chu in his activist insistence that *t'i* was not enough, that the classics *and* railroads were needed in China, but when he seemed to suggest that *t'i* and *yung* were where one found them, and that he found *t'i* in Chinese learning and *yung* in western, he showed how little the neo-Confucian logic met his case. For Chang's sum of a *t'i* from here and a *yung* from there never added up to be Chu Hsi's indivisible entity, a *t'i*—in—*yung* or *yung*—in—*t'i*. Chang was pleading for a coupling of concepts on the authority of an imprecise analogy with an earlier dichotomy, which had really referred to an internal symbiosis, not an externally-contrived aggregation.

In short, Chang Chih-tung, without a conscious acknowledgment of what he was doing, changed the significance of the *t'i-yung* dichotomy in a very important way. Chu Hsi's emphasis had been metaphysical: *t'i* and *yung*, substance and function, jointly defined the one object. But Chang Chih-tung's emphasis was sociological. He was concerned not with the nature of things but the nature of cultures, and *t'i* and *yung* were separate in objective embodiment (as they were not for Chu Hsi) and fused only in mind. Man, that is, had something (Chinese) for *t'i* and something (western) for *yung*; while according to Chu Hsi, all 'somethings' had both *t'i* and *yung*.

Such, then, was Chang Chih-tung's use of an orthodox formula to characterize his effort, by a Sino-western syncretism, to preserve orthodoxy. It betrays a traditionalist's contribution to the wearing away of tradition. In fact, orthodoxy was not preserved by Chinese action taken under cover of the *t'i-yung* sanction; and an orthodoxy had to be mishandled, so that, in fancy, a belief in its preservation might be entertained.

As an easy, conventional conceit in Chinese thinking, the prescription of Chinese spirit plus western matter has never quite lost its appeal since Chang Chih-tung expressed it in his *t'i-yung* terminology. (Some western observers, too, are still setting China to rights with a bit of easy phrase-making —e.g. 'the grafting of the new scientific culture on the old stock of literary tradition . . .')[29] But in more rigorous, formal thought, the self-destructive implications of a *t'i-yung* defence of Chinese culture were soon exposed. There were thinkers who came to hold that if there was any *t'i* involved in combination with the *yung* of western applied science, it was western pure science, and western philosophy, literature, and art, not their Chinese counterparts. Or, in a further refinement, the applied science and industrialism which were *yung* from the standpoint of scholarship were *t'i* from the standpoint of general social reform.[30] This was how the catalytic power of science and industrialism, which Chang had ignored when he asked them in to protect his spiritual heritage, came to be recognized; and the very recognition of that power was one of the latter's subversive effects.

4. REJECTION OF *T'I-YUNG* AND REJECTION OF INNOVATION: WO-JEN

The traditionalists who in the very beginning, in the middle of the nineteenth century, failed to be persuaded by the official westernizers recognized the *t'i-yung* dichotomy for what it was, a formula for self-deception about the implications of innovation. If the western learning were let loose in China, the Chinese learning would not stay safely screened off and unsullied. And if the western learning came in because the Chinese deluded themselves that there could be two separate components to a culture, the western learning would speedily end the separation and expose the delusion— the new *yung* would become also the new *t'i*.

Wo-jen (d. 1871), one of the most inflexible anti-westernizers in a position of influence in nineteenth-century China, would not defend Chinese culture by accepting western culture as a complement, a *yung* to a *t'i*; he defended it by rejecting western culture as a rival, an alternative *t'i* to the traditional one. That is why we see Wo-jen tracing the origin of western values (which others wish to admit as *yung*) to Chinese history, and saying, in effect, that they had had their chance to become Chinese *t'i* and had been rejected.

In other words, he denied any conflict or, rather, any distinction between the specially Chinese and the generally valid by alleging that all possible value-choices had already been posed and settled in Chinese history; he maintained that the Chinese inheritance was good, and that it ought to be sustained not just because of its particular 'Chinese-ness' but because of its universal rightness. His ideas accorded with comprehension that if elements of western culture were admitted, eventually the grounds for clinging to Chinese culture would seem more and more exclusively particularistic, and the *t'i-yung* rationalization, which was supposed to keep the sense of Chinese identity unspoiled by foreign mentality, would only make that vitiation certain.

Thus, while Chang Chih-tung assumed a radical separation in the conditions of origin of the western and Chinese learning, Wo-jen assumed their identity. For Chang, western learning was a foreign development, a promising candidate for Chinese acceptance as *yung*; for Wo-jen, 'western' learning was a domestic development, a discredited candidate for Chinese acceptance as *t'i*. While Chang thought western learning could be accepted as means, Wo-jen feared it would usurp

Chinese learning's prerogatives as end, and he condemned the western learning, therefore, as an end already judged and rejected in the course of Chinese history. The western scientist, in Wo-jen's view, could not be an aide to Confucius—he was a fallen angel cast out by Confucius, and the relation between them was not collaboration but struggle.

So Wo-jen emphasized the distinction, the incompatibility, between the Chinese ideal of the 'human heart' and the western ideal of 'techniques'. He explicitly disavowed any effort to bring them together as complementary partners, for the Chinese had had the techniques and had left them go. It was a disgrace, he said, for Chinese scholars to study mathematics and astronomy, and, even if this were not the case, foreign teachers should not be used, since Chinese knew as much about these subjects as anyone else.[31] He and like-minded literati delighted to maintain that ancient China had known the prototypes of that scientific learning which the westernizers so uncritically admired. Astronomy and mathematics, it was alleged, derived from the *Chou-pi suan-ching* (a book which was thought to be of Chou Dynasty authorship) and the *Ch'un-ch'iu*. Chemistry derived from the *Shu-ching*, especially the *Hung-fan* ('The great plan') section, and from the Taoist Huai Nan-tzu. The part of physics which covers problems of solids, liquids, and gases was outlined in the *K'ang-ts'ang tzu* (a book by an eighth-century Taoist, Wang Shih-yüan, though it purported to be Chou). Mineralogy was expounded in the *Shu-ching*, optics and mechanics by Mo-tzu, and electricity was explained by Kuan-yin tzu, a Taoist supposed to have been a disciple of Lao-tzu.[32]

Wo-jen's intellectual position, of course, was shaped by social considerations. When he declines to exempt western science from the ban of the conservative Chinese, one hears not Wo-jen the abstract logician speaking, but Wo-jen the head of the *Han-lin yüan*, the spokesman for the most honoured masters of the ancient learning, men whose prestige and careers depended on the discrediting of the western learning, a potential rival. It was just this social sensitivity to the cold blast at the back, perhaps, which accounts for Wo-jen's feeling for the weakness of the *t'i-yung* rationalization. The social position of the Confucian gentry-literati-officialdom was tightly linked with the intellectual pre-eminence of Confucianism; no formula, embroidered with whatever Confucian pieties, which threatened to break the Confucian intellectual monopoly could expect general support from the old bureaucracy.

All question of vested interest aside, western 'matter' could not, in fact, be broken to the service of Chinese Confucian 'spirit'. And the intellectual inadequacy of the *t'i-yung* formula as a principle for a viable syncretism is no better illustrated than by its general rejection among the pillars of the old society. For to say that Wo-jen saw the logical fallacy in the *t'i-yung* rationalization is only to say that he saw its social perils; if the literati, whose pre-eminence was as traditionally *Chinese* as the classics they guarded, were really imperilled by innovation according to a *t'i-yung* formula, a formula which ostensibly protected tradition, then the formula was illogical indeed.

In their opposition to modern technology, were literati like Wo-jen (or, for that matter, less literate poor people, like the mass of Boxers in 1900) really any different from Oxford dons with rural sympathies or Luddite labourers, deploring in their various ways the industrial revolution in nineteenth-century England? In other words, do we need to find, in and around the *t'i-yung* controversy, a constant sensitivity to cultural rivalry, a brooding awareness of alien menace to the autonomy of Chinese civilization? Perhaps it is enough to explain away the opposition to material innovation as nothing especially Chinese, nothing involving a conflict of civilizations, but as simply a local specimen of a ubiquitous type of reaction or nostalgia. And if that is so, then the cardinal avowed assumption of *t'i-yung* reasoning is sound: when western techniques are brought to China, as *yung*—no matter how much, in the natural course of events, they shock the obscurantists who are always with us, for whom novelty is always unsettling—these techniques will not compromise the individuality of the Chinese essence. If Europe was not less European for the spread of railroads, notwithstanding the fact that some Europeans lamented Arcadia or feared for their pigs, then China would not be less Chinese for the spread of railroads, the opposition of some Chinese, elegant literati or fearful peasants, equally notwithstanding.

There is, of course, a good deal of truth in this. Some of the early Chinese hostility to machines was simply a plausible reaction of pre-industrial people to the spectacle of industrialism, not necessarily a Chinese reaction to the threat of westernization. Fears were freely expressed, and not peculiarly Chinese fears, of the stimulation of social unrest by the substitution of machines for men in many occupations; and rationally conceived attacks were made on the value of railroads (e.g. scouting the claims of 'self-strengtheners' that railroads would aid the national defence, and suggesting rather that they might turn out to be royal roads for invaders), without the emotional implications of the history of railroads being allowed to intrude in the argument.[33] The existing Chinese culture was certainly due to be shaken up by modern industrialism, but western culture had been fed into the same machines in recent times and been almost indescribably transformed as well. It would seem, on the basis of this comparison, that *t'i-yung* theory should not be seen as defensive rationalization, since Chinese had no need to feel, even vaguely, that western culture was one-up.

And yet, how convincing is the answer which convincingly explains that the question never needed to be asked? The question of whether China was submitting to westernization cannot be exorcized in this way. It stubbornly existed; it *was* asked. For, even though much opposition to innovation can be accounted for in general anti-modernist terms, *defence* of innovation always did more than just meet that general protest. *T'i-yung* and other, later syncretisms, as we shall see, were Chinese apologetics (including demonstrations that Chinese need not apologize) in a dialogue with the West.

To speak of apologetics is not to suggest that Chinese thinkers, in vindicating the worth of Chinese culture against western pretensions, were saying anything untrue. What is true is no less true because apologists insist upon it. But apologists are no less apologetic because what they insist upon is true; it is the insistence that counts.

In short, we can call the *t'i-yung* rationalization a fallacy, as we have suggested, because the *yung* of modern techniques could not defend the Chinese *t'i*, as advertised, but only change society so that the old *t'i* would have a rival instead of a shield; and we can call this fallacy a rationalization, an explanation of cultural borrowing which explains away the attendant sense of indebtedness, by referring still to this 'live' quality of ostensibly dead material things. For industrialism had social implications behind it as well as before it. There had to be a proper social matrix for the inception of industrialism, and this the West had provided, never China, where the bureaucratic structure, with its anti-scientific and anti-capitalist intellectual aura, had never, like western feudalism, been undermined from within. Because the West could nurture industrialism, the shock of its change at the monster's hands was less emphatic than the Chinese shock or was absorbed, at least, with different questions asked, along with some of the same.

Both Wo-jen and Swift—to reach back for an example— could claim, each for his own culture, that experimental science was not a high traditional value. But only Wo-jen could hope to support his protest (and thus inevitably did so) by describing acceptance of this putative value as originally foreign to his culture. The anti-modernist Swift, however he might decry the fact, could hardly deny that western civilization itself had finally hatched that wretched enthusiasm for scientific achievement; whatever else scientists had to contend with in Europe, they were necessarily spared any serious allegation, of a xenophobic nature, that science came with the stamp of alien culture. Wo-jen, however, while wryly claiming the scientific achievement, could plausibly, in the name of indigenous Chinese culture, disavow the enthusiasm. And Wo-jen's foes, who felt this enthusiasm in some measure, had to reject his disavowal and claim legitimate Chinese standing for scientific practice. The question of its foreignness could not be waved away.[34]

Thus, the widespread use of the *t'i-yung* formula in China

as an intellectual cloak for industrialization suggests that the ground had not been prepared within, in Chinese social history, for industrialization's acceptance as a value. This lack of preparation, and the social factors behind it, are the reasons for failure of material 'self-strengthening' in nineteenth-century China. Chinese officials, *t'i-yung* enthusiasts as well as sceptical conservatives, made a shambles of their modernizing efforts, by and large, even in their primary field of military power, as the Chinese fiasco in the war with Japan, 1894–5, attested.

And so *t'i-yung* was a fallacy in a twofold sense. The halting persistence of Chinese *t'i* inhibited the Chinese acceptance of *yung*, which was supposed to help the *t'i* to persist without a halt; and the grating injection of western *yung*, though it pointed to social chaos instead of to a smooth new industrial social order, doomed the indigenous social order which was the base of the Chinese *t'i*.[35] But it was not the fallacy in intellectual theory which made a mockery of social hopes; it was rather the Chinese social condition which required that some theory be devised, and which made it certain that the first one, at any rate, would promise an easy syncretism that could not be brought about.

5. REJECTION OF *T'I-YUNG* AND SEARCH FOR A NEW RATIONALIZATION: THE CLASSICAL SANCTION

Wo-jen, refusing to settle for a syncretism of Chinese ends and western means, tried to save Chinese tradition by staking everything on it. Anything, he felt, which westerners were presumptuous enough to offer and westernizers blind enough to accept as a complement to Chinese civilization had already been found wanting by that civilization; and, indeed, the latter could hardly expect to be unaffected in admitting scientific techniques, when it had taken its present spiritual form by frankly demeaning them.

Now, Wo-jen's devising of a Chinese precedent for modern western science is more familiar to us as a tactic of the opposite camp, the syncretists. No theme is more hackneyed in modern Chinese intellectual history than that of proud discovery of modern western values in pre-modern Chinese history. Chinese thinkers have found this by all odds the easiest way to acknowledge the prestige of certain western values, when they feel they must, without thereby casting reflections on Chinese history. Sun I-jang (1848–1908) for example, a traditionalist who nevertheless bowed to the persuasiveness of western science, believed, as Wo-jen did, that Mo-tzu's ideas were very close to modern conceptions of physics,[36] and Hsüeh Fu-ch'eng discoursed with pleasure on Chinese priority in astronomy, mathematics, and various inventions.[37]

When *t'i-yung* innovators resorted to this searching for precedent, they were less consistent in their reasoning than the Wo-jen school of obscurantists in two ways. First, in supporting their case for innovation by maintaining that western science was really Chinese anyway, they tripped themselves up; for their basic argument, of course, was that science, non-Chinese but manageable by Chinese, could be accepted by Chinese without embarrassment because it was merely utilitarian. And second, the miscellaneous character of the specimens which the precedent-seekers retrieved favoured the reactionaries rather than the progressives. If Chinese examples were a scattered lot, and found mainly in the odd by-ways of Chinese thought, this would be consistent with Wo-jen's assertion that they lacked value and were found out early. But when westernizers, on their side, were forced to scour Chinese history for their discoveries (some of which were obviously painfully worked-at), they had to explain away the difficulty of their search, while their opponents could rest their case on it. Why, one might ask (and nineteenth-century Chinese did so), if western ideas are commended to Chinese minds by their allegedly Chinese lineage, should this lineage be so hard to trace? If science was valuable, as the westernizers admitted, and if ancient China had known this value, as the westernizers tried to establish, then it was embarrassingly obvious that the Chinese critical faculty had become terribly dulled somewhere along the way. Why else would China in the nineteenth century have to make such a new beginning?

The *t'i-yung* rationalizers, if they diluted their reasoning with appeals to precedent, could never answer that question. And on their own proper ground, they had less feeling than the reactionaries for the ominous potentialities of western methods imported solely 'for use'. Nevertheless, although the reactionaries might well plume themselves for sensing the logical inadequacies of that particular rationalization for innovation, their conclusion—that the innovation must be stopped, rather than the rationalization changed—was unsound. For they were obscurantist in failing to realize that innovation was inevitable, and that some rationalization, logical or not, was a psychological necessity. This may not have been crystal-clear in the eighteen-sixties, when stand-patters like Wo-jen were harrying 'self-strengtheners' like Tseng Kuo-fan, whose premises Chang Chih-tung was later to systematize. But by the eighteen-nineties, after years of bitter lessons, it was hard to deny that drastic changes, under foreign auspices if not Chinese, were on the way for China.

Among those who saw this clearly were the late nineteenth-century reformers of the *chin-wen* ('modern text') school of K'ang Yu-wei (1858–1927), who undertook to attain the goal of the *t'i-yung* school—westernization with honour—while avoiding the basic fallacy in the *t'i-yung* formula. The *chin-wen* school made no attempt to separate *t'i* from *yung* (and thereby doom China to the drain of Chinese *t'i* into western *yung*) but tried, rather, to link *t'i* and *yung* in the Chinese learning. The reformers would not leave the Chinese learning alone as *t'i*, with nothing of *yung* about it, and thereby condemn it; they would rather reinvigorate it, making the values of the modern West not a complement to the Chinese tradition but an integral part of it. In short, K'ang Yu-wei would keep western values (which Wo-jen would not do), but would find them *inside* Confucianism (which Chang Chih-tung would not do).

Instead of saying, like the obscurantists, that Chinese tradition should dispense with western values, or saying, like the *t'i-yung* school, that Chinese tradition should be supplemented with western values, the *chin-wen* school said that

Chinese tradition should possess western values. And it does possess them, said the *chin-wen* reformers, as the Chinese would realize if they only went back to their *authentic* Confucianism, which had long and sadly been under eclipse.

CHAPTER V

The Chin-Wen *School* and the Classical Sanction[1]

1. NEW VALUES INJECTED INTO CHINESE HISTORY: K'ANG YU-WEI

ALTHOUGH K'ang's reformers believed as little as the obscurantists that a Sino-western civilization would be cleanly partitioned between Chinese essence and western utility, they shared with the official westernizers of the *t'i-yung* school a willingness to proceed towards some such civilization. Indeed, they improved on that willingness. On the spectrum of attitudes toward westernization in nineteenth-century China, *chin-wen* stood as a mean not between implacable anti-westernizers and *t'i-yung* Confucian officialdom, but between the latter and the Protestant missions.[2]

The officials saw themselves as padding their civilization, a pearl of great price, with useful western ideas. China was still alone, they felt, in possessing intrinsic value. The missionaries, however, while perfectly ready to spread useful ideas, were far from ready to accept these Chinese strictures on the culture of the West as a whole. Religious missionaries, after all, could hardly agree that the West was simply materialistic, that practical techniques were the only respectable products of western history. If Confucian officials disparaged western values in the non-material sphere, Christian educators returned the compliment. Not only science, they insisted, but western political and ethical values must come into China and displace their Chinese counterparts.

Between these two groups, there stood the reformers. Before their brief moment of political influence in the summer of 1898, when they prepared decrees for the Emperor to issue (and the Empress-dowager soon to rescind), they conducted school and study-projects neither official nor Christian, though some aid came to them from both those quarters.[3] The reformers disparaged neither the western spirit nor the Chinese spirit, but prized them both and tried to believe them identical. Intellectually alienated from much of what passed for Chinese ideals, yet invincibly Chinese themselves, they strained to establish that mind and heart, in spite of appearances, had not been divided in China by the meeting of East and West.

The reformers, it must be apparent, had more disaffection to explain away than had the liberal, *t'i-yung* officials. The latter, in their confidence of the value and staying-power of the 'essentials' of Chinese civilization, were only a shade less complacent than the outright reactionaries. Old school modernizers felt simply that China was weak; and the weakness was only relative to an evil western strength. But once they had taken 'self-strengthening' to be a Chinese ideal, properly Chinese because supposedly harmless to the Chinese essence, the essence itself became subject to criticism if it seemed to inhibit the programme designed to protect it. And so a younger generation, no more anxious than their elders to break the tie of history, but even more sorely troubled by the gathering wave of disasters, diplomatic and military, which China suffered in the later nineteenth century, came to a paradoxical conclusion: to preserve the Chinese spirit, they must change the spirit as well as the tools of their Chinese civilization. Even before the *chin-wen* school became influential, this necessity had come to be dimly seen. As early as 1878, Kuo Sung-tao (1818–91), the first Chinese minister to England, had observed that overseas students from Japan seemed to be emphasizing political over scientific studies; and he fluttered the ranks of his staid official contemporaries by suggesting that there was more to *yung* than ships and soldiers, and that self-strengthening might have to apply to the Chinese polity (which was presumably an expression of the Chinese spirit) as well as to the world of base material techniques.[4]

The only way in which the reformers could reconcile their traditionalism with their condemnation of the Chinese way of life was to strip from the latter its cloak of tradition. China was not only somehow weak, they felt, but somehow wrong. To escape the consequences of this admission, they tried to show that it was not the genuine principles of Chinese culture which were wrong. These had been perverted, distorted, or suppressed. And if these true principles were asserted again, China could have what the West had, and still be true to itself. The values which the missionaries saw as the issue of European progress and Christian faith, K'ang Yu-wei would make Chinese.

All Chinese traditionalists, whatever their opinions on westernization, had to agree that Confucius was the sage of Chinese culture, and Confucianism its very essence. But if the tables could be turned on the self-deceptive, ostensibly Confucian despisers of the West, and contemporary Chinese culture be described as un-Confucian, then innovations in a wholesale measure, by no means simply in the material sphere, might not discredit the Chinese essence but make for its rediscovery. Accordingly, when K'ang recommended sweeping changes in Chinese society, he presented his views in three great works of Confucian exegesis. In the *Hsin-hsüeh wei-ching k'ao* (On the false classics of the Hsin learning), he challenged the authenticity of certain texts of the Confucian canon (especially the *Tso-chuan*), texts which he wished to see superseded by others more 'exploitable' (especially the *Kung-yang chuan*, one of two long-overshadowed alternatives to the *Tso-chuan* as the key to the meaning of the *Ch'un-ch'iu*, the 'Spring and Autumn Annals'). In the *K'ung-tzu kai-chih k'ao* (On Confucius as a reformer), he drew on his revised Confucian canon to interpret Confucius as a progressive, not a conservative, in his own day. And in the *Ta-t'ung shu* (Book of the great harmony), he made Confucius the prophet of progress to a utopian Confucian future, towards which the West, with its modern values, was also on its way. K'ang set a course for Chinese history in the stream of western optimism, and he called it a Chinese stream. When K'ang, building on the foundation of the 'Han learning' of the seventeenth and eighteenth centuries, seemed to discredit the *kuwen* ('ancient text') classics of the orthodox Confucian canon, among which the *Tso-chuan* was included, as forgeries by Liu Hsin (d. 23 B.C.), and when he heavily over-interpreted the early Han *chin-wen* ('modern text') classics like the *Kung-yang chuan* ('*Kung-yang* school' and '*Chin-wen* school' were familiarly interchangeable tags) which he believed he had rehabilitated, all the impressive western values fell into their Chinese places.[5] And science, the twin of progress, was a special favourite which would make the Gobi a part of China, the mountain-top a city, and banish the pains of illness and of toil.[6] Here was no foreign-spawned, patronizingly accepted *yung*, but the life's-blood of a professedly Confucian system.

2. PASSING OF THE *CHIN-WEN* SANCTION

Another eclectic utopian, inspired by the visions of K'ang Yu-wei, was T'an Ssu-t'ung, one of the 'six martyrs' to the reform movement who died in September, 1898, after the 'hundred days of reform'. T'an attempted to syncretize Christianity, the Buddhism of the *Hua-yen* (Lotus) Sutra, and *chin-wen* Confucianism. If man approached social questions with Christian love—in its Chinese form *jen-hsin*, benevolence—then the 'great peace' envisaged in the *chin-wen* school's favourite classic text, the *Kung-yang chuan*, would come into being, with freedom and equality, no differentiation between peoples, and no separation of nations from one another.[7] Like K'ang, T'an leaned a bit to the Chinese side in his universalism, and in the *Jen-hsüeh* (Study of benevolence), T'an's major work, he saw an all-encompassing Buddhism leading the way to unification of the world's religions, and the ancient *ching-t'ien* or 'well-field' idea doing the same for the world's polities, and the non-phonetic Chinese script, which could be all sounds to all men, making for a single world of learning.[8]

In this work, T'an set up a striking parallel between western and Chinese histories. The Papacy killed Christianity in the West, he said, and Luther revived it. Confucianism, done to death in China by the false scholarship of authoritarians, needed a Luther, too.[9] This suggestion that the Chinese reformers had had their western counterparts recurred frequently in reformist writings, and Liang Chi'-ch'ao, in his biographical tribute to K'ang written in 1901, expressed it with simple clarity: 'My teacher is the Martin Luther of Confucianism.' [10]

But the invocation of K'ang as the Chinese Luther was an ambiguous argument, which the *chin-wen* Confucian reformers pointed first at their conservative opponents, and then turned in on themselves. On the one hand, it supported metaphorically the essential position of the *chin-wen* school; for, as Luther claimed to be only restoring the pure Christianity of the Gospels and the Fathers, which had long been distorted by its self-styled representatives, so K'ang could maintain that he, also, had cut through the fog of centuries and restored the doctrine of the real Confucius of the earliest days. And if K'ang's Confucius, the prophet of progess, was the genuine article, then the fruits of progress, which had seemed to be solely western fruits, could spring from the roots of Chinese tradition.

But, on the other hand, the K'ang-Luther analogy could suggest the equivalence of China to Europe in quite a different manner. Instead of forcing the Chinese to contemplate western success, and to find its principle, through tortuous reasoning, in an 'authentic' Chinese past, it could lead him to dwell on western failure, the age of darkness before Luther came, and to feel that China, not unrespectably, develops in parallel fashion. In other words, there need be less emphasis on Chinese deviation from the right way and more on the Chinese advance towards it, an advance which Europeans, with their own dark ages, had been forced to make painfully, too. And K'ang could be a Chinese Luther, not as a rediscoverer of an ancient truth, but as a hero of freedom of thought, who breaks the grip of a smothering, mindless orthodoxy.[11]

This analogy of stages of progress remained, when the

classical sanction lost its force, to cover a Chinese sacrifice of traditional Chinese values. If the West had once been benighted like China, and 'Reformation' and 'Renaissance' were all that were asked of China, then there was an implication of parallel histories and of China redeemed from the tense conflict of special Chinese attachments and the force of generally compelling ideas. Neither intellectually stubborn, out of concern for the dignity of Chinese history, nor flatly submissive to Europe, China could grow into modern times with self-respect. The idea of progress was both a break with conventional Confucian conceptions and a means of explaining the break away.

T'an died before the doctrine of social progress—with Confucian orders to that effect no longer being relevant—was clearly extracted from the *chin-wen* reasoning. And K'ang, as long as he lived, never lost his *chin-wen* convictions: that the stages of progress were Confucian stages, and that the values of progress, modern values, were really values because the sage had once conceived them. But with Liang we see Confucianism trailing off to its twentieth-century ruin; for he comes to accept the second meaning of the K'ang-and-Luther analogy, and insists that what China needs, and can have with no indignity, is *not* a commitment to a pure Confucianism, but a break with it.[12]

Historical evolution, in the basic principle of the *chin-wen* Confucianists, was a universal progress from the 'age of chaos' (as Confucius called it) to the 'great peace' or the 'great harmony'. Confucius, it seemed, had licensed China to listen to new ideas. But the new ideas were so many, and so clearly subversive of the stable Confucian society, that it soon was merely fanciful for moderns to claim the Confucian imprimatur.

And so the classical sanction seemed only for a moment to deny the conflict between home and the world in modern China. But it gave a new direction to the Chinese search for a formula which might succeed. Since Confucianism could neither exclude nor absorb western ideas, since neither *t'i-yung* nor *chin-wen* could really save the Chinese *t'i*, then Chinese thinkers must cease to feel that equivalence with the

West was staked on it. And a new possible defence for China, a new sanction for innovation, could be salvaged from the *chin-wen* doctrine. For if evolution is the way of the world, as the *chin-wen* school had taught, an ancient *t'i* is properly superseded. Men may turn, if they lose the heart to compare the values of Europe and China, to comparing their histories, and see a morphological analogy between the life of China and the life of the West. These may seem to evolve with similar sequences, as the dismal stages of their pasts are succeeded by stages to a brighter future, as their bondage to intellectual orthodoxies gives way to intellectual freedom.

CHAPTER VI

The Modern Ku-wen Opposition, Reactionary and Revolutionary, to Chin-wen Reformism

I. THE REACTIONARY *KU-WEN* ATTACK

THE *chin-wen* school, as its name indicates, was not eclectic in the field of Chinese choices. Though even more aware of western incursions than Tseng Kuo-fan had been, the reformers failed to respond as he did, and, far from burying an ancient domestic intellectual conflict, they revived it. Han dynasty scholarship had finally accepted the so-called *ku-wen* Classics as the really authentic texts, and the rival *chin-wen*, in the third century A.D., went into eclipse. The Han Learning of the early Ch'ing, to a large extent, reversed this judgment, and K'ang Yu-wei, for his generation, kindled the conflict anew.

Yet, K'ang's truculence was not inconsistent with the peaceable eclecticism of Tseng Kuo-fan. For Tseng saw the West as a common rival of all the Chinese schools, and meant to distinguish the West from China as matter is distinguished from spirit. But K'ang had no hopes of separation, and preferred to see peace between civilizations, with the West and China sharing common values. With peace abroad, a battle at home was possible. And for a semblance of peace abroad, a battle at home was necessary. Orthodox Confucianism of the *ku-wen* school could never appear to shelter western values.

It was the need to accommodate western values, then, which impelled the reformers to revive the *chin-wen* scholarship. Since that was the case, since the reformers' scholarship was hardly 'pure', it was impervious to attack by the pure scholarship of *ku-wen* conservatives. When the classical sanction faded, when Chinese rebels ceased protesting that Confucius was their master, it was not the *ku-wen* scholars who effected that development. For the issues now were not the same as in the *ku-wen–chin-wen* conflicts of earlier centuries. Social facts, not textual critics, were the damaging antagonists of the modern *chin-wen* school.

The serious question for these latter-day *chin-wen* scholars was whether their doctrine was really compatible with western experience. They had seized on the *chin-wen* scholarship not as simple Confucianists, who wanted only to know the truth about what their sage had said; they had acted rather as westernizers, for whom the *chin-wen* doctrine *had* to be true if they were to be Confucianists at all. Western values possessed the younger minds, and the harder they found it to cram their new knowledge into K'ang's Confucianism, the less they cared about any Confucius, either the one who spoke through the *ku-wen* texts or the one who spoke through the *chin-wen*.

Thus, when the reactionary *ku-wen* traditionalists attacked the reformers on textual grounds, they were engaging in an irrelevant battle. 'Irrelevant' does not mean unsound. On textual issues, for assertions such as these—that Confucius composed the Six Classics, that Liu Hsin forged the *Tso-chuan*—the *chin-wen* scholarship was certainly open to grave indictment.[1] But K'ang's mistakes were more important than other men's corrections, and the indictment had no significance for future Chinese history. For the *ku-wen* critics never answered the real question which the *chin-wen* school was asking: not, 'What does Confucius say?' but, 'How can we make ourselves believe that Confucius said what we accept *on other authority?*'

Therefore, although the lines were drawn as at earlier

times, there was an air of unreality about the textual conflict. For *chin-wen* Confucianism was a different idea before and after the western invasion of China. And a hostile *ku-wen* argument, which might have been telling against an eighteenth-century *chin-wen* scholar of the Han Learning, was an answer later to a dead question. The Confucian canon was simply not the issue. Liang Ch'i-ch'ao attested to this in 1902, when he abruptly ceased, in his reformist writings, to exhort his readers to care about the Classics.[2] And the keener members of the *ku-wen* camp realized this as well. Yeh Te-hui (1864–1927), brushing past the question of what Confucius said, seized quite certainly on what K'ang meant, though K'ang himself was always in the dark:

> K'ang Yu-wei, secretly proposing to be a 'reforming Luther' in his own life, desired to clear away the Six Classics, and composed first the *Wei-ching k'ao*; and he desired to stir up the imperial regime, and went on to compose the *Kai-chih k'ao*.[3]

2. THE REVOLUTIONARY *KU-WEN* ATTACK

The *chin-wen* school was reformist in political action, never anti-dynastic, and it blamed Chinese for distortion of the genuine Chinese tradition. But other dissidents in the last years of the empire were revolutionaries. For them, the Manchu usurpers of Chinese power were fair game, in cultural attacks as well as political. If it had to be acknowledged that the contemporary West, intellectually and politically, was far in advance of China, the blame could be heaped on the Manchus, and the Chinese spared.[4]

Therefore, anti-Manchu revolutionary nationalists had no need to arraign Confucian 'heretics' for Chinese ills and every reason to consider that K'ang's diagnosis was counter-revolutionary. In his *Po K'ung-chiao i* (Refutation of the 'Confucian Religion'), Chang Ping-lin (1868–1936), a virulently anti-Manchu revolutionary, skilfully defended the *ku-wen* Classics against the *chin-wen* textual criticism.[5]

Yet, though *ku-wen* scholarship may seem proper in revolutionary circles, as a symbol of the denial of reformism, the great majority of *ku-wen* scholars were consistent conservatives, whose loyalty to the orthodox *ku-wen* canon was an affirmation of the *status quo*; and there was a peculiar complexity about Chang Ping-lin's position. For he came by his *ku-wen* opinions honestly, as a cultural conservative himself, defending the old literary style and the traditional materials of the old imperial examinations.[6] He was an important contributor to the Shanghai monthly *Kuo-sui hsüeh-pao* (1904–11), which defended the Chinese cultural heritage against the 'European wind and American rain', the storm of western ideas, and inveighed against 'ignorant, illiterate self-styled scholars' who puffed up the West and contemned China.[7] He did not derive his conservative views in classical scholarship from his revolutionary political views. He seems, rather, to have derived the latter from his concern to save the 'Chinese essence'. And in this, he parted company with most of his fellow traditionalists.

He saw more clearly than they that change must come to the Chinese scene; and if traditionalism was not to be sentimentality alone, and intellectually indefensible, he must hold, he knew, a rational theory which would keep the Chinese past from seeming discredited by the change. But he was wrong to think that Manchu-baiting was a serviceable theory in the twentieth century. It could seem to protect the reputation of traditional Chinese culture, but it would help to end its existence.

For the institution of the monarchy, the ultimate target of the anti-Manchu revolutionary movement, was as traditionally Chinese as Confucianism itself. The *chin-wen* school, it is true, in attacking the accepted Confucian canon, was culturally subversive, opening the way for cultural drift; when the Classics could be doubted, anything could be doubted. But it was hardly striking a blow for tradition to reject the *chin-wen* heresy and to spare the Classics by condemning the throne. When the imperial system could be doubted, anything could be doubted. Who could be sure of any rule, when almost the oldest rule of all was broken?

My older uncle was drunk, and angry about the revolution most of the time. . . . He would stare at the relatives, and say ironically: 'But, excuse me, we have the revolution.

What difference does it make who is the oldest in the family? What can I have to do with the marriage of my brother, Tan Tsi-pu?' [8]

3. THE CLASSICS AND HISTORY

In the last analysis, did Chang Ping-lin even spare the Classics? He felt that he did, of course, as he reaffirmed the authenticity of the *ku-wen*, orthodox canon and proclaimed his respect for the Han scholar, Liu Hsin, whom K'ang Yu-wei and his *chin-wen* followers had vilified as the arch-forger.[9] The *ku-wen* Classics, Chang loyally insisted, were *history*, not fiction, and *history*, not elliptical, mystical prophecy —as the Classics became in the rival interpretation. The *Kung-yang chuan*, the central text for the *chin-wen* school, which chose it in preference to the *Tso-chuan*, was philosophically exegetical in character and bore little obvious relation to any course of events; but the *Tso-chuan* was formally an historical narrative.[10]

'The Classics are all abstract words and not real history', said Liao P'ing (1852–1932), the last and perhaps most fanciful of the *chin-wen* Confucianists, who revered Confucius as a visionary, not as a scrupulous traditionalist.[11] Liao P'ing considered the Classics so far from history that he treated the *Ch'un-ch'iu* not at all as it appeared, a chronicle of the ancient state of Lu, but as a vision of the modern world, with Cheng standing for China, Ch'in for England, Lu for Japan, and Duke Ai of Lu for the Emperor Meiji.[12] But, 'The Six Classics are all history', Chang countered,[13] deploring (as orthodox scholars had done since later Han times) *chin-wen* invocation of Han apocrypha, the esoteric *wei-shu*, as keys to the Classics' alleged character of prophetic revelation.[14] He scouted the *chin-wen* claim that Confucius composed (not transmitted) the original Classics, and even the *Ch'un-ch'iu*, he said, the 'Spring and Autumn Annals', the one Classic which all Confucianists had always ascribed to Confucius himself, was not constructed by Confucius *de novo* but based on the records of Tso Ch'iu-ming, the historian of Lu.[15]

'*Liu ching chieh shih*', 'The Six Classics are all history.' . . .
A traditionalist in so many things, Chang was traditional in
his choice of words: this phrase was not his own. And yet,
however little he willed it, when Chang Ping-lin repeated
these words of Chang Hsüeh-ch'eng (1738–1801),[16] he made
them part of the history of the dissipation of Confucianism.
For *ching* and *shih*, the Classics and history, had a delicately
adjusted relationship in traditional Chinese thought, and
what one said about them in earlier times, even if later it
was literally repeated, had a different ring in the different
modern context.

The study of history had been the most characteristic
Confucian intellectual activity. 'Among all branches of
scholarly investigation, only in history is China developed
to the utmost; among all countries of the world, only in
China is history developed to the utmost'—thus Liang Ch'i-
ch'ao, with some rhetorical licence, has emphasized the
paramount importance of historical thinking in Chinese culture.[17] But this thinking was concerned typically not with
process but with permanence, with the illustration of the
fixed ideals of the Confucian moral universe. Su Hsün (1009–
66), father of the famous poet, painter, and statesman, Su
Shih (1036–1101), expressed it very well. How do *shih* and
ching, he asked, history and the Classics, differ?

Ching stresses the underlying Way and fixed principles
(*tao* and *fa*); *shih*, facts and words. Without assimilating history to itself (*te shih*), the classical canon cannot make evident its [standards of] praise or blame; without assimilating
the Classics to itself, history cannot decide its course of appreciation and disparagement. A Classic is not a matter-of-fact
record of a particular age, and history is not a changeless
design for all generations. Different in essence, they are
actually supplementary in function.[18]

History, then, by this reckoning, is a record from which a
universal, timeless, abstract morality is distilled from particular, temporal, material events. The classical canon is the
respository of those abstract principles which make such a
reading of history possible. Su Hsün, whose treatise on this

subject was in the form of inquiry into the nature of history, obviously had to call *shih* and *ching* correlative, not identical: not all histories were Classics. But if the nature of the Classics had been his point of departure, as it was later for Chang Hsüeh-ch'eng in discussing this relationship, Su Hsün would have found 'The Six Classics are all history' an admissible statement. For he, no less than Chang Hsüeh-ch'eng, saw the Classics as eternal principles *made manifest*, in action (history), not couched in 'empty words'. The idea of *shih* was indispensable to the idea of *ching*; and the idea of *ching*, as the ancient fountain-head of critical judgment—and not, therefore, subject to its appraisal—was indispensable to Confucian intellectual life. Before the twentieth century, to call the Classics history was never construed as a limitation on the Classics, but as philosophical description.

History, then, in the pre-western Confucian context, was regarded without ambiguity; it was the form in which absolute wisdom was cast, and not yet the clothing of relativism. Accordingly, Chang Hsüeh-ch'eng, in the eighteenth century, was not reducing the Classics to 'historical significance' (in the modern relativist terminology) when he emphasized their historical character, but was defining the way in which eternal truth was conveyed. The *tao* cannot be abstracted from its material realization, he said, and Confucius could not state in words the '*tao* of the ancient kings' but could only illustrate it through their history and their documents.[19] The Classics were made of historical material, but the Classics themselves were not simply materials for the history of an age; they were texts for the ages.[20]

In a day when that conviction of the permanent significance of the Classics went virtually unchallenged in Chinese intellectual circles (whatever the quarrels about exegesis), the problem of Classics and history could be taken up without calling into question the canonical character of Classics. Chang Hsüeh-ch'eng affirmed it; and Kung Tzu-chen (1792–1841), who was attracted to *chin-wen* opinions and appropriately, therefore, attacked Chang for his 'Six Classics are all history' pronouncements,[21] affirmed it, too. But when K'ang Yu-wei took up the *chin-wen* thesis and freighted it with western values, which then slipped out of their Confucian casing and openly won adherents on their own, the old counter-cry, that the Classics were history, was worse than ineffectual in restoring classical loyalties—it compounded the damage *chin-wen* claims had done them. For, once there was a readiness to listen to foreign voices, without concern for their qualifications by any Confucian standards, the Classics-history equation assumed an ominous ambiguity. If the Classics were not supreme arbiters in modern times, they were not for the ages; and to say, then, that the Classics were history was not to fix their character in eternity, since their title to eternity was spurious. It was, instead, to pin the Classics to the age of their composition, that age alone, and to read them rather as documentation of a stage of a history in process of change, than as final truths which were anciently established and immanent in events and which thereby divested the idea of history of the very connotation of process.

Chang Ping-lin in his later years bitterly conceded that the Classics had been reduced from persistent guide to historical source, that they could no longer be taken to dominate men throughout time, but had to submit instead to the scrutiny of men who allowed them only one time in history. The modern *chin-wen* scholarship, he said, though dying itself in the republican era, had been the fatal source of a still increasing corruption. The veracity of the ancient records had been impugned, such classical figures as Yao, Shun, and Yü were all supposed to have been invented by Confucian scholars, and the Chinese people were forgetting their origins.[22]

Thus Chang held that the great heresy was the denial, by *chin-wen* Confucianists and their inevitable successors, the emancipated non-Confucianists, that the Classics told historical truths; and he, still proclaiming that the Six Classics were all history, was the lonely defender of the faith. In thinking this, he separated himself a bit too clearly from the modern Confucian debacle. For Ku Chieh-kang (b. 1893), a young scholar in the nineteen-twenties who exemplified the heresy, set himself to demonstrate that the Classics, to a large extent, had been contrived by controversialists to express their own ideas, religious and political, and not to render honestly the actual history of ancient China;[23] and Ku confessed a debt to Chang Ping-lin. True, he confessed a debt to K'ang Yu-wei as well.[24] Thus Chang, who had meant to annihilate K'ang, was harried into his company. Their classical theories must have been given a new construction indeed.

Chang Ping-lin and K'ang Yu-wei, the *ku-wen* and *chin-wen* Confucian champions, had milled around an old field—and both had lost the war. Their positive contentions went unheeded; what the post-Confucianists found in both was a negative value. Ku Chieh-kang was inspired by K'ang to see in the classical canon a tendentious myth-making spirit, where an objective historical spirit had been imagined. But, unlike K'ang and the *chin-wen* school, Ku did not propose to criticize 'false Classics' in order to peel down to 'true Classics' of timeless transcendent importance. K'ang's *chin-wen* predecessor, Kung Tzu-chen, who 'read the Classics for their "great principle"', had protested that *ch'uan-ch'i*, tales of fiction, ought not to be called *ching*, Classics;[25] and while Ku Chieh-kang could appreciate this eye for forgeries, he rejected the implication that somewhere underneath lay an irreducible stratum of supra-historical truth.[26] That is where Chang Ping-lin came in to contribute to Ku's unorthodox detachment. For, while K'ang was right, thought Ku, in pointing out that the accepted Classics, by and large, were doubtful history, Chang was right in suggesting, nevertheless, that the Classics *were* history of a sort, rich though sometimes recalcitrant sources of real data about ancient China, not prophetic texts of a binding religious nature. The *ku-wen* school had won a faded laurel—the Classics were all history, all right—but (to put it another way) the Classics were not classics any more.

CHAPTER VII

The Role of Nationalism in the Disowning of the Past

I. THE ATTACK ON THE MANCHUS

WHEN nationalism swept the Chinese student world, in the first years of the twentieth century, inevitably the Manchus felt the blast of hatred. They were such obvious targets, and on two counts—as usurpers of the Chinese power, and as rulers of China in a bleak age of national degradation. But anti-Manchu feeling was only an effect of nationalism, only a manifestation, not its cause or its core.

The cause of Chinese nationalism, and the core of its content, was intellectual alienation from traditional Chinese culture.[1] Nationalism, as a meaningful concept on the Chinese scene, had not only a positive but a negative significance; in accepting the nation as the proper object of Chinese loyalty, the nationalist rejected the historic alternative, the 'culturalistic' reverence for the 'Chinese way of life', above and beyond all other loyalties. Theoretically, nationalists were free to make any intellectual choice, however unorthodox in terms of Chinese culture, if only it were nationally useful. Chinese civilization lags extraordinarily, European civilization must be adopted—such was the burden of a memorial, in 1894, to the powerful senior official, Li Hung-chang, from the *Hsing Chung hui*, the first political society of the nationalist, Sun Yat-sen.[2]

By the twentieth century, the Manchus were almost

impervious to attack on a culturalistic basis, for they had become the champions of the Chinese way of life. In the seventeenth century they may have seemed to pose a cultural threat to China (though in fact, even by the time of the conquest, in 1644, their Chinese education was far advanced). But as time passed, western culture became the only dangerous alternative. What survived of Manchu cultural peculiarities was mainly contrived, prescribed to keep the Manchus alive and distinct enough to enjoy the power which their cultural deference in larger matters had helped to preserve for them;[3] as long as the Manchus were anti-western Chinese culturalists could rally around the Ch'ing. And where their predecessors had flaunted the slogan, '*Fu Ming, mieh Ch'ing*' (uphold the Ming, destroy the Ch'ing), the 'Boxers' of 1900, xenophobic and culturalistic, rose to the cry, '*Fu Ch'ing, mieh yang*' (uphold the Ch'ing, destroy the foreigner).[4]

Thus, the Manchu cause and the traditional cause had become the same. But there was a brand of Chinese traditionalists, not sublimely confident, like the Boxers, but defeatist, like Chang Ping-lin, who chose to believe that the Ch'ing had thwarted the Chinese genius. It was a straw to clutch at, something to keep them from sweeping along to either cold iconoclasm or arid traditionalism. And so, as a gesture of respect for Chinese culture, they called themselves nationalists, and they re-issued, as supposedly nationalistic fare, seventeenth-century, long-outmoded culturalistic invectives against the Manchus.[5]

Chang condemned K'ang Yu-wei's invocation of a *Shih-chi* passage to indicate the allegedly common ancestry of the Chinese and the ancient Hsiung-nu (by extension, 'men of the north', Manchus). Chang accepted neither the Manchu —Hsiung-nu identification nor the Hsiung-nu—Chinese. And he rejected K'ang's Ch'ing—Ch'u analogy, whereby Ming-period Manchus and *Ch'un-ch'iu* people of Ch'u— racially akin to the Chinese, supposedly, but still culturally barbarian—were completely sinified in Ch'ing times and Han times, respectively. K'ang had hoped to score a point here, since the very founder of the Han dynasty, that first great imperial line which gave its name to the Chinese people for all subsequent generations, was a man of Ch'u. But Chang, on the one hand, was impossible to persuade that Han emperors and Ch'ing emperors had the same relation to the Chinese people they came to rule; and, on the other hand, he was unwilling to accept the Han—even if this imperial parallel could have been constructed—as *bona fide* patrons of the genuine Chinese spirit. He tried to give a racist interpretation of early Confucianism and claimed (for all the world like his *chin-wen* opponents, pushing another thesis) that China had lost *true* comprehension of the *Ch'un-ch'iu* in the Han period, when the racially exclusive national idea was filtered out of Confucianism, and foreigners like the future Manchus were authorized to sun themselves in the light of mistaken Confucian universality.[6]

Yet, right or wrong, the version of Confucius which had really mattered to China throughout her imperial history was a Confucius who distinguished between barbarism and barbarians; the former was irredeemably rejected, the latter —because men were educable—it was possible to redeem. Chang's racist attack on the Ch'ing dynasty of Manchus, who had long ago made the grade as a Chinese dynasty by the traditional cultural, if not the revolutionary national criterion of Chinese-ness, was no vindication of the Chinese past, but repudiation.

Rigorous nationalists like Liang Ch'i-ch'ao, who since 1902 had been proclaiming the need for a 'new people', opposed the specious nationalism of the easy anti-Manchus, for the latter seemed to proclaim (or their conclusions tended to encourage the belief) that the old people was good enough, if only the Manchu incubus could be taken off its neck. Therefore, although the ruin of the Manchus was certain if nationalism spread, as Liang intended it should, he refused to accept his own anti-Manchu conclusions, because the 'official', republican anti-Manchu appeared to reject his premises. Nevertheless, the new state, the republic of 1912, belongs in the history of the new people. Chang Ping-lin was iconoclastic and Liang was revolutionary, each in spite of himself.

2. CULTURALISM AND NATIONALISM AS COMPETITORS FOR LOYALTY

When nationalism began to flourish in Chinese intellectual circles in the earliest years of the twentieth century, it represented a bold attempt to sweep away the cant which had become all too obvious in the usual apologia for Chinese tradition. The dilemma posed by intellectual alienation from tradition and emotional tie to it still existed. But the nationalist dispensed with the effort to end the dilemma by somehow justifying Chinese tradition. He still hoped to establish the cultural equivalence of China with the West; but his ingenious way of accomplishing this was to deny that culture was the proper unit of comparison.

That unit was the nation. When the Confucian efforts of the *chin-wen* school subsided, and yielded the figure of 'parallel histories' for the syncretist to work with, the Chinese nation became his first concern. The ideas of progress and freedom of thought were his new possessions, but these, by themselves, were useless to guide him in intellectual choice. 'Progress to what, thought about what?' he must ask, before tampering with the Chinese tradition. To what end should change take place?

The end of change, he must answer, is the strengthening of the nation. For if the nation, not the culture, has the highest claim on the individual, then the abandonment of traditional values, if they seem to be indefensible, is a cheerful duty, not a painful wrench. And the laws of evolution, not Confucian now but social-Darwinist, exalt the nation as the highest unit in the struggle for existence, and proclaim that the past must die and should never be lamented.[7] The growing Chinese acceptance of the existence and authority of a Chinese nation worked a Nietzschean 'transvaluation of values' in Chinese culture.

We have seen that in the seventeenth century, Chinese had criticized the dominant metaphysics of the day without being philosophically revolutionary in their criticism. They had been critics also of the state of contemporary society, but here, too, as social critics, they were thoroughly Confucian: men had strayed from the fixed ideals of Chinese civilization. Their China was a world, a *t'ien-hsia*, in which traditional values claimed authority. But in the early twentieth century, anti-Confucian critics of the Chinese *status quo* traced disaster not to the flouting of fixed ideals but to blind and slavish respect for them, to the fixity itself; their China was a nation, a *kuo*, in which traditional values were impugned as tyranny.

This changing fortune of a civilization, this vast and perplexing history, was caught in miniature in the changing relation between the concept *t'ien-hsia* and the concept *kuo*. *T'ien-hsia* and *kuo* were time-honoured co-ordinates in Chinese political thinking. And co-ordinates they remained, while ever-increasingly heirs to Chinese history called its values into question.

T'ien-hsia signifies 'the (Chinese) Empire'—alternatively, 'the world'; as *t'ien-hsia*, China *is* the world. And *kuo* is a local political unit, a part of 'the Empire' in classical times, and in the modern world, 'the nation'. But the respective meanings of *t'ien-hsia* and *kuo* are not really revealed in these simple, self-sufficient English equivalents; for at either end of this history, the definition of either term implies a reference to the other, a comparison with the other. In the earlier time it was its contrast with *kuo*, the regime of power, which defined the *t'ien-hsia* as the regime of value. But the claims of value are absolute, and if their justice comes to be doubted, respect for these claims will seem the mark of servility, not civilization. It was its contrast, then, with *t'ien-hsia*—preconception, dictation—which defined the *kuo*, at the later date, as an area of untraditional free inquiry. Just as China persists but changes, the link between *t'ien-hsia* and *kuo* persists while something changes their connotations and the degree of esteem accorded to each.

What works these changes is something unchanging itself: the Chinese need of a China which no defeat may compromise. In the seventeenth century, the Manchus had conquered the Chinese political power, so China as *t'ien-hsia*, unimpeachable, civilization in the abstract, was the China which the vanquished exalted. But China came, in time, to face a new kind of conquest while still subject to the old. To many Chinese, by the turn of the nineteenth and twentieth centuries, China seemed to be losing her title to *t'ien-hsia*, her dignity as a culture. Abandon a hopeless claim, they urged, strengthen political power by changing cultural values, and from a Chinese defeat as *t'ien-hsia* snatch a victory as *kuo*.

Here is a brief excursus, then, into the traditional Chinese past of the subversive concept 'nation'.

i. The Tradition

The meaningless power of sheer egoism is braked by civilization, for every civilization has values, ends to be served. In traditional Chinese civilization the monarch, the *T'ien-tzu*, the Son of Heaven, had an end to serve, an ideal above him, and the anti-Manchu scholar, Huang Tsung-hsi, in his *Ming-i tai-fang lu* (1662), reminded him what it was:

At the beginning of life, each man acted for himself, each man planned for his own well-being. If there was public well-being in the empire (*t'ien-hsia*), he did not try to extend it; if there was public injury, he did not try to expunge it. The princely man emerged, who did not consider his own personal well-being to be the only well-being there was but endowed the empire with its well-being, who did not consider his own personal injury to be the only injury there was but set the empire free of its injury. . . .

Those who later became monarchs were not like that. They considered that the power of bringing well-being or injury to the empire issued entirely from them. They coolly accepted the idea that well-being in the empire devolved wholly upon them and injury in the empire devolved wholly upon others. They kept the men of the empire from venturing in their own interests, from venturing for their own well-being, and they considered their own aggrandizement to be success for the empire. At first there was a sense of shame, but at length there was equanimity, and they looked on the empire as a vast business enterprise to be handed down to their sons and grandsons to receive and enjoy unlimitedly. . . .

The ancients had held that the empire came first and the

monarch second. In general, a monarch's occupations throughout his lifetime were for the empire. Now, it was held that the monarch came first and the empire second. It was because of the monarch that nowhere in the empire was there peace. While he had not yet attained it (the empire), he scattered the sons and daughters of the empire, in order to further his own individual enterprises. He was never sorry, and said that naturally he had undertaken his projects for his sons and grandsons.

When he had already attained it, he clubbed and flayed the bones and marrow of the empire, and he scattered the sons and daughters of the empire, in order to provide for his own individual sensual pleasure. He deemed it natural, and said that this was the profit from his own business. If it was so, then he who encompassed the great injury of the empire was the monarch, and, were there no monarch, men all could attain their own private ends, men all could attain their own well-being. Alas, can this really be the way to establish a monarch?[8]

It could hardly be the way, not in a Confucian China; and Huang Tsung-hsi, with such searing phrases, hurls the imperative of morality at the ruler of *t'ien-hsia*, 'the empire', under-Heaven, the Chinese world. For the gauge of the *t'ien-hsia*'s peace or chaos is the joy or sorrow of its myriad people, not the rise or fall of its ruling house.[9]

Ku Yen-wu concurred in these views and published similar ones in 1670. But he sounded a more deeply philosophical note. For morality, in Ku's *Jih-chih lu*, is more than an attribute of the ideal ruler of the *t'ien-hsia*; it is the distinguishing mark, the *sine qua non*, of *t'ien-hsia* itself.

T'ien-hsia contrasts with *kuo* ('country', 'nation'). The latter connotes not only land and people but protection by military force. But *t'ien-hsia* is a conception of civilized society; it means far more than just a political unit held by *de facto* power. 'There being *t'ien-hsia*,' says Ku, 'it is desired to broaden the people's lives and to straighten the people's virtue.' [10]

There is destruction of *kuo* and destruction of *t'ien-hsia*. Between destruction of *kuo* and destruction of *t'ien-hsia* what distinction should be made? 'Change the surname, alter the style' (*i-hsing kai-hao*)—this is a description of the destruction of *kuo*. The widespread dominion of benevolence and righteousness (*jen* and *i*) decayed into the rule of beast-eat-man, men, leaders, eating each other—this is a description of the destruction of *t'ien-hsia*. . . .[11]

Culture and morality, then, the whole world of values, belong to *t'ien-hsia*. If men have a stake in *kuo* at all, it is only a political stake—'Those who defend the *kuo* are its monarch and its ministers; this is the design of the wealthy. . . .' But civilized man as man, by the very fibre of his human being, must be committed to *t'ien-hsia*—'but as for defending the *t'ien-hsia*, the mean common man shares responsibility'.[12] The civilization, not the nation, has a moral claim on man's allegiance.

This is good classical Chinese doctrine. A hundred generations have known, says Ku, that 'no one without benevolence has ever attained the *t'ien-hsia*'.[13] Mencius had said that first, and had said this before it: 'There have been men without benevolence who have attained a *kuo*.'[14] This, from Mencius —however much it might seem just a counsel of prudence, a warning to covetous rulers of *kuo*, ambitious of 'the empire', that tyranny would carry them only so far—could be more a statement of the ends of life than of the truths of political science. The implication was there, for later men to ponder, that men bent to power or men bent to standards. If they did the first, they were nondescripts living in a *kuo*; if they did the second, they were Chinese living in a Chinese way, in their *t'ien-hsia*, which was the world.

Ku Yen-wu understood this well when he echoed Mencius naturally, without acknowledgment, as he did in the phrase which has just been quoted, and when he wrote, himself, as follows:

When the superior man attains station, he desires to work out the *tao*, the Way; when the small man attains station, he desires to serve his own interests. The desire to work out the Way manifests itself in making *t'ien-hsia* of *kuo-chia*; the desire to serve one's own interest manifests itself in wounding men and destroying things.[15]

To '*t'ien-hsia* the *kuo-chia*', the passage says, to take a political power-unit and make it, with values, a civilization—or to take life, as the Confucianist wishes who knows that *t'ien-hsia* and China are one, and make it ideally Chinese.

Political China is *Chung-kuo*, the central *kuo*. But 'central in what?' is the classical question. And the traditional answer —whether the world was narrow, as in classical times, or vaguely wide, as in Ku's century—was *t'ien-hsia*, a world of standards, which the Chinese ideally upheld, to which barbarians ideally aspired. 'The ancient sons of heaven commonly lived in Chi-chou,' wrote Ku. 'Later men for this reason came to give Chi-chou the name of *Chung-kuo*.' And he quotes statements of the ancients that Chi-chou was central in the *t'ien-hsia*.[16] The world that was *t'ien-hsia* then, the total China of all the *kuo*, was *Chung-kuo* now in a larger world. And *t'ien-hsia* ideally still existed, the larger China of all that world, as long as the people of '*Chung-kuo*' deserved to be central, as faithful servants, not careless masters, of the ideals of civilization. Chinese in their *kuo* were barbarians among barbarians unless they took the yoke of an ideal way, the Chinese way, and set the styles for others. Then the world could be *t'ien-hsia*, not a congeries of *kuo*.

Huang Tsung-hsi and Ku Yen-wu could tell a Chinese emperor what he should do and a Chinese empire what it should be. The ideal was fixed, and Confucian reformism could go no farther than plead that it be adhered to. But the nineteenth century brought outside *kuo* forcefully into China, and some Chinese minds began to stir. Perhaps the Chinese empire should be something other than what traditional standards ordained. Perhaps new criteria had a higher claim, those of western success and Chinese necessity. Should not, perhaps, the vision of *t'ien-hsia* fade away, so that China might survive its fading traditional culture?

ii. The Transformation

In large part the intellectual history of modern China has been the process of making *kuo-chia* of *t'ien-hsia*. The idea of *t'ien-hsia* had indeed been identified with a Way, the

Confucian way, the major indigenous Chinese tradition, and when, for one reason and another, modern Chinese turned to foreign ways for China, the exaltation of nation over culture, of *kuo-chia* over *t'ien-hsia*, was one of their manoeuvres. Culture should be changed, they said, if the change would serve the nation. Such a criterion was intellectually and emotionally helpful. Using it, one could feel both justified in calling for a break with tradition and soothed while contemplating the tradition's decay.

And so Liang Ch'i-ch'ao, for one, in the early twentieth century, urged China to become new and to become a nation, to cease to be old and cease to pay homage exclusively to its culture. The literati had taken the culture as their preserve, and under their influence, said Liang, the Chinese had come to think of China as *t'ien-hsia*, the world, in which no other high culture existed, rather than as *kuo-chia*, a nation, which had a great deal to learn. Nationalism, patriotism, had been destroyed.[17] China, in short, must deem itself not a world but a unit in the world. Unless it chose to come down from its pedestal, its view of itself as *t'ien-hsia*, and to stand as a *kuo* among *kuo*, it would be smashed. And as a *kuo*, it had no standards thrust upon it. A given civilization adheres to certain values or it becomes something else; but a nation's choice is free, if the choice but help it live. Nationalism invades the Chinese scene as culturalism hopelessly gives way.

Thus, if *t'ien-hsia* meant fixed standards, a traditionally accepted ideal of civilization, as, from Mencius to Ku and beyond him, Confucianists had thought it did, then free choice and a pragmatic sanction, the denial of all that *t'ien-hsia* meant, came in with the *kuo* to which *t'ien-hsia* had always been in contrast. And that is how the old order changed, with an old cloak for the new content, the antiquity of the alternatives covering the newness of the choice. *T'ien-hsia* was challenged in the name of *kuo*, Chinese tradition was challenged; but the logic of the battle was a rigorous logic in traditional Chinese terms. For the old Confucianists and the new eclectics shared this one conviction—that culture stood with *t'ien-hsia*, and that culture changed in *kuo*.

3. THE REINTEGRATION OF TRADITION INTO NATIONALISM

When nationalism developed in China as the denial of culturalism, the latter changed in itself; for culturalism now, in its turn, had Chinese nationalism as something new to deny. Chinese culturalism had defined itself formerly as the alternative to foreign barbarism. But now, with the rise of nationalism, when the weight of intellectual opinion was making Chinese 'barbarism' the real alternative, a calculated intemperance seemed to replace the old complacency of spokesmen for tradition. 'Better to see the nation die than its way of life change,' said Hsü T'ung (1819–1900); and Ku Hung-ming (1857–1928), for whom, as for Hsü, the Boxers' practically ideal anti-foreignism in cultural matters outweighed their political hopelessness, protested that footbinding should be sacrosanct, as an important element in the Chinese spirit.[18] One can sense a note of defiance here, a willingness to shock, and a grim decision to stand on principle, though the principle be out of fashion.

Such men as these were quite correct in believing that nationalism and culturalism were irreconcilable, and that the rise of nationalism was somehow linked with the disintegration of Chinese civilization. But there is a complication in the picture.

We have ascribed to nationalism freedom to dispense with the cultural loyalties which are the sum and substance of culturalism. Nationalism thus becomes, it appears, the basis of a cool iconoclasm; without feeling tied by a special cord to earlier Chinese values, a restive modern Chinese generation can abide by what it conceives of as general standards, which lead it to western examples. For the traditional culture need not be protected. Its claims have been explained away. When nationalism follows culturalism, necessity, not precedent, has the right to govern choice.

Yet, if we examine the actual content of nationalistic expression in China, we see that this definition is too abstract.[19] An absolute breach between the *chiao* and the *min*, doctrine and people, 'essence' and nation, is not ruthlessly enforced. On the contrary, there are nationalists who insist on loyalty to the old. They prescribe fidelity to what history has established as Chinese. They will never admit that a Chinese who is careless of Chinese tradition can be a Chinese nationalist. Yen Fu (1853–1921), for example, objected to nationalistic opinion which damned the traditional family as a bad influence on Chinese society and as the nation's rival for loyalty. Yen declared flatly, in 1914, that love of country derived from familism (*chia-ting chü-i*), and that the latter's basic principle was *hsiao*, filial piety, one of the cardinal Confucian virtues and a witness to the abiding place of the old values in the national spirit.[20]

Traditionalism, then, retains a place in nationalism. But in that case, where is the nice distinction between Chinese nationalism and Chinese culturalism? When loyalty to the past is so clearly one of its features, can nationalism really contribute to a deliverance from the past? How do the following sentiments, from a Chinese Nationalist (Kuomintang) handbook of 1934 (a year when Confucian sacrifices were officially reinstated), clash with the culturalism of Chang Chih-tung?

A nation must always remain faithful to its own history and its own culture in order to maintain an independent existence on earth. For a people to keep faith with itself and progress courageously, it ought not to renounce its own old civilization lest it become like a river without a source or a tree without roots. While wishing to assimilate the new knowledge of western civilization, we ought to give it for a base the principles of Confucius. The whole people must learn the doctrine and conform to the thoughts of Confucius.[21]

That statement, with its apparent reaffirmation of the culturalistic *t'i-yung* philosophy, actually shows the difference between the *nationalism* which celebrates a traditional way of life and the *culturalism* which does the same. For Chang Chih-tung was an absolutist, not a relativist, in his convictions about Confucius as a base for western knowledge. He saw value, absolute value, in the Chinese *t'i*. In his inherited way of life (or in that part of it which he cordoned off, yielding to the West the world of 'practical utility'), he found not only the appeal of affinity but the appeal of assurance.

It was not just *his*—it was right. And it was its rightness which justified the allegiance he was moved to assert. Chang, like all true culturalists, did not see the *t'i-yung* formula as universally applicable, *mutatis mutandis*; not just *any* nation's national essence, its *t'i*, was entitled to preservation, with a foreign *yung*, perhaps, to shield it. The Chinese learning, for Chang, had more than mere traditionalism to enjoin its preservation.

Thus, Chang retained a philosophical attachment to Confucianism, the heart of the Chinese *t'i*. But nationalists had a romantic attachment, not a primary belief in Confucianism, but a belief in the need to profess belief. The nationalistic passage quoted above, so near on the surface to culturalism, which attributes absolute value to the culture to which it refers, is really a statement of cultural relativism; and the latter is a tenet of romanticism, which denies the contention of rationalists that abstract value should be the sole criterion in intellectual choice. Romanticism insists indeed (as one writer has put it), on the possibility of valid difference without necessarily approaching or receding from a single norm of excellence.[22]

One must note the anonymity in that Kuomintang pronouncement. Who should remain faithful to its own history and its own culture? 'A nation'—i.e. every nation. As a nationalist literary group, closely linked with the Kuomintang, insisted in 1930, a work of art must emphasize the 'vital conscience of the race'.[23] China must be loyal only as other nations must, each to its own culture.

This note of relativism, so unfamiliar to Chinese minds in the halcyon days of the Empire, was sounded clearly by Liang Ch'i-ch'ao, writing as a nationalist in 1915. It was disastrous, he said, for a nation to break with its past. It must act in keeping with its national character, which is manifested in language, literature, religion, customs, ceremonies, and laws. For a nation dies when its national character is obliterated. That happened, said Liang, to Korea and Annam. So many Chinese elements entered their cultures that their national characters could never be more than half-developed. Hence, they fell into subjection.[24]

It is easy to see the distinction between such an appeal for traditionalism and the earlier, culturalistic one. It had been the assumption of Chinese civilization, in the old days, that if Annam and Korea adopted a certain amount of it, to that degree were they civilized. Traditionalism had not been a blind charge on the Chinese, not an imperative (*'we must'*), but an axiom (*'how could a reasonable man think otherwise?'*). For modern nationalists, however, traditionalism was no longer necessary in the primary sense of the word, as axiomatic, but in the hortatory sense: it must exist if an end is to be achieved. Traditionalism was no longer an end in itself, self-justified.

Its end is nationalism. It must exist in nationalism, shorn of its claim to value as it is, in order that nationalism may exist. The sense of community which is essential to nationalism depends on people's acknowledgment of a common past. And the common past must be prized if a man is to let it forge a bond between himself and his fellow-nationals. Otherwise, why should it matter?

Yet, the fact that traditionalism had to be 'worked at' in Chinese nationalism, instead of exerting a natural charm, reminds us why nationalism swept into favour. The reason was that the tradition had lost its natural charm; Chinese thinkers, however reluctantly, had lost their faith in its continuing value. And nationalism justified emotionally the departure from tradition, which was already justified, only too well, by intellectual conviction.

Chinese nationalism, therefore, began as a paradox, a doctrine with increasingly obvious internal tensions. The nationalist protected tradition so that he might *be* a nationalist and be able to attack it. And a tradition requiring protection instead of compelling belief became increasingly open to attack. In the search for a credo in modern China to bring special and general needs into one intellectual line, to keep the irreplaceable and irrefutable from drastic confrontation, simple nationalism failed to provide the final resting place; for nationalism, which tried to preserve the authority of the waning Confucianism which it had attacked and succeeded, was not at rest itself.

CHAPTER VIII

Emphasis on General Validity: (1) As a Defence of Tradition

I. 'SELECT THE BEST IN EAST AND WEST'

CHINESE nationalism came into being with two prescriptions for the Chinese thinker which were hard to reconcile. He was to have a special sympathy for the Chinese past, and he was to review the Chinese past with a disinterested critical honesty. A decision to combine the best which the West and China offered seemed the most suitable way to meet the requirements of this complex point of view. The willingness to pool the resources of the two civilizations was to be a genuine willingness, without the reservation of the culturalistic *t'i-yung* westernizers, who always grudgingly added that the western best was a poor one.

This formula seems to call into play the iconoclastic potentialities of nationalism. Ostensibly, value alone shall be the concern of the thinker. This is clear from the fact that 'best', a culturally neutral value-term, describes the object of the thinker's search. The importance of tradition as an influence on judgment seems completely denied, for whatever part of the Chinese heritage which a western 'best' displaces is just as commendable on traditional grounds as what remains.

Nevertheless, just as the past retains significance in Chinese nationalism, though the latter was designed to deny it, so it intrudes in this formula, making the 'best' equivocal. In the apparent need to specify the origins of values, a continuing conflict between universal and particular is tacitly admitted though outwardly denied. Men are to choose, of course, solely according to the dictates of universal reason; but the suggestion is insistently offered that our objective thinker will doubtless find the East as well as the West a repository of values from which he may draw.

Now, if value-judgment were being rigorously applied in a simple, impartial search for the best, such insistence that the West *and* China shall inspire the brave new culture would be irrelevant. For the traditional Chinese values which a modern could reaffirm would be those which conformed to his own standards, i.e. those to which he would subscribe even if he knew nothing of tradition. Therefore, the only motive which a Chinese could have in celebrating the beauty of blended values would be a desire—entirely foreign to the world of value—to see China and the West as equal partners. The supposed commitment to value alone, to the generally acceptable, masks a concern with its special, historical origins.

2. EXAMPLE: TS'AI YÜAN-P'EI

For the first two decades of the twentieth century, an important educator, Ts'ai Yüan-p'ei (1867–1940), was an influential advocate of values-across-the-sea. His fundamental conviction was that truth has no national boundaries. Truth, that is, belongs to the man who knows it, who may be and should be Chinese, even though a particular article of truth has perhaps been discovered in Europe. Value, being universal, is *a fortiori* Chinese; if the Chinese only 'select the best', they are true to themselves.

Ts'ai, then, asking only for an appreciation of truth, was ready to settle for a composite culture based, ostensibly, on a commitment exclusively to abstract validity. Yen Fu, the conservative translator of many philosophical western works, went only so far as to say that if the ancient sages could have survived to modern times, they would have dismissed neither western learning and culture nor the Chinese ideals of 'investigation of things' and 'extension of knowledge.' [1] But in Ts'ai's appeal for syncretism, he meant truth to be absolutely its own sponsor. It was unnecessary for the 'sages' to grant it the freedom of China; truth had its freedom naturally, and Ts'ai had no scruples in 1918 against introducing John Dewey to a Chinese audience as a 'greater thinker than Confucius'.[2]

Therefore, when Ts'ai stressed the importance of the principles of the French Revolution, liberty, equality, and fraternity, it is particularly significant that he related liberty to the classical principle of Righteousness (*i*), equality to the principle of Reciprocity (*shu*), and fraternity to Benevolence (*jen*); and that for liberty he pieced together a mosaic of gems from Confucius and Mencius—for equality, Confucius, Tzu-kung, and the *Ta-hsüeh*—for fraternity, Confucius, Mencius, the Sung neo-Confucianist, Chang Tsai, and assorted sage-emperors and sage-ministers from the *Shu-ching*.[3] For his philosophy, unlike the *chin-wen*, did not demand of him that he legitimize cultural borrowing by a reference to the Classics. He sought only the best from East and West—but with a wish to see the East as a genuine partner.

One can see that desire, too, behind his advocacy of 'world education', something broad enough, he urged, to allow expression to the best in man.[4] Though there were political frontiers, scholarship, he said, a web of interrelations, was public; there were no intellectual frontiers.[5] Living in a particular culture, he implied, was too severely limiting. Implying this, he simultaneously attacked both Chinese ethnocentrism and Chinese self-abasement. For, if China ought to throw her values into a common pool, so ought the West, whose culture was just as limited. And in this spirit he envisaged the 'world-citizen', a man with rights and duties, tempering Nietzsche's egoism with Mencius' and Mo-tzu's altruism.[6] The middle course was the road to take, the best in each culture must be chosen and brought together.[7]

Was this a traditional Chinese appeal for 'harmony' or the recourse of one who saw his tradition imperilled? I think the latter, that Ts'ai's zeal for universality, his eagerness to see both the West and China sacrifice their individualities, was a balm for cultural defeatism. If general validity was all, then reflections were cast on no one's history by intellectual choices, no culture won or lost. China could choose selectively from the storehouse of its past or from the storehouse of the West, without lapsing into either a petrifying imitation of its own manners or a soul-destroying imitation of western manners.

But there was a flaw in the premises of Ts'ai's appeal for the reign of sweet reason. He was magnanimously willing to sacrifice what the West had already killed—the power of traditional Chinese culture to contain the Chinese mind. The westernization of China was becoming a fact; the 'sinification' of Europe was out of the question. Ts'ai had proclaimed that the cultures should meet, but he meant halfway. The West had to sacrifice, too. Westerners were supposed to acknowledge the value of Chinese things, and acknowledge value not just with their critical faculties, as the western collectors of Sung landscapes did, but with their creative faculties, as the Chinese did who went to Paris to learn to paint like Matisse. Yet, the West would be obliged to sacrifice only if a significant amount of the Chinese heritage was universally commendable to modern minds. Values acceptable to general modern humanity *had to be* found in the special Chinese past. The lack of concern with anything but quality, broadly conceived—the emancipation from the less than broad individual history—was an illusion.

Thus, when Ts'ai described the modern age as the age for blending eastern and western cultures, and spoke of China as naturally adopting the 'strong points' of the West, he went on to couple his appeal for a 'western' point of view in contemporary Chinese painting with an obviously balancing reference to a (hypothetical) Chinese inspiration for early western art (' . . . If those western artists were able to adopt our virtues, shall we, withdrawn, be unable to adopt the westerners' virtues?').[8] Two points are of interest in this single simple argument—first, the quest for a Chinese counterweight to the modern western weight in the scales of value; second, the turn in the quest to western antiquity, not to modern times.

Ts'ai's theory, then—'best in East and West'—with its surface commitment to general validity alone, but its inner, perhaps defeatist commitment to a share in validity for the historically Chinese, was an incantation which some nationalists used to stave off suspicion that traditional Chinese civilization was petering out, and in no condition to set the terms of its modification. As such, it hastened the day when the tradition's ruin could no longer be concealed. For compulsion *a tergo* to admire a heritage, even the compulsion of one's own nostalgia, instils a doubt that the heritage attracts on its own merits. As their reassertion of old values became thoroughly deliberate and smacked of artifice, Chinese were driven to make other adjustments to the modern world, or were confirmed in them.

The trouble was not, of course, that in traditional Chinese culture there was nothing worth admiring. No suggestion could be more outlandish. To speak of a culture's modern transformation is not to deny the lustre of its great past achievements nor even the discovery of permanent truths in its past. It means only that a new generation finds it impossible to govern action by its own precedents, though the precedents may be honoured, and that as traditionalists, in these circumstances, become more self-conscious, their commendation of past values seems ever less convincing. The fact is, simply, that a European who admired traditional Chinese achievements remained just a European with cosmopolitan tastes, not the synthetic Sino-European whom Ts'ai envisaged; while the Chinese who admired western achievements might pass through cosmopolitanism and synthesis together and become a western convert. It is a matter of difference of tone. When Toulouse-Lautrec or Gauguin made a painting in an oriental vein, it was pastiche, a foreign-dialect story. But when a painter who signs himself Zao Wou-ki (b. 1920) paints a Paul Klee, it is a token of serious commitment, a story in a foreign language.[9] Neither the westerners nor the Chinese use the Esperanto which Ts'ai commends, so hopefully.

Like the *t'i-yung* recipe for synthesis of Chinese and western civilizations, the pure-value formula, 'select the best in East and West', has a persistent emotional appeal which age cannot wither nor custom stale. The more Chinese thinkers are forced to operate in a western intellectual atmosphere, the more the illusion of freedom—the freedom implicit in value-judgment—is insisted upon, in some quarters, to compensate for the reality of force. In a world in which balance is actually lost, the sense of balance may perhaps be recovered by an expression of will, a free construction of a morally pleasing eastern-western symmetry. Thus, Fung Yu-lan (b. 1895) speaks of bringing rationalism (European) and mysticism (Chinese) to the melting point together, so that a universal philosophy may be compounded out of two particular, historical ones, with the strength of each as remedy for the weakness of the other.[10]

Now, with Fung as a Chinese philosopher, represented by this fragment, where does the emphasis lie? Is he primarily the philosopher, seeking peace between mysticism and rationalism? Or is he more profoundly the Chinese, sensitive to an ever-increasing cultural penetration and seeking peace between China and the West? In a man of Fung's superb philosophical attainments, such a drastically oversimplified comparison of Chinese and western philosophies must be culturally significant. It is the Ts'ai Yüan-p'ei mentality still, striving to consolidate an embattled historical China by diffusing it into the neutral air of universal value.

In a contemporary writer more crudely obvious than Ts'ai or Fung, we see this mentality in its fullest condition of strain and paradox. The quintessence of wisdom, political, economic, and cultural, ancient and modern, Chinese and foreign, is not only commended to China—it is attributed to China, and to China alone, in the form of Sun Yat-sen's 'Three People's Principles'.[11] So the universal synthesis redounds to the credit of an individual China, which ostensibly had lost itself in that very universal.

3. 'MATTER' AND 'SPIRIT': THE *T'I-YUNG* RATIONALIZATION *IN EXTREMIS*

For many Chinese, the first World War deferred or ruled out any realization that evaluative eclecticism, however judicious and intelligent, was simply verbalism, not a practical deflection of the western cultural tide. On the level of value, the West fell open to devastating scrutiny; and there seemed such a sharp improvement in China's chances, before any value-selection board, for a mighty share in the synthetic ideal that the problem of western invasion could seem to be solved, by possibly valid denunciation, when the problem was really still intractable. For history is just not made by selection-boards. Western culture might lie exposed in the depths so often assigned to it, and Chinese traditions still not escape a transformation under western influence.

However that may be, Chinese traditionalists were immensely cheered by the western debacle. A mass of post-war Chinese apologetics is summed up in the gloating statement of the erstwhile evolutionist, Yen Fu, in his stubbornly classical style, that three hundred years of European progress had brought only 'profit self and kill others, diminish incorruptibility and banish shame'.[12] But the revival of confidence among Chinese traditionalists could not dispel the modern challenge. To recapture his assurance that whatever was happening ought not to be happening might redeem a traditionalist from failure of nerve, still without affecting its ultimate, outer cause.

Nevertheless, in the nationalists' dedication to an impartial search for the best in East and West, it was refreshing to seem able to be impartial on the Chinese side. Before the War, many of the nationalists who insisted most firmly that China and the West had equal title to whatever was best for modern men had disowned their past more in sorrow than in anger. After the War, they were more than pleased to rediscover it and, instead of defensively pleading 'no contest', to proclaim again their triumph over the mechanistic West. In the early 'twenties, in a sprawling debate on 'science and the philosophy of life', many scholars belaboured one another, making science king, or cutting it down to size as a false pretender, dangerous in its falseness, to absolute dominion. To the Opposition, the West was matter—China, spirit.[13]

Matter could be used, spirit was essential, and *t'i-yung*

analysts were abroad again in the land. Their finest flowers appeared in the writings of Ch'en Li-fu (b. 1900) and in the *China's Destiny* attributed to Chiang K'ai-shek where the West was loftily authorized to disclose the secrets of merely material power, while China was beatified for its spiritual achievement in traditionally neglecting the search.

We have already suggested, however, that nationalistic eulogies of the Chinese essence were only a counterfeit of culturalistic confidence in it. The nationalist-traditionalist impulse was for Chinese to be Confucian because Confucius was Chinese, not because he told the simple truth. If nationalists, with latter-day *t'i-yung*, still made absolute claims of general validity for their special Chinese spirit (commending it, as it were, to all mankind), their descent from culturalism was nevertheless exposed in the simultaneous relativism of their pleas for the *national* essence, their emphasis, in a time of foreign borrowing, on *China's* obligations towards what had been proved Chinese. It was a particular urge for balance with the intrusive, seductive West, described by them as materialist, which impelled conviction (quasi-culturalist, or universal) about Chinese spirit—not conviction which led to balance.

Thus, the *t'i-yung* formula of men like Ch'en Li-fu and Chiang K'ai-shek differed in meaning, because it differed in context, from the *t'i-yung* formula of Chang Chih-tung. The latter, in urging that western learning be introduced as material *yung*, had addressed himself to traditionalists, who seriously doubted that western learning would really protect the Chinese *t'i*. And they were right to be sceptical. For when the nationalists at a later time revived the *t'i-yung* rationalization, they were forced to confront iconoclasts, the 'new youth' of the 'Chinese Renaissance', who doubted that the *t'i* deserved protection.

CHAPTER IX

Emphasis on General Validity: (2) As an Attack on Tradition

I. CONFUCIANISM, CHRISTIANITY, AND CHINESE SELECTIVITY

THE most aggressive school of Chinese thought in the nineteen-twenties was not *t'i-yung* traditionalism, which distinguished science from Chinese spirit, but iconoclasm, which touted science as the proper basis of a new spirit for modern man. For all their anti-Confucianism, the iconoclasts were no less committed to a special Chinese context of thought than their opponents, hostile critics of western civilization. However grudgingly, most of the latter were reconciled to science and modern technology, and they meant to preserve the balance of cultures by including (or indeed, by emphasizing) the Chinese spiritual inheritance in their combinations of the best from East and West. And rebels against this Chinese spiritual inheritance meant to preserve the balance of cultures, too; but their balance was one of inadequacies, not goods. If with their anti-Confucianism they paid their bitter respects to old China, they scored off the West with anti-Christianity. The whole story of the growth of iconoclasm in modern China, of how it came to be possible for Chinese minds to drift away from historical Chinese values, is implied in the modern history of the Christian Church in China.

i. The Christian Failure to Infiltrate a Living Confucianism

Coming at the end of the sixteenth century to a proud, exclusive Confucian China, Christianity, for all its ecumenical pretensions, had been compromised by its character as a western institution. Ever since the days of Matteo Ricci, who died in Peking in 1610, many spokesmen for Christian claims of general validity have tried to break through the opposition which special Chinese attachments interposes—or not to break through but to will them away, denying significance to the particular origin, the discolouring, compromising, particular source, of the universal. Absolute reason, they imply, transcends historical relativities, and the Church is strange to no one. Europe has no claim on the Church and China no set against it. When the Church has no cultural bias, it should meet no emotional bar. For no Chinese is called to a western creed; man is called to the truth.

So Maritain says today that the Church knows no single civilization, 'no nation has pure hands'.[1] And the Sacred Congregation of the Propaganda, three centuries ago, instructed the Catholic missionary

. . . not to seek for any reason to persuade peoples to change their customs, as long as they are not openly contrary to religion and morality. Indeed, what could be more absurd than to transplant France, Spain, Italy, or some other part of Europe to China? It is not that which you are to import, but the Faith, which neither repulses nor scorns the usages and customs of any people, as long as they are not perverse, but which desires that they be guarded with all the respect which is their due.[2]

One Christian assumption, then, has been that any particular cultural wrapping can cover the core of a universal truth. Yet, this assumption, which should have precluded any Chinese emotional need to balk at Christian foreignness, was but a net to catch the wind. It was meant to persuade a Chinese that the truth belonged to everyone, but the assumption could simply confirm the Chinese in his predisposition to see truth in what belonged to him.

Thus, the early Jesuits in China, in their fear, for their

religion, of its fatal indictment as a western, passing thing, hopefully expressed it as a sort of 'perennial philosophy'. Its truths were supposed to be evident even in the Chinese Classics, if the Chinese would only look. Revelation, the emphasis on what was *sui generis* to the religion, was deliberately shadowed in mysticism, in the insistence that truth is free of temporal, historical context. And this tactic, though born of a sound instinct that some sort of tactic was necessary, was self-defeating; in effect, it authorized the potential convert to see in the foreign church-organization, and in its foreign-composed Scriptures, at best vessels of the truth which must also exist in his own historical inheritance. It is hardly surprising, then, that a seventeenth-century Jesuit should have to record such a Chinese view as this—a friendlier Chinese view than most but not, for the Church, more promising:

. . . men who are most nearly perfect, either by the goodness of their nature or by their industry, best represent the universal nature of the first principle, and their excellence is to be one with it. Whence one must conclude that it is Jesus for Europe, Confucius for China, and Buddha in the Indies . . . Your law is like that which was given to us by Confucius . . .[3]

In summary, then, of the initial Christian problem: A claim of general truth is brought from the West to China. But the westerners see that the Chinese feeling for a special historical Chinese identity, unless it is made irrelevant, will inhibit Chinese acceptance of an outsider's general claim; for men do not change their minds just for the flooding light of allegedly abstract reason. And so the Christians insist that western history, though in some sense, clearly, a Christian history, is just an embodiment (not *the* embodiment) of a supra-historical value. Chinese history, the westerners say, embodies it just as much. Now, eager to harmonize truth and tradition, hating a breach between general and special intellectual appeals, a Chinese may welcome this invitation to keep the peace between them; but this very proposition, he feels, this very plea for Christianity on grounds of its general immanence, makes him justified in preferring the *status quo*. If it is the nature of universals to be immanent in particulars, if the essence of particulars is not their surface-characteristics but oneness of noumenon beneath phenomena, then the Chinese particular, Chinese history, *before the intrusion of the Christian universal*, must have that value in Chinese garb, without Christian colouration. Christian cultural relativism is a poor servant, in the last analysis, to the Christian religious absolute. When, to make his religion proof against Chinese ethnocentrism—to make it, in short, essential—the westerner sees his western culture as fleeting and superficial, the Chinese notes the sacrifice, and accepts it, and stands pat. There is no conversion, no outward turning. If he looks at all for what the westerners see as truth, he looks within.

ii. *The Christian Failure to Succeed a Dying Confucianism*

Though Christians might deny, then, that Christianity was intrinsically western, the Church did no better in China for that. But if the Christian religion would not be allowed to make its peace with Chinese culture, there was yet one recourse left to the western Chinese spokesmen. They could cease to conciliate. Instead of trying nervously to keep Christianity culturally antiseptic (so as not to clash with historic Chinese loyalties), they could openly flaunt their 'foreign' stigma, accept the Chinese tradition as the implacable foe it was, and contribute to and rejoice in its destruction. If Chinese culture blocked them, Chinese culture-change, perhaps, would sweep away the bars.

The compulsion to choose between these tactics—an attack on Chinese culture or an attempt to plant the Christian message within it—has haunted the Christian effort in China through all its modern history. The inadequacies of each suggest the other. Thus, in the very beginning, we find Matteo Ricci, pioneer spokesman for a Christian-Confucian syncretism (which should appease the Chinese historical conscience), trusting not only to that device; he tried, too, to blast the Chinese pretension that Chinese culture had unquestionable general validity, to force the Chinese intellectually to acknowledge—with whatever emotional reluctance

—the higher value of western culture, and of Christianity, coming in tow as a part of it. Ricci, first, explaining his religion in Confucian terms, admits the prestige of Chinese civilization and smuggles Christianity into it. But Ricci, on the other hand, vaunting the western arts and sciences, shakes the Chinese bias against anything foreign and makes it possible for Christianity not to be pre-judged. 'Do not begin with religious polemics', ran a friendly Chinese counsel, he reports. 'Your mathematics alone', they said to him, 'will take away all credit from the fabulous fantasies they (the Chinese) hold on natural phenomena . . .; and how shall they put confidence, for affairs of the other world, in those who are so grossly deceived in the affairs of this life?' [4]

Why has this expectation—that secular westernization in China would smooth the path for a western religious message—been disappointed, up to now? Why should anti-Christian feeling have become particularly marked in the nineteen-twenties, and particularly in the ranks of those most disaffected with Chinese traditional ways? At a disadvantage, admittedly, in the seventeenth century, when traditional Chinese society was yet unimpaired, Christianity should have benefited, presumably, from the later assault on traditional society and from the anti-Confucian iconoclasm attending it. But when Christianity could no longer be damned as foreign (for modern China accepted so much that was foreign), why was it still its fate to be rejected? 'Considering the vast amount of money, personnel, thought, and devotion that has gone into the Christian schools and colleges in China,' wrote a western Christian missionary, surveying the wreck of missionary efforts in the hour of communist triumph, 'our intellectual failure is remarkable.' [5]

Several factors may have had a part in this, but there is one reason sufficient, perhaps, to account for it. Christianity has failed thus far in any general sense to succeed Confucianism, I suggest, because restless Chinese, for all their turning to western ways, still felt a compulsion to own the ground they stood on. Iconoclasm was impossible unless it left unweakened the Chinese sense of cultural equivalence with the West. Only if its old rival, western Christianity, were dispatched with it, could Chinese Confucianism be thrown to the modern western lions.

Culture embraces all the fields of human choice, both those involving value-judgments and those involving scientific judgments. Valid conclusions of science (as remarked already, in another connection) are empirically demonstrable, hence ultimately irresistible. But the necessary supplanting, in the main, of modern Chinese scientific practice by modern western scientific practice—which is the key to the West as *industrial civilization*—leads Chinese to seek compensation in another test of alternatives. In a field where general judgments cannot be empirically proved, where choice is still possible, the special Chinese commitment shows itself; since Christianity (the West as *Christian civilization*) is rejectable, Christianity is rejected.

Confucianism must go. But if Christianity, expendable Christianity, is singled out as its western analogue, then Chinese history need not suffer in comparison with western; when Christianity alone is Confucianism's opposite number, then a surrender of Confucianism to industrialism need not seem a surrender of China to the West—if Christianity only surrenders too. In rejecting Christianity, the modern Chinese, even as he abandons the central tradition of his own history, wills that the central western tradition be comfortingly drained as well. For when Chinese Confucianism and western Christianity are packaged together and consigned to oblivion, China can seem redeemed.

Science, then, industrialism—as 'modern' civilization, not as 'western'—may seem to wait in the end, a universal fate, for both a superseded Confucian China and a superseded Christian Europe. And if the fate is really universal, it is properly Chinese. For all the newness of general convictions, the special feeling for China is not outraged, after all.

Chinese hostility to Christianity in the nineteen-twenties often appeared in a context of nationalism, as an identification of missionary activities with foreign political pressure. Nationalism involved an important degree of rejection of Chinese tradition, the 'anti-imperialist' attack implied the association of Christianity with the West: there is nothing here to confuse the picture of Chinese 'spirit' and western 'spirit' balanced in rejection, with Chinese equilibrium as the longed-for concomitant. And the modern swing to Christianity on the part of some Chinese traditionalists corroborates the picture, too. Resisting the secular modernism of the iconoclasts, whose growing power they recognize with growing concern, such traditionalists tend to accept what their opponents had long been establishing as the definition of alternatives for moderns—scientific materialism on the one hand, Christianity and Confucianism, with little discrimination, on the other. As long ago as 1902, an erstwhile Confucianist had appealed for freedom of thought in this revealing fashion:

Whence comes the movement to preserve the Confucian doctrine? It comes from the fear of the incursions of Christianity and a belief that this is the way to resist it. To my way of thinking, this anxiety is out of date. . . . As the strength of science daily waxes, the strength of superstition daily declines. As the frontiers of freedom daily expand, the frontiers of religious domination daily contract. Today the strength of Christianity in Europe is only one or two-tenths of what it was in centuries past.[6]

iii. In Summary

In the seventeenth century, Chinese opposed Christianity as un-traditional. In twentieth-century China, especially after the first World War, it was the principal anti-Christian cry that Christianity was un-modern. In the early instance, then, Christianity was criticized for not being Confucian; this was a criticism proper to Chinese civilization. In the later instance, Christianity was criticized for not being scientific; and this was a criticism from western civilization.

Thus, the changing character of Chinese opposition to Christianity reflected the progressive disintegration of traditional Chinese civilization. But it did more than indicate the fact of disintegration, it exemplified the process. After an unimpressive beginning in the early modern period, Christianity assumed a great and important role in Chinese history

—important, but vicarious. Chinese came to require it, not as something to be believed in, but as something to be rejected. Modern Christian missionaries have made outstanding contributions to the westernization of China, but in this, their secular, secondary success, their religious cause was lost, at least for a time, at least as long as waning traditions survive enough to be regretted. For men do not change their intellectual commitments coolly. When Chinese traditionalism crumbles into iconoclasm, it costs the Chinese dear; and he prefers, as far as possible, to pay in a foreign coin.

It may appear that Christianity here has been represented as a problem only for Chinese intellectuals, whether steadfast or delinquent in their expected Confucian loyalties. Would these considerations seem academic to the Chinese masses? After all, when peasants (as distinct from literati) expressed anti-Confucian sentiment during the T'ai-p'ing Rebellion, their leaders taught a garbled Christianity, a travesty of the original, to be sure, but still not *anti*-Christianity as a hostage for anti-Confucianism.

It is true that, throughout history, for Chinese in conscious social conflict with a Confucian ruling group, an intellectual parallel tended to be constructed; rebellions were often ideologically coloured by the going alternative—Taoist, Buddhist, or Christian—to the Confucian professions of the masters jointly of high culture and high estate. But if Christianity's chances in China for sweeping penetration were of this symbolic character, depending on fission in Chinese society, then the chances were dimmed by the intellectuals' dilemma. For because of their peculiarly strategic position in Chinese society, the desertion of intellectuals from the ruling order was probably more essential to a successful revolution in China than to revolution anywhere else, and an anti-Confucian, hence anti-Christian leadership descended on the anti-Confucian, hence potentially Christian twentieth-century rebels from below. And the potential Christianity had not burgeoned very much. A Christian symbol of social protest had possibly always been less appealing than the promise of radical content that issued from certain intellectual circles, from the years of the first World War, the Russian Revolution, and the May Fourth movement, 1919, in China.

2. THE PRESSURE OF ICONOCLASM AGAINST NATIONALISM

We have seen that there were nationalists who were willing to innovate, but whose earnest desire was to let the tradition down gently. Nationalism also sheltered a group which felt it possible, under nationalism's auspices, to spare the tradition nothing. If a man would see things honestly, they felt, in the clear, cold light of universal judgment, his release from tradition was unconditional.

Ch'en Tu-hsiu (1880–1942), a leader and mentor of the young intellectuals who gathered under such meaningful banners as *Hsin ch'ing-nien* (The new youth) and *Hsin ch'ao* (The new tide, or 'Renaissance'), was an iconoclast with the best of them. Although something may come down from the ancients, he said, though it be approved by sages, imposed by the government, and accepted by the people—if it is impractical it is without value and should be suppressed; and with this as his general principle, Ch'en cut a wide swathe through Chinese culture, solemnly indicting his fellow-countrymen, and demanding correctives, for servile obedience, lethargy, uncombativeness, ignorance and superstition.[7]

But as an enthusiast for European qualities, Ch'en refused to accept his release from Chinese tradition at the hands of nationalism. He was wary about nationalism as a foe of tradition, for he feared that nationalism would let tradition in by the back door.[8] Many of his students and disciples, however, did combine political nationalism and cultural iconoclasm in the May Fourth movement of 1919 (which politically was a surge of feeling against the Japanese expropriators of Shantung province, etc., their World War allies, and their Chinese official creatures—and culturally, against the temper and institutions of China, which had allegedly made her such easy, helpless game). And in later periods of political crisis, student-patriots continued to link these nationalistic political and iconoclastic strains of thought. In the decade of the nineteen-thirties, in anti-Japanese student circles, the old education was stigmatized as 'poison left over from feudalism'.[9]

This brand of patriotism was unpopular with official nationalists, who suspected a student affinity with communism. The suspicion was well-founded. For the desertion to communism of the younger generation of Chinese intellectuals was apparent during the war against Japan, and signs of it had been noticeable in the nineteen-twenties.

In so far as nationalists really thought as Ch'en did about Chinese tradition, they overloaded their nationalism with iconoclastic content and became quasi- or actual communists. For communism, as we shall see, appeared to be able to absorb a higher degree of anti-traditionalism than simple nationalism was able to do, and yet justify a Chinese, emotionally, or historically, in breaking intellectually with his Chinese past. And there, in communism, they met Ch'en Tu-hsiu, one of the founders of the Communist Party of China. He had refused the sanction of nationalism for his anti-traditionalism, but he could not, as a Chinese, do without any sanction at all.

3. THE SOCIAL COMPULSION ON NATIONALISM, BOTH TO CONTRIBUTE TO AND DENY THE STERILITY OF TRADITION

As long as an iconoclast could believe that nationalism sanctioned iconoclasm unreservedly, as a prerequisite to the strengthening of the nation, he could remain a nationalist. But when he observed that nationalism seemed to encourage the preservation of tradition as a museum-piece, he was forced to re-think his position. One thing was clear—nationalists killed tradition in one way or another, whether they cast it out or congealed it. Why, then, the iconoclasts must ask, should men as modern as they themselves pay lip-service to a tradition in which all nationalists must really have lost their confidence?

Actually, in their diagnosis of sterility in the traditional thought and art which persisted in a nationalistic China, the iconoclasts implied a decision about its causes. The charge of sterility suggested that the new traditionalists had no primary intellectual or aesthetic commitment to what they were doing, but only a social commitment; this was the reason why what they produced lacked value, and equally the reason why they continued to praise and produce it, its aesthetic or intellectual weakness notwithstanding.

The practice of ascribing a role in class struggle to the traditional classical literature goes back at least to the war-time periodical *Hsin ch'ing-nien*, with its slogan of 'opposition to feudal aristocratic literature, approval of popular realistic social literature'.[10] The association of adjectives here shows that realism had become not an aesthetic but a social issue. The zeal for the written use of colloquial language (*pai-hua*) which characterized the *Hsin ch'ing-nien* group was evidence of this; it was largely zeal to make fresh ideas, which the social crisis called for, the matter of literature—ideas which ordinary language would communicate unobtrusively but which literary, classical language would wall off in a separation of art from life. Ch'en Tu-hsiu spoke with scorn of modern practitioners of classical styles as having skill only in 'imitating the old and deceiving men', their works being 'eight-legged', or without content, completely unrelated to the society or the culture of the present day.[11] But new language (new, that is, in the claims made for it as the proper medium for serious literature) was put to the service of new themes, appropriate to the quest of a new society. Hardly had Hu Shih (b. 1891) issued his *pai-hua* manifesto, through *Hsin-ch'ing nien* in 1916, than poems began to appear like *Jen-li-ch'e fu* (Rickshaw boy), by Ch'en Yin-mo, injecting modern social content into a literature anti-classical in form.[12]

Incisive iconoclasts, then, like Lu Hsün (1881-1936), the most highly regarded Chinese writer of the twentieth century, used social analysis in directing the battle in the nineteen-twenties between a morally-motivated naturalism in the arts and what they condemned as 'art for art's sake', traditional Chinese art in particular. Elaborate concern for style was interpreted as a denial of the importance of content and a refusal to say what had to be said about the desperate problems of society. Science (said Mao Tun, b. 1896), the spirit of the modern age, impelled the writer to the search for social truth.[13] Traditional expression in the modern context, it was charged, was socially significant as an effort to establish form as a rival of content, not aesthetically significant as an effort to maintain that traditional form was the best vessel for content. Thinkers and artists must speak out, said the naturalists, and when thinkers and artists with a traditionalistic bias remonstrated that speaking out was vulgar, they were speaking out themselves. In their aesthetic purity, they took a stand on the social issues which they disclaimed as proper subjects of their concern.[14]

In believing that cultural traditionalism in modern China had a social purpose, the iconoclasts were surely right. But the fostering of tradition was hardly just a cynical manoeuvre in social policy. Traditionalism was, indeed, socially useful to nationalists in so far as they were anti-communists. It was also, however, psychologically necessary to nationalists in so far as they were non-communists, barred by their social requirements from the communist means of renouncing a moribund system.

Socially, nationalism was a formula for denying that class-warfare should exist. Chinese must all have solidarity as Chinese, the nationalist could say, and an affirmation that Chinese culture had a universal claim on Chinese loyalty would be a sign of solidarity. Since iconoclasm was linked with social protest (and who knew it better than the nationalists, emerging as critics of the gentry-literati from treaty-port positions of power, outside the control of the traditional society?), traditionalism, successfully nurtured, would be a palliative. This nationalist traditionalism, as we have already suggested, was not universalist, like the older Confucian traditionalism, but relativist and romantic; and in this (to borrow Mannheim's characterization of the romantic traditionalism of Burke, and of other Europeans in the several decades after the French Revolution) it was a conscious, reflective counter-movement to a systematic, anti-traditional 'progressive' movement.[15]

Accordingly, having thus been circumscribed in their range of intellectual choices by the social conflict between Chinese and Chinese, non-communist nationalists had to make the most of traditionalism in the cultural conflict between China and the West. Nationalist enough to feel alienation from their traditional culture, they had nowhere to go for compensation but socially impossible communism. Therefore, their only way to treat the malaise which alienation engendered was to deny the alienation. They had to try to believe in the contemporary value of Chinese tradition, and believe sincerely, not as a tactic. Modern Chinese traditionalists have been, not political manipulators in a smoke-filled room, but self-persuading devotees of a culture drying up.

4. THE CHARGE OF STERILITY AGAINST CREATIVE EFFORTS IN THE TRADITIONAL SPIRIT

There should be no mistake: this culture was nothing detached from the devotees, no autonomous abstraction growing old within itself, independent of the human beings who chose to live it. It was the very living it that withered it, that forced men to transform ideas even as the latter persisted. For other men, sensing a new tide of ecumenical and renovating industrial civilization, meant to abandon older Chinese ideas and to supplant them with a new learning, in an education which was not so much a basis for the family's prestige, as in the old Confucian-examination days, but a means of emancipation (a revolutionary freedom) from the family. Living in this changing social setting, with the iconoclasts' creed as alternative and the iconoclasts' questions as the spur to answers, traditionalists failed to keep tradition green. Back again in the world of painting, we can see the sands encroaching.

When science, though disparaged, was admitted under the *t'i-yung* or matter-spirit sanctions, care had to be taken that China should, in fact, preserve its traditions in the realm of spirit. In the field of painting, for example, a revolutionary group had founded an academy in Shanghai in 1913, dedicated to painting in oils by western rules. Since they boldly undertook not only *plein air* and still life but the nude, for the first time in Chinese painting (outside the subterranean realm of erotica), traditional artists could cry scandal with extraordinary vigour and even prompted a few arrests. But traditionalists knew that more was at stake than public morals. For the offending painters of nude models were emphasizing the main point in an anti-traditional manifesto. They were calling for painting after nature rather than the characteristic painting after masters, to which they imputed the decadence of Chinese art.[16]

In an effort to counteract such sentiment, which stabbed into Chinese culture more intimately and ruthlessly than any feeling for factories or steamships seemed to do, the *Chung-kuo hua-hsüeh yen-chiu hui* (Society for the study of Chinese painting) was founded in Peking in 1919, under the sponsorship of Hsü Shih-ch'ang, a political figure of scholarly and traditionalistic bent.[17] Its animating spirit was conveyed quite clearly by a somewhat later writer, in a sarcastic attack on universal criteria; he contended that the individual, historically bequeathed Chinese artistic techniques were a necessary corollary of the Chinese people's individuality:

Recently we have seen men who have made a bit of study of Chinese and western painting and thereupon rejoice to change the face of Chinese painting and make it resemble western painting; they advertise themselves as 'modern Chinese painters' or 'revolutionary Chinese painters', and they strongly condemn the defects of Chinese painting's emphasis on brush and ink, forgetting, on the other hand, that, given a world in which there already are Chinese people of such and such an aspect, then there must be Chinese painting of such and such an aspect. It is a pity that they can change the aspect of Chinese painting in its characteristic features and make it like western paintings, but they cannot change their own aspects and make themselves like western men—the revolution is not thorough—what an eternal shame![18]

What happens to a traditional aesthetic when it is perpetuated as a symbol of something outside its field? The painter Wu Hu-fan (b. 1894), a devotee of the art of Sung, Ming, and early Ch'ing, has left us some useful testimony. He has taken no interest, he says, in new or western techniques of painting because he feels that new things can grow only out of old. They must have roots.[19]

This statement is unexceptionable. It is clearly true, as Sapir has remarked, that an individual is helpless without a cultural heritage to work on:

He cannot, out of his unaided spiritual powers, weave a strong cultural fabric instinct with the flush of his own personality. Creation is a bending of form to one's will, not a manufacture of form *ex nihilo* . . . the creator from out of a cultural waste gives us hardly more than a gesture or a yawp . . .[20]

In undertaking to work within a tradition, then, Wu made a legitimate decision, and one, moreover, with more promise of value than the undisciplined eclecticisms which other modern artists have embarked upon. We are all familiar with that sort of social coloration of aesthetic purposes which has led so many Chinese painters to do their bit to select the best from East and West, thus to redeem China from either sterile imitation of its own past or servile imitation of the West.[21] ('I then picked out the finest points in western art and applied them to my Chinese techniques . . . thereby blending the East and West into a harmonious whole. . . .')[22]

But Wu Hu-fan himself, it becomes clear, was far from free from social motivations, which led him to see in his traditional forms something quite different from what his traditional masters had seen in them; he emerges as a spokesman for just that course of sterile imitation which has driven other contemporary painters to their hopeless symbolic syntheses, and still others to outright rebellion. For, although his concern with 'roots' implies an interest in development and in the relation between past and present, Wu's interest is in the past itself, a past which he sees as sharply distinct from the present.

One of his paintings is a landscape, with a girl dressed in

ancient Chinese costume in the foreground. When asked why the girl could not have been dressed as Chinese women dress today, he replied.

If I did that, the style would change and in a few years the picture would look old-fashioned and ridiculous. My pictures are not painted for people of today only, but for those who will look at them during a thousand years.[23]

A credo like this reveals the ravages which the West has wrought in traditional Chinese art and, by implication, in traditional Chinese thought in general. Creativity requires, as Whitehead says, a combination of reverence for the society's symbols with freedom of revision;[24] it presupposes a state of tension between a fresh imagination and the weight of tradition, a tension which leads to development within a tradition. 'Even while the hand makes its alterations, the ear hearkens to the deeps of the past. . . .'[25] But how was there to be development within the Chinese artistic tradition when the West stood across its path? The West, it seemed, had anticipated the possible new departures, and Chinese painters who might have been tempted to apply their fresh imaginations to Chinese tradition, and to create their own ideals of value within a stream of invincibly Chinese cultural history, were caught up short when they recognized that now their results might testify to Chinese cultural abdication. Back in their groove, where once they had valued tradition generally as the spur to creativity, now they set a general value on tradition because only there could they find their special Chinese bearings, and special associations and general assurance had to seem united.

The search for roots, then, really meant the search for the old flowers. Development, and with it the hope of creativity, were sacrificed to an idealization of the past, and one undertaken for reasons not solely aesthetic. Wu Hu-fan's statement on costume seems totally illogical unless one sees that the past is idealized and far removed from the plane of the present. For if a change in the fashion tomorrow would be sufficient to render ridiculous the painting of a woman in the costume of today, what principle, except the idealization of the past, could authorize the painting of the costume of yesterday? The present must be ephemeral, and the past, the ancient past of the authentic China, eternal.

When traditionalists lost the will to develop tradition, and sought instead to repeat it, they changed its content. They no longer saw it, with a spontaneous aesthetic vision, as a world of beauty which could pique them to new discoveries. They saw it rather as an antithesis to the West, and development could only weaken it in that capacity. The strength which tradition should have brought them was lost, for they put themselves under the ban:

An automatic perpetuation of standardized values, not subject to the constant remodelling of individuals willing to put some part of themselves into the forms they receive from their predecessors, leads to the dominance of impersonal formulas. The individual is left out in the cold; the culture becomes a manner rather than a way of life, it ceases to be genuine.[26]

Therefore, when western pioneers appeared to be astride all avenues of development, Chinese traditional thought went stale. Traditionalists, seeking to avoid a conflict between historical affection and acknowledgment of value, drained the contemporary value from what they perpetuated. The conflict grew sharper, and it became inevitable that some Chinese should try a course of outright iconoclasm ('. . . We meet poets of this kind at the end of any age, poets with a sense of the past only, or alternatively, poets whose hope of the future is founded upon the attempt to renounce the past . . .')[27] and see where it took them. It took them, in some numbers, to communism.

CHAPTER X

Communism

I. COMMUNISM'S APPEAL TO THE RACKED CHINESE INTELLECTUAL

WHEN conservative Chinese nationalists felt the social compulsion to use their traditional legacy for all it was worth, they weakened its claim to intellectual persuasiveness and made western intellectual alternatives more compelling than ever. But raw intellectual conviction had never been enough to sustain a western-oriented Chinese iconoclasm, and if nationalism was unable to cover a ruthless rejection of traditional Chinese values, the step to communism would be taken by those who were socially free to do so. The very western origin of the communist call to revolt, instead of putting a psychological hurdle in the way of Chinese acceptance, smoothed the path, for it guaranteed that the pre-communist West, the West which had impinged on China, was as firmly rejected by its own critics as by the most hidebound Chinese traditionalist. A Chinese who wishes to be confident, then, of the equivalence of China and the West need not fall back on a desperate traditionalism, since anti-traditionalism, under communist aegis, would serve his purpose. Instead of being the laggard, following in western footsteps, a communist China, with Russia, could seem at the head of the queue.

2. RESIDUAL TRADITIONALISM

But the communists found that a complete disavowal of old China was psychologically impossible even for them. Occasional statements attest to this. The poet Ai Ching remarks that the May Fourth movement went too far in destroying the images of the past.[1] The philosopher Ai Ssu-chi calls for a search for evidence of dialectical materialism in traditional Chinese philosophy.[2] And the important party-statesman Liu Shao-chi, writing that the thought of Mao Tse-tung is the best expression of Marxism applied to a given nation, adds, 'It is as Chinese as it is thoroughly Marxist.'[3]

In saying this, Liu seems to show some private leaning, unconnected with the force of publicly plausible argument, for the statement does not issue logically from a communist assumption, affirmed by Liu himself, according to which the 'Chinese-ness' of Chinese communist doctrine, its particularity, is irrelevant as long as its Marxism, its universal truth, is established.

The assumption which Liu states and which makes Mao's 'Chinese-ness' irrelevant is the frequent assumption, familiar to us, of men who reveal their special involvement in the issue of conflict of cultures by their very disavowing of the issue: only general validity matters. For Liu says:

As regards historical heritages, whether Chinese or foreign, we neither accept nor reject them without discrimination, but accept critically what is valuable and useful and discard what is valueless and inapplicable, basing ourselves on Marxist dialectical materialism and historical materialism.[4]

Now, this is roughly the principle behind the dutiful Chinese response to Comintern manifestos of cultural cosmopolitanism, and in 1952 commemoration of the 'four cultural giants', Avicenna, Leonardo, Hugo, and Gogol, was carried on in Peking, even as in Warsaw or Prague.[5] But in 1953, when the annual chorus of cultural giants had a Chinese in the line, the ancient poet, Ch'ü Yüan (*patriot*-poet, always, in communist appreciations), there was a noticeably greater Chinese fervour in this supra-national celebration.[6] With a similar mingling of universal and particular strains, Chou Yang, a contributor to a symposium at the First All-China Conference of Writers and Artists, in July, 1949, had said that communists respect and humbly welcome the fine, useful legacy of all native and foreign traditions.[7] But here, too, although the general specification 'useful' supersedes the special commendation of tradition, he went on wilfully to reintroduce a special tie to China; for any foreign forms, he said, once they had been used to depict Chinese struggles and been accepted by the masses, would have inevitably changed into a Chinese national and people's form of art.[8]

3. CONCESSION TO TRADITIONALISM: RATIONAL TACTIC OR EMOTIONAL COMMITMENT?

Should such concern for the 'Chinese spirit' be explained not as a kind of emotional manifestation but simply as a tactic to lure the people, the less-advanced thinkers?

We must note at the outset that a concern with what is viable does enter indeed into the communists' analysis of problems of innovation. Chou Yang observes that the old-form drama ('the main pillar of feudal literature') still commands a huge audience. This drama is an important legacy of Chinese national art, he remarks. It is closely linked with the masses, who know it and love it, and yet the old ruling class has used it as a tool to deceive and drug the masses. It is the communist duty, therefore, both to preserve and revise it. As the political consciousness of the masses increases, their liking for the old-form drama will diminish, but the watchword in revision must be practicality.[9]

Here, then, is a seemingly clear statement that old forms have *ipso facto* no claim on Chinese, but, for tactical reasons, the communists should preserve them and sweeten their content. The old-form drama, it is suggested, can be used to give the masses, not the interpretation of history generally contained in it, one 'saturated with the ideology of a feudal ruling class', but a new and scientific interpretation[10] (just as an old tale, that of Wu Sung, the tiger-killer, is told in a popular 'egg-book' for the peasants—to illustrate Mao's warning that 'imperialism is like a revenging tiger which we must destroy, or it will destroy us').[11]

Elsewhere, the same writer reports that the Liberated Area literature most popular with the masses is that which preserves close ties with national and popular-traditional literature.[12] And Chou En-lai is another who holds that traditional forms have their communist uses. If any form of the old literature or art has taken root among the masses, it has a claim to survive and deserves communist reform. Any attempt to eliminate and replace the old forms of expression, he believes, would surely fail.

Chou is not of the opinion that everything in the old literature and art is good and should therefore be preserved. He is far from suggesting that all Chinese should be conservative admirers of the past. But neither does he think that everything in the old literature and art is bad and should therefore be discarded. Such an attitude, he says, is one which totally disregards the Chinese national traditions and the sentiment of the Chinese people and which is therefore wrong. It is wrong in the sense that it would keep the communists from their primary objective of popularizing literature and art.

Thus, Chou seems to indicate that the communist concession to traditionalism is after all no more than a conscious stratagem. But he goes on to dispel that illusion. For he holds that unsparing denunciation of the old is wrong also in a second sense: it does not fit in with the Chinese communists' historical point of view.[13]

Chinese communist theory, then, is not something to which, intrinsically, the claims of tradition are extraneous. We cannot interpret the communists' tenderness to the particular claims of the Chinese past simply as an artful manipulation of traditionalistic sentiments, to the end of eventually drawing the people past them to a coldly utilitarian iconoclasm. On the contrary, on Chou En-lai's testimony, communist theory demands concessions to the Chinese past not in the interests of its success but as a condition of its existence. The theory is concerned with tradition in its own right, not as a sop to the feelings of the backward.

4. CLASS-ANALYSIS

Communism in China, like simple nationalism, permits iconoclasm while sheltering an impulse to restore a tie with the past. But it is a source of strength to Chinese communism that this impulse is not an embarrassment to it, something either to be smothered or uneasily tolerated, with a nagging sense of inconsistency. As Chou En-lai has indicated, communist theory does not merely suffer the restoration of such a tie, it demands it.

In the communist explanation of history in terms of class-struggle, ideas are represented as ideologies, not compelling acceptance for their abstract value but themselves compelled into existence as expressions of class-interest. Chinese communism, then, can authorize the rejection of the content of an historical heritage while it preserves the urge to inherit. *The* Chinese tradition can be scrapped; but a Chinese tradition exists which can be prized.

The anti-gentry and anti-Confucian T'ai-p'ing rebels (active 1850–64), whom the communists regard with critical affection as precocious children, but immature,[14] tentatively came to class-analysis of Chinese society and introduced the idea, or the feeling, that Confucian tradition was not Chinese tradition but gentry tradition. With this in mind, T'ai-p'ings could advocate the introduction of steamships, railroads, and other such products of western material culture without resorting to the *t'i-yung* type of doctrine which appealed to some of the intelligentsia of the same period, the Confucian official self-strengtheners. The latter, understandably not acknowledging any schism in Chinese society, saw the cultural alternatives as Chinese or barbarian and agreed to a supplement for Confucian culture, a western material shield for Chinese spirit. But the rebels, alienated, ready to reject Confucian culture, saw the alternatives as Chinese or gentry, a people to which they belonged or a class from which they were barred, and could feel that what they were shedding was not of themselves.

One index of change in Chinese culture since the rebellion is the degree in which the intelligentsia has moved over to the T'ai-p'ings' position and made it explicit. An aggressive note of social grievance, not the regretful one of intellectual disenchantment, has been sounding most clearly in expressions of anti-traditionalism. When Confucian tradition (and so much else that goes with it) is consigned to a class, then China, a nation, not a class, has no necessary historical commitment to it. China's natural historical commitment is to its own history.

Who is China? The gentry is not China, say the communists; it is a class, and the gentry-culture is a class-culture. In the feudal society of the past two or three thousand years (runs a rather loose communist analysis), thought had two poles, Confucian and Taoist. Confucian thought was an educational tool of the governing class and therefore emphasized rites. Taoist thought was escapist, a way out for failures in the feudal society.[15] In Chinese literature (according to another communist statement), the true tradition is popular; it does not lie in the court literature or the literature of the leisure class, which has passed for traditional.[16] For China is the non-gentry, comprising all those whom the communists loosely designate as 'the people', who, by their numerical predominance, can identify China with themselves. The tradition which is China's, which is to be appreciated and not disowned and which iconoclasm cannot touch, is the tradition of the non-gentry, one which has always existed but has always been submerged and scorned, or its meaning falsified, as long as the social and cultural domination of the gentry persisted.

Thus, the 'new, correct interpretation' of Chinese history makes the T'ang poet, Po Chü-i, a mainstay of the 'people first' tradition which always existed in China, though it was sometimes obscured.[17] An older poet, Hsi K'ang, one of the 'Seven Sages of the Bamboo Grove' of the third century A.D., is edited by Lu Hsün in the twentieth and acquires the patent of popularity ('feudal era . . . tyrannical government . . . Confucian dogma/patriotic poet . . . spirit of the people . . .', runs the citation, by one of Lu Hsün's admirers).[18] And farthest back of all is the *Shih-ching*, the traditional Classic of Odes or 'Book of Songs', now dismantled as a Classic in the old

sense but reconstituted in the new, with popular novels, not
ritual codes, joining it in a canon. It is as a gem of people's
literature that a communist sees it, with its sense of struggle
and indignation; he, despite the calculated insensitivity of
Confucian interpreters, finds the saving mark of popular protest in poems reflecting opposition to buying and selling in
marriage, to the 'feudal religion of rites', etc.[19] Certainly Mao
Tse-tung is not above referring to the *Shih-ching*—as in this
bucolic reference to China's need of friends, in Mao's tribute
to Stalin, 1939 (the occasion being the sixtieth birthday of
that sentimental gentleman from Georgia): 'It is said in the
Book of Odes, "When the birds coo, they are seeking friend-
ship". That is exactly the predicament we are in.' [20]

The people's tradition, then, is the Chinese past which can
be reclaimed, while what had been represented as the Chinese
past (when it was only gentry) is freely disowned or undergoes
a *C*-change. The T'ai-p'ings themselves become for the communists a part of a living Chinese tradition which supplants
the spurious Chinese tradition of the official spokesmen for
gentry China.

And like the world of social protest, the world of science
is a natural one for communist raids on the Chinese past.
Ancient Chinese inventions or suggestions of the future, like
versions of the compass, seismograph, distance-measurement
gauge, and armillary sphere, have been proudly emphasized
as national achievements.[21] And the lore of Chinese medicine
is especially combed for the enrichment of western medical
science.[22] This is a people's tradition in the course of construction. For science, so little esteemed in the Confucian
official tradition, was 'people's' by default.

5. 'ICONOCLAST-NATIVIST' SYNTHESIS

Such is the formula which the communists use to keep special
and general commitments together. An alternative Chinese
tradition intervenes between the classical Chinese tradition,
which they excoriate, and the western tradition; for the latter
would rush in to fill the vacuum left by the removal of traditional (gentry) China, if this 'people's China' were not un-

earthed to fill it. The class-analysis which disposes of traditional Chinese values as 'gentry' or 'feudal' disposes of a prospective successor, western values, as 'bourgeois'.

The communists seek, in effect, to find a synthesis to displace the western antithesis to the rejected Confucian thesis. China should embrace neither the traditionally celebrated Chinese values nor the modern western ones in whose name the former were first attacked. Thus, the well-known literary figure Kuo Mo-jo speaks critically both of Chinese feudal scorn for the novel as a literary medium and of bourgeois appreciation of the novel when capitalist civilization entered into it, after the May Fourth movement of 1919.[23] The influence of 'obsolete, semi-imperialist and semi-feudal' literature and art is to be exterminated.[24] The May Fourth movement remains a glorious tradition, but its revolutionary thought must be distinguished from its 'reactionary' thought, such as Hu Shih's and Ts'ai Yüan-p'ei's ideas[25]—ideas, that is, of liberal intellectuals, whose anti-traditional critiques (acceptable enough in themselves, perhaps, to their communist former colleagues in the movement) might be represented as mere surrender to western 'cultural aggression', the counterpart of imperialism, in the communist view of the world. Chou Yang states the communist theory clearly. Formerly, he says, Chinese considered the forms of the feudal literature as old. This is correct, but to consider those of the bourgeois literature as new is an error. The latter concept originated from an inclination to worship the West blindly, and this inclination, to put it bluntly, was a reflection of semi-colonial ideas.[26]

In the fine arts, similarly, there is condemnation of complete traditionalists and complete westernizers. Traditional Chinese painting is called '*shih-ta-fu*', literati-official (the term is used tendentiously here, not as a scholarly classification aiming at technical precision), and associated with *pa-ku*, or 'eight-legged essay', that symbol of all that was stylized and stereotyped in the old imperial China.[27] And the modern movement in western art is called the product of a capitalist-class ideology, whose basic tenet is that no such thing exists, that fine arts, literature, philosophy, and science are 'spiritual' manifestations, having no relation to the material conditions of society.[28]

Mao Tse-tung has told us (and he was not the first) what communists think of such a contention. In 1942, in an address which has been accepted as practically an official directive in aesthetic matters, he declared:

All culture or all present-day literature and art belong to a certain class, to a certain party or to a certain political line. There is no such thing as art for art's sake, or literature and art that lie above class distinctions or above partisan interests. There is no such thing as literature and art running parallel to politics or being independent of politics.[29]

It is this approach which enables the communists to 'see through', as they would put it, or be liberated from, as an observer may conclude, both traditional China and the modern West. For it is precisely in the name of the purity of art, says the communist critic, that Chinese perpetuate traditional Chinese art ('imitate Sung, resemble Yüan', he quotes the slogan of this school) or chase after the European moderns.[30]

After the May Fourth movement (the argument runs), 'capitalist painters' either displayed an extreme 'revive-the-old' spirit, in order to quash the revolutionary movement, or (running dogs of the impressionists?) surrendered to the art of capitalist countries. The reactionary spirit was especially strong in the two decades after the Kuomintang coup of 1927. *'Sung Yüan chia fa'* (the rule of the Sung and Yuan masters) were widely advocated; in communist opinion, the great monument to this tendency was the Burlington Art Exhibition of 1936, sponsored in London by the Chinese government. As for the surrender to the West, the founding of the *T'ien-ma hui*, a society to advocate impressionism, in Shanghai in 1921 is cited. In 1931, a passion for post-impressionists, fauves, and surrealists swept the art circles in the big Chinese cities, but this phase petered out when the patriotic fervours of the anti-Japanese resistance movement began to take hold.[31]

As it steers between these two shoals, then, which class-analysis helps it to mark out and avoid, what does the Chinese communist aesthetics value? It has only contempt for the eclectics who use traditional Chinese brush-technique for realistic pictures or who try to paint 'atmospheric life-movement' pictures in oils. These painters, who imagine that they produce a new art, neither Chinese nor western, are simply mired down, it is charged, in the futile *t'i-yung* reformism.[32] This is not the compromise which the communists seek.

What they value in painting is realism.[33] Realism has the virtue, for modern Chinese, of seeming to be a mediant between the idealistic values of the classical Chinese painting most honoured in the traditional canons of criticism and the non-representational, architectural values (among others) of the modern movement in the West. Dispensing the benison of 'realism', communists can retrospectively bleach selected classical art into people's art, which is obviously non-western and can be called 'non-feudal'. Sometimes the urge to see 'socialist realism' as the culmination of the great tradition of Chinese painting makes a communist critic generous with the purifying stream, and Chinese landscape paintings in general are said to exemplify fundamental realism, or strivings towards it, at least.[34] But the redemptive quality of realism may (probably characteristically) be ascribed more selectively, as in one writer's tribute to the 'northern' tradition of the Sung academy—the emperor Hui-tsung himself is praised—as the inspiration of a precious heritage of realistic masterworks.[35] Now, the academic painters had indeed been more detailed than others in their representations of objects. But both the northern school and the southern school of pre-modern Chinese painting had, in actual fact, subordinated realism to formal considerations. For the academics, while less absorbed than their intuitive 'southern' colleagues in transcendence of detail, in problems of immanent form in nature, arranged their detailed natural objects without naturalistic intent, in patterns of formal abstraction, in which the closely observed figures had the effect of setting off the formalizing qualities of the empty space around them. The Hui-tsung sort of 'realism', then, was surely a far cry from the 'socialist realism' of modern representationalists. But there was a sense in which this court tradition could be salvaged for the people: its traditional opponents (at least theoretically —we have seen how eclectic catholicity could mitigate their judgments) had been *shih-ta-fu* painters—'literati-painters'— gentry.

There is a more direct way to pluck this flower, the people, from the nettle of the past; the work of craftsmen, with the blessed anonymity of the humble, may be singled out as the main line of tradition.[36] It is in this connection that the famous frescoes (Wei-T'ang dynasties) in the rock-cut Buddhist temples of Tun-huang have been given the full communist devotional treatment, including commemoration in two sets of postage stamps (in the 'Our Great Motherland' series) of the most widely used denomination.[37] The painter, Hsü Pei-hung, who had gone earlier to Tun-huang for painting inspiration,[38] elicits admiration on interesting grounds: he has fought, it is said, against formalistic or abstract art from abroad, and against the dead hand of the literati-painters of China.[39]

Among art-forms less ambitious than painting, woodcuts of homely scenes have been given tremendous encouragement; their popularity had mushroomed during the war, especially among young artists who were moving away from the Chinese tradition and were influenced not by Sung examples of the woodcut, but by Soviet.[40] The communists have also fostered simpler peasant arts, techniques called 'scissors-cuts' and 'knife-cuts', silhouette designs of flowers, birds, insects, people, or scenes from well-known stories. And the judgment passed on them by one communist critic is this: 'The decadence of China's old-style literati or of the so-called "modernists" has not touched them.' [41]

This compulsion to find a middle-ground in art between old Cathay and new Paris symbolizes a general compulsion in modern China. The need to find a new tradition at home and a new principle of critical selectivity abroad shows that it costs something for a Chinese to scrap the old tradition at home and invite in the West, costs something to the Chinese communist as well as to any other. The need for compensation implies an attachment to the old tradition, an attachment on the part of communists which is not belied but evinced in their repudiation of that tradition. They introduce class-analysis, not joyously to kill the traditional Chinese culture, but in the latest of a series of efforts, all of which have previously failed, to exorcize the spectre of decay.

Communism in China can hardly be defined as a rarefied intellectual refuge from an introspective despondency; earthy social protest is behind it. But the breakdown of traditional Chinese society is the result of the western impact, the same western incursion that ruffled and finally ruined Chinese confidence in China's intellectual self-sufficiency. The question of cultural loyalty comes alive only with the question of social upheaval.

To suggest, therefore, that Chinese communism has a role to play as a device for an intelligentsia in its effort to escape an intellectual dilemma is not to deny but to confirm the fact that Chinese communism has come to the fore because of awesome social pressures. Alienation from Chinese tradition is inseparable from restlessness in Chinese society; and a revolutionary effort to cure the malaise which alienation engenders is the inescapable counterpart, in intellectual history, of the effort, by revolution, to pass through social restlessness to a social equilibrium.

CHAPTER XI

Western Powers and Chinese Revolutions: the Political Side of Culture-change

THE West which drew intellectual responses from China in the course of the last hundred years or so provoked political responses as well. Treaty ports both established the cultural conditions of Chinese nationalism and served as its political targets. And the Chinese path to nationalistic communism has been a long march from a point of self-sufficiency, both intellectual and political, through a deepening slough of western double dominance, to what is hoped to be a point of release to equal standing, or more than equal, with the West again. But the past is not recaptured, experience of the western intrusion can never be blotted out. The present point of Chinese politics and Chinese culture is new. For what emerges now is not the traditional order, but a sense of compensation for its loss.

In pre-Treaty days, Chinese literati had established an attitude towards western thought, but they failed to stabilize it, and in the western century, from the eighteen-forties on, the corrosion of Chinese cultural tradition gradually led to a phase of communist thought. Chinese literati had also established a position against western power, but this, too, gave way, and the enforced change in their diplomatic practice led to a phase of communist polity. This diplomatic practice of Chinese leaders had formed a part of their cultural tradition. The change in one was part of the change in the

146

other. China's becoming a 'people's republic', in alliance with communist Russia against the political power of western nations and erstwhile Chinese leaders, is the same process as Chinese culture's becoming a 'people's culture', ranged against western intellectual power and the Chinese literati tradition. This is the political side of Chinese culture-change.

It is said that the ancient Roman triumvir Crassus had both a private fire department and a private arson squad, and that he made many talents out of using the two in judicious combination. To an interesting degree, western powers in China, and perhaps elsewhere, appear to have played the part of Crassus in the last century. Their material interests seemed best secured when the Chinese government had a fire lit under it, the fire of at least partly western-inspired domestic rebelliousness; for in such a precarious situation, no matter how much they would ordinarily wish to withhold concessions from foreigners, Chinese rulers would have to make concessions, or confirm them, in order to qualify for the foreign aid which alone could save them at home. For both sides, there was one condition to the smooth working of this protection-system: the Chinese government should not become so helpless before its domestic foes that effective foreign aid must overtax the foreigner or over-encumber the Chinese client; the former will not dispense more than his stake is worth, the latter will not repay more than he stands to lose.

In its ideal form, as a point of reference for our comprehension of later modifications, the system was established in 1860. The T'ai-p'ing Rebellion against the Ch'ing dynasty had already been raging for ten years. Nevertheless, the Manchu government had tried quite naturally, in the ancient manner, to be successfully anti-foreign and anti-rebel at the same time, and it had been reluctant to extend or even confirm the foreign privileges in China granted in the eighteen-forties, in the wake of the Opium War. But though the traditional Chinese world may have seemed the best of all worlds to the ruling group in China, it was no longer a possible one. For when the government was defeated by the

Anglo-French forces in the second western war against China (1856–60), and thereby weakened in its resistance to the rebellion, it was established for the next century that either domestic dissidents or foreign intruders had somehow to be accommodated. Both internal threats and external threats of despoliation could not be fought off at once.

Since in 1860 the foreigners sought only the dynasty's capitulation, while the T'ai-p'ings sought its extirpation, the dynasty's one recourse was to suffer the evil of foreign aggrandizement at China's expense, and to try to turn the loss to account; when it was hammered home to the Ch'ing that they had no hope of two victories, they became grudgingly reconciled to accepting the one defeat (and the lesser one) which could be put to use in staving off the other. New treaties, more favourable to foreign interests than the old ones, were concluded with western nations in 1860, and thus the latter, especially Britain, were bound to the service of the Chinese government by virtue, in effect, of their owning shares in it. British intervention in the civil war was soon forthcoming. It was worth the while of a western power to preserve the government which at last it had taught to be tractable.

The T'ai-p'ings, who had never been allies of the foreigners even when they shared the same Manchu enemy, now served the foreign interest by persisting in their enmity while the West abandoned hers. For the British, however easily, perhaps, they might have crushed the Ch'ing forces themselves and even taken over the government, were better suited by a client government—dependent, yet able to play the larger part in its own defence—than by the prospect of wars against a possibly unified, anti-foreign nation-at-arms. No Chinese government would yield bounty to foreigners unless pressures were being exerted upon it. The British had exerted their share (and would do so again, when usable rebels lay not so close to hand), but once their point had been made, it seemed more politic and probably more profitable to let the task of pressing the Ch'ing devolve on the excellent T'ai-p'ings, who were usefully dangerous but far from invulnerable, and whom the dynasty could never conciliate except by conniving at its own destruction. The British, therefore, by a relatively small expenditure in the form of aid to a Chinese agent, instead of a large expenditure in the form of suppression of Chinese independence, could work their will in China. The Ch'ing regime, in its T'ai-p'ing-induced extremity, sold out to foreigners what it once had fought to keep.

The situation, then, concerning the foreign stake in China may be summarized, *in a preliminary fashion*, as follows:

Foreign claims in China may be honoured by unpopular governments, which can be used, or by popular (i.e. generally accepted) governments, which must, however, be menaced or forced. For a government representing a general Chinese will would have to oppose foreign intrusion, but an unpopular government would be relatively docile, since acquiescence is the only key to acquiring from foreign sources the force that is needed to counter the force of opposition at home. Therefore, liberal western nations, often providing the inspiration for Chinese protests against Chinese rulers, tend to support discredited Chinese regimes; to see a regime discredited, then to step in as its only hope—that is the way to buy it. The West drains power from the Chinese ruling circles so that the West, for a *quid pro quo*, can give it back to them.

This is the ideal pattern for the western use of leverage against Chinese governments (a pattern depending on the logic of events, not on assumptions of flawlessly rational, cunning forethought in foreign chancelleries). But the pattern dissolves with the passing of time, for the situation is never static. Either the Chinese government, using its bought protection to good advantage, becomes domestically less in jeopardy, hence less inclined to continue to pay for protection; or on the other hand, the jeopardy grows, precisely on account of the government's possession by foreigners, and there is no longer a sort of tame loyal opposition, a steady but moderate resistance to the regime, which the powers can easily and perpetually exploit. They prefer to invest in a Chinese government which is always a little off balance. But either the government eventually tries to dispense with the

West and to right itself (e.g. the Boxer movement, 1900), or it threatens to lose its balance completely and require more western succour, lest it fall, than its services seem to its western sponsors to warrant.

The latter description applies to warlord-foreign relations during the 'Nationalist Revolution' of the nineteen-twenties. From the foreign point of view, Chinese political forces were in an uneasy equilibrium. Chinese hostility to the Peking regimes of puppet warlords was indispensable to ensure their dependence on foreign powers, for the warlords had to replenish abroad the support they squandered at home. However, especially after May 30, 1925, nationalist hatred of the Peking cliques fed on the foreign support of them, and the hatred increased out of all proportion to the foreign aid lent to Peking to counteract it.

Obviously, for the powers, this had reached the point of diminishing returns. The foreigners might well find themselves the receivers of an entirely bankrupt regime, faced by a solid phalanx of Chinese opposition, so that only a total foreign commitment to war against the Chinese nation could protect the West's prerogatives. The ground the warlords stood on might vanish to a pinhead, and foreigners, instead of enjoying the favoured position of arbiter in a civil war, would find themselves faced with a full-fledged national war.

Some foreigners were willing to face this prospect. They saw China as it appeared in the middle nineteen-twenties, a land of two camps: nationalist or 'Bolshevik' (i.e. Kuomintang and communist parties together in an anti-imperialist, nationalist united front), and anti-nationalist. Seeing no hope for themselves in the first camp, the united front, these foreigners stood ready to bail out the warlords, whatever the cost. Other foreigners, assuming, like their compatriots, that Chinese nationalism was implacable, doubted it could be thwarted by the essentially limited western forces which properly might be charged with such a task. As long as Chinese nationalism was so gloomily assessed, as solid and inflexible—as long, that is, as the *North China Herald* continued to inveigh against the raging Bolshevik, Kuomintang leader Chiang K'ai-shek—the foreign community could see indeed only two alternatives: either invade China properly, or cut losses and get out.

But by the spring of 1927, when the insight was gained that not all nationalists were Bolsheviks—in short, to put it coldly, when the foreigners realized that civil war was still a possibility—a third, the old and the best, alternative emerged. The West could support a Chinese government strong enough to bear some of the burden of its own support, yet threatened enough from within to need foreign aid. When the Kuomintang, with foreign connivance, broke with the communists in 1927, the western powers had a new agent, neither uselessly weak, as the warlords had become, nor solidly, nationally secure (hence very hard to deal with), as Chiang K'ai-shek had seemed to be becoming.

Yet, the arrangement between Chiang and the West was not precisely the old one. The foreigners had to settle for a *faute de mieux*, retention of their treaty rights, but with some infringements and promise of others. There was not simply a change in hirelings, with the foreigners turning from one to another internally-jeopardized regime (as they had done in 1912, for instance, when the Chinese Republic was born). For Chiang was authentically a nationalist, and in the course of its struggle against warlords and foreigners, Chinese nationalism, in these twentieth-century parlous times for Chinese culture, had acquired so strong a position as a moral imperative that a new regime had to appear to be following its dictates. The foreigners were either changing an impossible control-system or they were not. If they were, they had to give their Chinese government such concessions as would prevent the communists simply capturing the title to nationalism. If they were not, they would make of the Kuomintang government just such an isolated, dependent warlord regime as those they had abandoned as bankrupt.

The West could mitigate the anti-foreignism of Chinese rulers by declining, otherwise, to bolster them against Chinese dissidents; that was like old times. But Chinese rulers could force the reduction of foreign pretensions by declining, otherwise, to break their alliance with dissidents (the most intransigent of anti-imperialists), an alliance which could prove for the foreigners a most expensive mischief; that was new. In effect, the West held up the spectre of communism to curb the Kuomintang, and the Kuomintang held up the same spectre to curb the West.

The Kuomintang's terms and the foreigners' terms were figuratively spelled out, each to the other. Implied the foreigners to the Kuomintang: 'If you want to get anything, stop trying to get everything, hence break with the left extremists; or we will block you ourselves with all our strength, or leave you, at best, with no aid from us, to your ultimate communist reckoning.' Implied the Kuomintang to the foreigners: 'If you want to keep anything, stop trying to keep everything, thus forcing us into our communist alliance, which threatens to cost you dear.' In February, 1927, retroceding their concession at Hankow, far up the Yangtze, the British seemed to be heeding the other's warning. In March, at Nanking, nearer the sea, the Kuomintang seemed to be doing the same, as it dissociated itself from what it described as communist violence against foreign nationals. In April, at Shanghai, the foreign stronghold and the nationalists' goal, where a clear-cut decision had to be made, the Kuomintang and the foreigners met, extremes were softened, and the communists, by joint agreement, ruined.

A communist remnant survived, becoming a serious force again in the next decade. The Kuomintang government fought communist rebels, but in 1937 these factions formed their second united front. For a Japanese threat had intervened, a foreign menace of such proportions that civil war could not lend itself to foreign exploitation, but could only be set aside.

The British, principal targets of Chinese nationalism from 1925 to 1927, had hoped at best to hold their own in China, and would never really have ventured, at that late date in Sino-British relations, on full-scale war. Therefore, they could be reached by the Kuomintang, a bargain struck, and Chinese nationalism to some extent politically indulged, at the expense of its solidarity. But when the Japanese, not the

British, posed the challenge to Chinese nationalism, a Kuomintang-foreign bargain was hardly possible. Since Japan was fully prepared to war on China and to monopolize power, not to share it, Chinese nationalism could be indulged not by bargaining but only by resistance; and real resistance precluded civil war. The British and Chiang K'ai-shek had had something to offer each other—relief from the prospect of communist expropriation. But the Japanese and Chiang had nothing to offer each other. Chiang could not force the Japanese to any self-denial, since whatever he had to sell they were ready to seize without incurring obligation. And the Japanese had no leverage on Chiang, since whatever part of his power they might save from communist raids they meant to pre-empt themselves.

Therefore, though the Japanese blatantly used the communist threat as a blackmail weapon to force Chiang to their side, in the end they lost him because they changed the rules for intervention in Chinese revolutions. What they wanted (and found in other quarters) was a Chinese agent to facilitate a wartime foreign conquest and the exercise of nakedly foreign rule, not a Chinese agent to facilitate a peacetime foreign remote-control. Chiang, in order to save the chance to break the communists in his own interests (not Japan's) in a later bout, had to join with the communists to clear the ring of the Japanese. As an anti-communist nationalist, he had to keep Japan from handing over the patriotic cause to the Chinese communists, from making nationalism and communism synonymous in China.

In short, Chiang's dearest wish was to eliminate both communists and Japanese from China. He deferred his pursuit of one of these satisfactions in order to seek the other, whose postponement would be fatal.

But with the entrance of the United States into the war against Japan, both of these ends for the first time seemed attainable together. A breach of the united front would no longer of necessity deliver Chiang to Japan, nor must it compromise his nationalism fatally, since the national objective, Japan's defeat, would presumably be provided for. So in the nineteen-forties civil war was prepared again for

China, even before the end came to the general, national war.

Like other modern Chinese civil wars and pressures of dissent on the central government, this civil war was relevant to the preservation of a foreign stake in China. But the situation was complicated, in that the stake was more political now than economic. With Japan's defeat, the United States emerged as the strongest western power in the Far East, and what the United States wanted was the political support of a dependable Chinese government. By American definition, that meant a non-communist government.

But when such support was the prize the United States sought, no manner of aid to the embattled national government could guarantee that the prize would be delivered. To Chiang K'ai-shek, because of the difference in kind of the foreign stakes involved, the United States seemed to lack what Britain had held in leverage against him in 1927—the priceless option to withhold the aid with which he could break the left. It had been entirely possible for Britain to utter a plague on both their houses in the early nineteen-twenties, when communists and Kuomintang had seemed equally ready to confiscate the British assets. But it was inconceivable that the United States, whose treasure in China was of a different kind, could abandon Chiang to the communists.

Therefore, it was easy for Chiang to withstand American pressure for Kuomintang reforms. For the Chinese revolution which reform was supposed to block was just as dark a *bête noire* to the United States as to the rulers of China; and the latter, then, rather than dissipate through reform the advantages they wished to save against revolution, assumed that sufficient foreign support would always be forthcoming, no matter how much the need increased as domestic corruption strengthened the rebels' hand.

And so the Kuomintang, in its capacity as a foreign instrument, went the way of the Peking governments of some twenty years before, forfeiting popularity until the only strength it could offer its foreign sponsor was the strength the latter gave it. But this time there was no place for the foreigner to jump, no other possible Chinese protégé, and the opposition to the West's candidate got out of hand. The United States aided the only contender whose triumph would serve her purpose—a contender, however, whose chances of triumph were hopelessly prejudiced by the very inevitability of American aid.

By 1950 the wheel had come full circle. The West had exploited domestic threats to Chinese governments so as to redress the domestic balance and receive a *quid pro quo*. But domestic threats, partly because of the western intervention, grew so strong at last that rebels became the government, while the erstwhile government, with its American ally, became the threat. The Kuomintang, or the United States looming behind it, was converted into the ominous threat which made inevitable Russian aid to China for a time, as a prop to the threatened regime, and equally inevitable the Chinese payment of a *quid pro quo*—a phase of political submission, if nothing else—no longer to the West, but to Russia.

Conclusion: a New Vocabulary or a New Language?

ERHAPS the warlords of the early Republican period were only recent versions of the end-of-Han or end-of-T'ang warlords. Perhaps the Nanking government of Chiang K'ai-shek was the Ch'in or Sui type of unifying, ephemeral dynasty which paves the way for a longer-lived bureaucratic centralized regime. Maybe China is forever China, as the saying is, absorbing everyone, and nothing has been new in a crowded century except ephemeral detail, spilling over a changeless paradigm of Chinese history.

If such assumptions held, then the Chinese communists would be not simply somewhat traditionalistic, but traditional; and while being traditionalistic by no means necessarily implies the continuing vitality of rooted values (it may mean the opposite, as we have seen), being traditional implies just that. Chinese civilization may have been broadened (according to this reading of history), its vocabulary enriched in the course of the dialogue between modern China and the modern West, but Chinese civilization remains its old self, still expressed in its own language.

Yet, if it is only the Chinese vocabulary which has been affected, only the detail and not the style of intellectual life, then the effects of the meeting of China and Europe would be the same for each in quality; for cultural diffusion has worked both ways, and Europe as well as China has accepted ideas from the other. But something is wrong with such a conclusion—I think we must feel it. When Needham, in a work pointing out the richness of science in pre-modern China, states the problem of modern culture literally in terms of language ('. . . while the progress of the world has forced Chinese scientists and technologists to be bilingual, the converse has proved so little true . . .'),[1] the metaphor of language is suggested irresistibly: what the West has probably done to China is to change the latter's language—what China has done to the West is to enlarge the latter's vocabulary.

I. VOCABULARY CHANGE IN EUROPE AND CHINA: ART AND IDEAS

Modern Europe has absorbed Far Eastern elements into its art history, either as exoticisms or as assimilations, without giving itself away to any strong external attraction. Rembrandt in his painting in a Rajput manner or Toulouse-Lautrec in his 'Japanese' prints may seem to be swallowing whole an Asian style, but really such exotic works depend for effect on traditions native to the artist; the point of these productions is in their novelty, their piquant revelation of virtuosity, not in their purely aesthetic qualities as they might have been judged in their own milieus where work in these genres was not a sport. In the more important category of assimilation, the great school of French impressionism was strongly influenced by the Oriental print, represented in Europe by the Japanese *ukiyoe*, whose ideals of draughtsmanship and dramatic portrayal were filtered down through Degas (with Hokusai behind his ballet scenes) to the Goncourts, Manet, and Whistler.[2]

Yet, impressionism was undeniably European. That is, the development of its aesthetic and its vogue in Europe were expressions of a European dialogue. In the background were the suggestive pronouncements, the productive conflicts of taste of classicists, romanticists, realists. The line to impressionism ran through Ingres, Delacroix, and Courbet, while the *ukiyoe* was a branch feeder, supplying impressionists with assimilable ideas which helped them to extend a European history.

This was turn-about and fair play. Hokusai had been touched by western influence in perspective and chiaroscuro.[3] But Japanese art was not *bouleversé* by Hokusai. With some western-derived vocabulary, he spoke the language and developed the theses of Chinese and Japanese aesthetics. And as in Tokugawa Japan, so in early-modern China, where a few Chinese artists borrowed western practices, some for exotic effect and some for enrichment, and went on about their business of being Chinese artists, cut off from the wide-spread unseen roots which had thrown up these surface, amusing ideas. 'Having had talks with the western scholar, Lang Shih-ning, I can now make Chinese drawings in the foreign style.' [4] It was the enjoyment of an obvious trick amidst the accepted Chinese order, not conversion to the underlying, not so accessible, foreign aesthetic purpose.

Similarly, in the realm of general ideas, we find Voltaire acknowledging the influence of Confucian secularism, as strained through the Jesuits' reports on China, but Voltaire's anti-clericalism was a western issue; his Chinese evidence weighed in a conflict whose lines were drawn already in European history. [5] And on the other side of the coin, in so far as Matteo Ricci's Christianity was congenial to the Chinese literati to whom he appealed, it was usually accepted as confirmation of Confucian dispraise of the Buddhists. Like Voltaire's Chinese, Ricci, to many of his admirers, was the honest broker, the impartial witness from outer space, who enlivened a native contest. [6]

2. LANGUAGE CHANGE AND THE PROBLEM OF CONTINUITY

There is a common feature in all these cases of western influence on China and Japan up to a century ago, and of Chinese and Japanese influence on the West in any century: the contacts were predominantly intellectual, not social as well. The effect of ideas in diffusion, the degree of their dis-arrangement of their fresh intellectual environment, depends, it seems, not on their disembodied character as abstract ideas but on how much of their mother societies they drag with them to the alien land. As long as one society is not being conclusively shaken up by another, foreign ideas may be exploited, as additional vocabulary, in a domestic intellectual situation. But when foreign-impelled social subversion is fairly under way (and that has been so in China, not in the West, and in China only in the nineteenth century and after), then foreign ideas begin to displace domestic. This change of language in a society may be described objectively as new choices made under conditions of total invasion, not of purely intellectual insinuation. It may be described subjectively as new choices made under conditions of increasing intellectual strain, the strain of efforts by main force to naturalize the alien truth and rationalize the native inheritance, the strain of steady divergence between general and special intellectual quests.

If this strain has been more rending in modern China than in modern Japan, and if accordingly Japanese modernization has been far less inhibited than Chinese, this may well confirm existence of a connection between the disruptive impact of a total foreign society and the shattering psychological effect (when such it is) of foreign intellectual penetration. For Japanese society, with its feudalism evolving into indigenous capitalism, was perhaps rather fired by the West than derailed; while Chinese society, with its bureaucratic character leaving it fewer potentialities for capitalist development on its own (and, correspondingly, leaving its political leaders with less intellectual flexibility than the Japanese, whose feudal origins made their status rest on assumptions of birth rather than on assumptions of possession of a given intellectual corpus), was struck a blow from the side.

Before the Opium War and the subsequent growing Chinese apprehension about the encroachment of western society, western ideas might certainly run foul of the more-than-ordinary Confucian suspicion of novelty, or of the simply different standards of value of literati in their own society, as yet unreconstructed. However, if western ideas got past these hazards, they were accepted calmly, as worthwhile borrowings, detached from their context of origin and perfectly assimilable to the Chinese inheritance. This is precisely the expressed ideal of many modern Chinese borrowers. But the very expression of the ideal, reiterated so often, belies its modern fulfilment—this is one indication that Chinese society is not, in fact, in its old situation, untampered with, when intellectual agitation at the occasional innovation could be less acute.

In the old situation, innovations from the West, like seventeenth-century cannon or effective western naval vessels or Copernican astronomy, could be slipped into the Chinese language as simply new vocabulary. But in the nineteenth century, when western society hovered close behind the intrusive western science and technology, Chinese admirers of the latter seemed to fear a change of language, and to allay the fear they sometimes invoked the seventeenth-century precedents.[7] These famous precedents, however, had themselves been permitted to exist without elaborate invocation of precedent (Ku Yen-wu's *Jih-chih lu*, with none of the urgency of later statements acknowledging foreign values, said simply, concerning astronomy, that men of the western regions were good at it and had been so from ancient times; their techniques, Ku quietly remarked, were not the same as the ancient Chinese methods but were more effective and therefore widely employed in recent times).[8] Indeed, it was this easy acceptability of the precedents in that safely and soundly authentic Chinese past which enabled the worried innovators of the nineteenth-century's China to say that their minds were at rest.

They were, in fact, restlessly torn, held by the warmth, repelled by the confinement of home. Before the total western invasion, value-change could be vocabulary-enrichment, without requiring historical justification.[9] And this pre-invasion era, then (being perfectly Chinese, borrowings and all), could be a storehouse of historical justification for a later day, when society and language were changing together and foreign offerings had to be admitted as valuable, while purged as far as possible of their alien connotations.

It is a difference in social conditions, therefore, which determines the different psychological conditions of borrowing. That is why it is inexact—yet understandable—to weigh off an ancient Chinese statement of some intellectual principle against the modern western statement of the principle. Western recognition of the Chinese statement and

Chinese recognition of the western have different sorts of repercussions. Interested, perhaps, with his cultural horizons broadened, but his attention steadily fixed on the problems of knowledge at hand—problems coming down to him from his own, non-Chinese intellectual history—a western scientist may hear that the modern 'complementarity principle' (whereby two diamentrically opposed statements can validly be made about the same thing) was exemplified in Chi-tsang's (549–623) Theory of Double Truth.[10] But a modern Chinese thinker, if he is moved at all to note an affinity between complementarity and the Double Truth, is unlikely just to be interested in cultural correspondences. He will have been persuaded of the prestige of a modern discovery and of the non-Chinese intellectual tradition in which it takes its place. His cultural horizons have not been broadened, but removed to another plane.

And that is why, too—change in language and enrichment of vocabulary being such quite different processes—it would seem mistaken to base any predictions about modern Chinese communism on the experience of Six Dynasties and T'ang Buddhism. The Indian homeland of Buddhism had not impinged on China socially; the contact was only intellectual, and while Chinese society had some throes of its own in Buddhism's early Chinese centuries, from the end of the Han to mid-T'ang, and the foreign creed seemed a serious menace then to the Confucianism appropriate to a normally operating Chinese bureaucratic society, the revival of this normal operation confirmed Chinese Confucianism as the master of an originally Indian Buddhism, which settled into a modified but invincibly Chinese background.[11] But communist ideas come to China from a western world which unmistakably has impinged socially on China, and the old saw about China's absorbing everything should be buried once and for all. Modern China, with industrialism pressing from without and planted within, seems frankly implausible in the role of unmoved mover.

Some compulsion seems to exist in many quarters to see Chinese communism not, indeed, as a foreign creed tamed down to traditional Chinese specifications (and certainly not as a foreign creed untamed and successfully destructive), but as Confucianism with another name and another skin but the same perennial spirit. Canonical texts and canonical texts, bureaucratic intellectual élite and bureaucratic intellectual élite—nothing has changed, allegedly—except, possibly, everything.

For the substance of the respective orthodoxies must count for something, and Confucian harmony is not Marxist struggle, Confucian permanence is not Marxist process, Confucian moralism is not Marxist materialism. And the rationalizations of the intelligentsias' power count for something, and Mencius' cool account of the way of the world—that those who work with their hands always support those who work with their heads[12]—is not the pious Maoist profession that the workers inspire the intellectuals who, simply by chance of their having education in a society still largely illiterate, necessarily take the official posts at first in a complicated system. Nor is the educated man's prestige as an amateur in Confucian society the prestige of the technically specialized product which Chinese communist education is seeking. Marxist classics, communist bureaucracy, even Huai River water-control are not so suggestive of old China exclusively that all Chinese history since the Opium War, with its social upheavals and intellectual agonies, should be reckoned just sound and fury. The categories of Chinese communist thought are not traditional. This is the salient fact. And it is belied neither by some communist taste for traditional achievement (Tun-huang frescoes or the odd phrase from a Confucian classic), nor by some communist casting in traditional roles.

Observers who tend to emphasize the traditional character of the Chinese communist regime often wish to refute the claim that communism has simply been thrust on China by foreign force and connivance. It is the continuity of Chinese history which they meant to assert, quite rightly, against theories of Moscow gold or American professors as the makers of modern China. Yet, the continuity of Chinese history, including its current communist phase, can be affirmed without our explaining the latter as the Confucian eternal return. Revulsion against the landlord system, the family system, the Confucian education has been building up for a long time in China, certainly not just since yesterday in doctrinaire directives. Though communists in power have helped such ideas along, their sources are deep in a century and a half of unplanned western action on the earlier social structure that was offered up to the contact. And what of the intellectual side of Chinese continuity? Old forms with genuinely new content (like the *t'i* and *yung*, *t'ien-hsia* and *kuo*, *ching* and *shih* dichotomies) establish continuity convincingly, at least as well as new forms with allegedly old content would do—and convey the reality of change better. If, as I have meant to do throughout this narrative, one interprets intellectual history as a history not 'of thought', but of men thinking, one will not see a bloodless Confucianism imposing itself by identity on a similarly abstract communism, but Confucian generations giving way, living, feeling and easing the strains. The Confucian tradition, transformed and abandoned, has led directly to the communist version of Chinese change of mind, not by preserving itself immanent in communist doctrine, but by failing in self-preservation, leaving its heirs bereft and potentially strange in their own land, and thus commending that latest doctrine as an answer to a need.

Notes

INTRODUCTION

1. Cf. the discussions of 'prehensions' (whereby everything somehow absorbs what is outside itself into its own being) and of the 'fallacy of simple location' (i.e. 'the belief that it is adequate, in expressing the spatio-temporal relations of a bit of matter, to state that it is where it is, in a definite finite region of space, and throughout a definite finite duration of time, apart from any essential reference of the relations of that bit of matter to other regions of space and to other durations of time'), in Alfred North Whitehead, *Science and the Modern World* (New York, 1937); *Process and Reality* (New York, 1929); and *Adventures of Ideas* (New York, 1933), *passim*. Elsewhere, in *Modes of Thought* (New York, 1938), 26, Whitehead says of every 'actual thing' that 'its nature consists in its relevance to other things, and its individuality consists in its synthesis of other things so far as they are relevant to it'.

2. R. G. Collingwood, *An Autobiography* (Harmondsworth, 1944), 25.

3. *Ibid.*, 27. Cf. Susanne K. Langer, *Philosophy in a New Key* (New York, 1948), 1–2: 'A question is really an ambiguous proposition; the answer is its determination. . . . Therefore a philosophy is characterized more by the *formulation* of its problems than by its solution of them. Its answers establish an edifice of facts; but its questions make the frame in which its picture of facts is plotted. . . . In our questions lie our *principles of analysis* and our answers may express whatever those principles are able to yield.'

4. For this distinction between Voltaire and Condorcet as rationalists, see Duncan Forbes, 'James Mill and India', *The Cambridge Journal*, V, No. 1 (Oct. 1951), 20–1. For Herder, see Ernst Cassirer, *The Problem of Knowledge* (New Haven, 1950), 203–4.

5. Collingwood, who defends the concept of the question-answer synthesis as the substance of ideas, also states the complementary concept, the definition of ideas in terms of alternatives.

See *An Essay in Philosophical Method* (Oxford, 1933), 106–9, where he states that every philosophical statement is intended to express rejection of some definite proposition which the person making the statement regards as erroneous. A philosophical assertion, whenever it affirms something definite, also denies something definite. '. . . if we cannot understand what the doctrines were which a Plato or a Parmenides meant to deny, it is certain that to just that extent we are unable to grasp what it was that he meant to affirm.'

6. Cf. Anthony Thorlby, 'The Poetry of Four Quartets', *The Cambridge Journal*, V, No. 5 (Feb. 1952), 298: 'The critical dilemma of this generation was nicely expressed by Mr. Allen Tate when he repeated the Christian Creed in answer to the question of what he believed, and added that the real question was what it meant to believe this.'

7. Paul Hazard, *European Thought in the Eighteenth Century, from Montesquieu to Lessing* (New Haven, 1954), 4–6.

8. Quoted passage by de Maistre, cited in Karl Mannheim, 'Conservative Thought', *Essays on Sociology and Social Psychology* (New York, 1953), 148–9.

9. Kingsley Martin, 'Rangoon Reflections', *The New Statesman and Nation*, XLV, No. 1142 (Jan. 24, 1953), 84–5.

10. Jean Hippolyte, *Introduction à l'étude de la philosophie de l'histoire de Hégel* (Paris, 1948), 20. Cf. Oswald Spengler, *The Decline of the West* (New York, 1934), 105: '. . . history is not the mere sum of past things without intrinsic order or inner necessity but . . . an organism of rigorous structure and significant articulation, an organism that does not suddenly dissolve into a formless and ambiguous future when it reaches the accidental present of the observer. Cultures are organisms, and world-history their collective biography.'

Cf. also Cassirer, *The Myth of the State* (New Haven, 1946), 73, where he compares Hegel as a spokesman for traditionalistic historicism and Plato as the founder of the opposing philosophical school in western thought. Hegel maintains, 'The striving for a morality of one's own is futile and by its very nature impossible of attainment. In regard to morality the saying of the wisest men of antiquity is the only true one—to be moral is to live in accordance with the moral traditions of one's own country.' Plato's view is that tradition follows rules that it can neither understand nor justify; implicit faith in tradition can never be the standard of a true moral life.

Elsewhere, too, in *The Problem of Knowledge*, 13, Cassirer sees history as a particularistic category, when he links Descartes' 'unhistorical temper' to his achievement in conceiving a *mathesis universalis*.

11. Herbert Luthy, 'Montaigne, or the Art of Being Truthful', *Encounter*, I, No. 2 (Nov. 1953), 43.

12. Richard McKeon, 'Conflicts of Values in a Community of Cultures', *The Journal of Philosophy*, XLVII, No. 8 (April 13, 1950), 203.

13. See Franz Boas, *The Mind of Primitive Man* (New York, 1938), 236–8, 249, where he writes of the ubiquitous tension between conscious rationality, implied in readiness to change, and emotional tenacity, implied in resistance to change. This is the tension between (in our terms) general and special commitments, which comes when men are confronted with the fact that certain ideas exist for which they cannot give any explanation except that they are there. Boas refers to the 'mental agonies that accompany the freeing of the mind from traditional opinions that have a sentimental value'. 'We try to justify our adherence to inherited or otherwise conditioned principles by trying to convince ourselves that these principles are the correct ones.'

James Baldwin, in *Notes of a Native Son* (Boston, 1955), 6–7, 165, writes movingly of the same problem from a slightly different point of approach; he describes not so much the shock of realization that one's history may not culminate in rationally chosen values, but the disturbing, irrepressible consciousness that what one values may lie outside his history. When one's own historical associations seem unchoosable, choices seem alien: '. . . I was forced to recognize that I was a kind of bastard of the West; when I followed the line of my past I did not find myself in Europe but in Africa. And this meant that in some subtle way, in a really profound way, I brought to Shakespeare, Bach, Rembrandt, to the stones of Paris, to the cathedral at Chartres and to the Empire State Building a special attitude. These were not really my creations, they did not contain my history; I might search in vain forever for any reflection of myself. I was an interloper; this was not my heritage. . . .'

'For this village, even were it incomparably more remote and incredibly more primitive, is the West, the West onto which I have been so strangely grafted. These people cannot be, from the point of view of power, strangers anywhere in the world; they have made the modern world, in effect, even if they do not know it. The most illiterate among them is related in a way that I am not, to Dante, Shakespeare, Michelangelo, Aeschylus, Da Vinci, Rembrandt, and Racine; the cathedral at Chartres says something to them that it cannot say to me, as indeed would New York's Empire State Building, should anyone here ever see it. Out of their hymns and dances come Beethoven and Bach. Go back a few centuries and they are in their full glory—but I am in Africa, watching the conquerors arrive.'

CHAPTER I

1. See Siu-chi Huang, *Lu Hsiang-shan, a Twelfth Century Chinese Idealist Philosopher* (New Haven, 1944), for a comparative discussion of these schools and for bibliographical references in Chinese and in translation.

2. T'an P'i-mu, *Ch'ing-tai ssu-hsiang shih-kang* (Historical outline of Ch'ing thought) (Shanghai, 1940), 10–11.

3. Hou Wai-lu, *Chin-tai Chung-kuo ssu-hsiang hsüeh-shuo shih* (Intellectual history of modern China) (Shanghai, 1947), I, 5.

4. T'an, 53.

5. *Ibid.,* 33.

6. Yen Yüan, 'Ts'un hsüeh pien', *Chi-fu ts'ung-shu* (1879), *ts'e* 275, 1.12.

7. Tai Chen, 'Meng-tzu tzu-i su-cheng', *An-hui ts'ung-shu*, 6th Ser. (Shanghai, 1936), *ts'e* 10, 1.11.

8. Hou, 8.

9. Liang Ch'i-ch'ao, 'Chung-kuo chin san-pai nien hsüeh-shu shih' (History of Chinese scholarship in the last three hundred years), *Yin-ping-shih ho-chi* (Shanghai, 1936), *chuan-chi*, XVII, 6. [Hereafter, YPSHC: CC.]

10. Ch'ien Mu, *Chung-kuo chin san-pai nien hsüeh-shu shih* (History of Chinese scholarship in the last three hundred years) (Chungking, 1945), 20.

11. Ku Yen-wu, *Jih-chih lu* (Shanghai, 1933), I, 18, 108, 114.

12. *Ibid.,* 121.

13. T'an, 1.

14. *Ibid.,* 2.

15. Ku, I, author's preface, 1.

16. T'an, 1.

17. Franz Rosenzweig, 'The New Thinking', *Franz Rosenzweig,*

His Life and Thought, trans. Nahum Glatzer (Philadelphia, 1953), 192.

18. R. I. Aaron, *The Theory of Universals* (Oxford, 1952), 25. For an interesting reference to this relation between generalization and particular instance, made by the musicologist, Donald Tovey, in terms of the musical 'form' and the musical 'work', see Aaron Copland, *Music and Imagination* (Cambridge, 1952), 63.

19. Ernst Lehrs, *Man or Matter* (London, 1951), 65–6.

20. Cf. George Sarton, *Introduction to the History of Science* (Washington, 1931), II, 194; A. C. Crombie, *Augustine to Galileo* (London, 1952), 11; Paul Sandor, *Histoire de la dialectique* (Paris, 1947), 65. It should be noted that there is a question in the minds of some recent scholars about the degree of nominalism in Abelard's thought. However, for our purposes here, the important thing is to define pre-Baconian nominalism, not to attribute it to any particular thinker, and Abelard may still be cited for purposes of illustration.

21. John U. Nef, 'The Genesis of Industrialism and of Modern Science, 1560–1640', *Essays in Honor of Conyers Read*, ed. Norton Downs (Chicago, 1953), 217; Whitehead, *Science and the Modern World*, 62.

22. Collingwood, *An Autobiography*, 22.

23. For Bacon, see Basil Willey, *The Seventeenth Century Background* (London, 1950), 25; for Ku, see Hou, I, 181, 186.

24. The example of Bacon has been introduced into the discussion not because his standing as a philosopher of science is secure, but because he gave the critique of idealism a turn towards science. He is, therefore, a fit subject for comparison with the Chinese thinkers who, like him, rejected the idealism of intellectual predecessors, but who failed to proceed in his direction. Scientific thinking has, of course, left Bacon far behind. It has been pointed out that he was notoriously wide of the mark in his illustrations of scientific method in the *Novum Organum* [Lawrence J. Henderson, *The Order of Nature* (Cambridge, 1917), 27], and Einstein implicitly criticizes the extremes of Baconian induction when he speaks of a 'philosophical prejudice'—the faith that facts by themselves can and should yield scientific knowledge without free conceptual construction [Albert Einstein, 'Autobiographical Notes', *Albert Einstein: Philosopher-Scientist*, ed. Paul Arthur Schilpp (Evanston, 1949), 49]. But we may cite Whitehead's moderate estimate of Bacon to confirm the latter in his place as an immediately post-idealist spokesman for science, as distinct from

the Ch'ing empiricists: 'The explicit realization of the antithesis between the deductive rationalism of the scholastics and the inductive observational methods of the moderns must chiefly be ascribed to Bacon. . . . Induction has proved to be a somewhat more complex process than Bacon anticipated. . . . But when you have made all the requisite deductions, Bacon remains as one of the great builders who constructed the mind of the modern world' [Whitehead, *Science and the Modern World*, 62–3].

25. Margaret L. Wiley, *The Subtle Knot, Creative Scepticism in Seventeenth Century England* (Cambridge, 1952), 18.

26. For examples, see note 7, above; 'Meng-tzu tsu-i su-cheng', Preface, 1b; 'Tung-yüan wen-chi', *An-hui ts'ung-shu*, 6th Ser., *ts'e* 10, 8.13.

27. Tai, 'Tung-yüan wen-chi', *ts'e* 35, 9.9.

28. Yen, 4.8b.

29. *Ibid.*, 1.1b.

30. T'an, 55.

31. E.g. Liang, 'Tai Tung-yüan sheng-jih ni-pai nien chi-nien hui yüan-ch'i' (The origins of the conference to commemorate the two hundredth anniversary of the birth of Tai Tung-yüan), *Yin-ping-shih ho-chi, wen-chi*, XIV, 40.38 *et seq.* [hereafter, YPSHC: WC], where Tai's affinity with modern science is proclaimed. Liang also related the Yen-Li school to the pragmatism of James and Dewey, which was associated with the use of scientific method; see Liang, 'Yen-Li hsüeh-p'ai yü hsien-tai chiao-yü ssu-ch'ao' (The Yen-Li school and the contemporary educational thought-tide), *ibid.*, 41.3. Hsü Shih-ch'ang (1858–1939) made a more extreme statement of the eternal and universal significance of the Yen-Li teachings; see Mansfield Freeman, 'Yen Hsi Chai, a Seventeenth Century Philosopher', *Journal of the North China Branch of the Royal Asiatic Society*, LVII (1926), 70.

Hsiao I-shan, *Ch'ing-tai t'ung-shih* (General history of the Ch'ing period) (Shanghai, 1927), I, 763 and 797, finds a spirit very similar to that of modern science in Ch'ing scholarship, especially in Ku Yen-wu and the Han Learning. Hou Wai-lu, I, 165, similarly finds a strong tendency towards modern science in Ku and the Yen-Li school.

32. Joseph Needham, *Science and Civilization in China*, 7 volumes, in process of publication.

33. Needham, I (Cambridge, 1954), 43.

34. So seen by Needham, I, 4.

CHAPTER II

1. Cf. Plato's *Republic,* a consistent model for a timeless, permanent social order. Plato held that philosophy, as soon as it turned from the study of nature to set up standards for human things, was at war with the state, potentially; and to banish the chance of conflict between the state, which has the authority, and philosophers out of office, he made the philosophers rulers of the Republic. See Werner Jaeger, *Paideia: the Ideals of Greek Culture* (New York, 1943), II, 71.

2. For the link between constancy of the social structure and constancy of taste, see Levin L. Schücking, *The Sociology* of *Literary Taste* (New York, 1944), 64.

3. For Swift's humanistic attack on 'originality', see the famous passage about the 'modern' spider (bringing dirt and poison, spun and spat wholly from himself) and the 'ancient' bee (pretending to nothing of his own, but ranging through nature to make honey and wax, or sweetness and light), in *An Account of a Battel between the Antient and Modern Books in St. James' Library* (first published in 1704). For his antipathy to science, see *Gulliver's Travels,* Part III, Chapter V ('The Grand Academy of Lagardo'), directed against the Royal Society, the citadel of science, which was challenging the humanities as an intellectual fashion. The conflict between science and letters was already established as a literary theme, e.g. in Shadwell's seventeenth-century play, *The Virtuoso* (i.e. scientist), in which the rhetorician Sir Samuel Formal remarks of Sir Nicholas Gimcrack: 'He is an enemy to wit as all Virtuosos are'; see C. S. Duncan, 'The Scientist as a Comic Type', *Modern Philology,* XIV, No. 5 (Sept. 1916), 92. For the necessarily ephemeral quality of a *combined* literary and scientific amateurism in that century and the next (because of the complexity, on the one hand, of Newtonian physics, which heralded the end of scientific communication between the generally cultivated humanist and the necessarily specialized natural scientist; and because of the philosophical implications, on the other hand, of Newtonian physics, which rendered the gentleman's tribute to Newton a tribute not so much to science as to order), see B. Ifor Evans, *Literature and Science* (London, 1954), 22–5, 72, and J. Bronowski, *William Blake, 1757–1827* (Harmondsworth, 1954), 145. For Swift's distaste for utilitarian criteria, and the contrast on this issue between Swift and such anti-traditionalistic 'moderns' and devotees of science as Bacon and Locke, see Miriam Kosh Starkman, *Swift's Satire on*

Learning in 'A Tale of a Tub' (Princeton, 1950), 72, 9, and Walter E. Houghton, Jr., 'The English Virtuoso in the Seventeenth Century' (part 2), *Journal of the History of Ideas*, III, No. 2 (April 1942), 215; and, for his corollary disdain of the business interests, Bronowski, 40. As a confirmation of the coherence of these various antipathies, see W. Arthur Lewis, *The Theory of Economic Growth* (London, 1955), 70–1, for an analysis of the stimulation of specialization by trade, of intellectual diversity (with attendant individual narrowness) by specialization, and of communal intellectual progress by intellectual diversity.

4. Cf. Fei Hsiao-tung, *China's Gentry: Essays in Rural-Urban Relations* (Chicago, 1953), 75: 'In Chinese traditional society, the intelligentsia have been a class without technical knowledge. They monopolized authority based on the wisdom of the past, spent time on literature, and tried to express themselves through art.'

5. It should be noted that the formalistic 'eight-legged essay', with its strong emphasis on rhetorical skill and literary culture, became a prominent feature of the examination system in the early Ming period. It was Ku Yen-wu's opinion that it took its final form some time after the *Ch'eng-hua* period (1465–87), but an essay of 1385 has been preserved which has all the features of the developed form. See Suzuki Torao, 'Kobun hihō no zenku' (The development of the forms of *pa-ku wen*), *Shinagaku*, IV, No. 1 (July 1926), 35–7; for specimens of the style, *ibid.*, 30–1, 35–6; and for T'ang and Sung predecessors, *Tz'u-hai*, I 325.

6. Etienne Balázs, 'Les aspects significatifs de la société chinoise', *Asiatische Studien*, VI (1952), 84.

7. Albert Chan, in his unpublished Harvard doctoral dissertation, *The Decline and Fall of the Ming Dynasty, a Study of the Internal Factors* (Oct. 1953), 113–14, notes that sub-officials, *li*, were a class quite distinct from that of officials, *kuan. Li* were employed by *kuan* to look after public works, among other things. In the *Yung-lo* period (1403–24), sub-officials were forbidden to take the examinations for metropolitan degrees.

8. On this suggestion that the cultural prestige of office in China (its economic value is another subject) depended on the external associations of bureaucracy, cf. C. Wright Mills, *White Collar: the American Middle Classes* (New York, 1951), 247: 'The rationalization of office and store undermines the special skills based on experience and education. It makes the employee easy to replace by shortening the training he needs: it weakens not

only his bargaining power but his prestige. It opens white-collar positions to people with less education, thus destroying the educational prestige of white collar work, for there is no inherent prestige attached to the nature of any work; it is, Hans Speier remarks, the esteem the people doing it enjoy that often lends prestige to the work itself.'

9. Kenneth Bradley, 'Personal Portrait: Sir Andrew Cohen', *London Calling*, No. 745 (Feb. 11, 1954), 13.

10. Noel Gilroy Annan, *Leslie Stephen: His Thought and Character in Relation to His Time* (Cambridge, 1952), 36–8. The opinion is G. M. Young's.

11. Matthew Arnold, *Culture and Anarchy* (London, 1920), 31.

12. Victoria Contag, 'Tung Ch'i-ch'ang's *Hua Ch'an Shih Sui Pi* und das *Hua Shuo* des Mo Shih-lung', *Ostasiatische Zeitschrift* (hereafter, OZ), IX, Nos. 3–4 (May–August, 1933), 86. The term, *shih-ta-fu*, derives from the title of certain clerical aides to the aristocracy in antiquity.

13. The *Han-lin t'u hua yüan*, to give it its full Sung title, was actually founded by the minor dynasty of the Southern T'ang (923–36). See Taki Seiichi, 'Shina e no ni dai chōryū' (The two main currents of Chinese painting), *Kokka*, 458 (Jan. 1929), 3.

It should be noted, however, that A. G. Wenley has expressed doubts that a *hua-yüan*, by that name or by variants of it, in fact existed in the Sung dynasty, although various contemporary and near-contemporary sources refer to it. Mr. Wenley infers from a study of the *Sung-shih* that not a *yüan*, or official academy, independent of other government departments, but *hsüeh*, or schools, under various superior departments, existed then. See A. G. Wenley, 'A Note on the So-called Sung Academy of Painting', *Harvard Journal of Asiatic Studies*, VI, No. 2 (June 1941), 269–72.

14. Contag, 92.

15. Osvald Sirèn, *A History of Later Chinese Painting* (London, 1938), I, 24.

16. Charles O. Hucker, 'The "*Tung-lin*" Movement of the Late Ming Period', *Chinese Thought and Institutions*, ed. John K. Fairbank (Chicago, 1957), 137–8. For an account of a Ming court painter (Liu Chieh, 1522–66) whose style was that of the Sung Academy and who was appointed an officer in the Imperial Guard, see Sirèn, *Early Chinese Paintings from the A. W. Bahr Collection* (London, 1938), 91.

17. Hu Man, *Chung-kuo mei-shu shih* (History of Chinese art) (Shanghai, 1950), 151.

18. Herbert A. Giles, *An Introduction to the History of Chinese Pictorial Art* (London, 1918), 181. For Shen Shih-t'ien as the very embodiment of the refined 'Wu taste' in sixteenth-century and subsequent opinion, see Tempō Imazeki, 'Shin Sekiden jiseki' (Biographical note on Shen Shih-t'ien), part 1, *Kokka*, 457 (Dec. 1928), 349–50.

19. Contag, 88.

20. Sirèn, *Later Chinese Painting*, I, 7.

21. *Ku-kung shu-hua chi* (Palace Museum collection of painting and calligraphy) (Peiping, 1930), *ts'e* 1, plate 15.

22. Contag, OZ, IX, 5 (Oct. 1933), 178.

23. Sirèn, *A. W. Bahr Collection*, 103.

24. Sheng Tsung-ch'ien, 'Chieh-chou hsüeh hua pien', *Hua-lun ts'ung-k'an* (Collection of treatises on painting), ed. Yü Hai-yen (Peiping, 1937), *ts'e* 3, 2.1.

25. Tanaka Toyozō, *Tōyō bijutsu dansō* (Discussions on Far Eastern art) (Tokyo, 1949), 69. For Tung Ch'i-ch'ang's admiration of Mi Fu, see *Ku-kung shu hua chi*, *ts'e* 1, plate 15, and Contag, 'Schriftcharakteristeken in der Malerei, dargestellt an Bildern Wang Meng's und anderer Maler der Südschule', OZ, XVII, No. 1–2 (1941), 49.

26. 'Lotus Flowers, by Liu (sic) Chih', *Kokka*, 315 (Aug. 1916), 38 (in English). In Giles, 187, there is a very similar story involving Wen Cheng-ming and a merchant.

27. Raphael Petrucci, tr., *Encyclopedie de la peinture chinoise* (Paris, 1918), 48. See introduction, vi–viii, for dating of the work.

28. Tsou I-kuei, 'Hsiao-shan hua-p'u', *Ssu t'ung ku chai lun hua chi k'o*, ed. Chang Hsiang-ho (Peking, 1909), *ts'e* 3, 2.4b.

29. Sirèn, 'An Important Treatise on Painting from the Beginning of the Eighteenth Century', *T'oung pao*, XXXIV, No. 3 (1938), 154. The reference is to Wang Yüan-ch'i (1642–1715).

30. For these references to the high standing of Tung Ch'i-ch'ang, see Naitō Konan, 'Tō Kishō Sai Bunki ezō' (Tung Ch'i-ch'ang's portrait of Ts'ai Wen-chi), *Tōyō bijutsu* (Far Eastern art), I (April 1929), 64, and Tajima Shiichi, ed., *Tōyō bijutsu taikan* (General View of Far Eastern art), XI (Tokyo, 1912), plate 16.

31. The *locus classicus* for the origins of the north–south dichotomy in Chinese painting is Tung Ch'i-ch'ang, *Hua Ch'an shih sui-pi*, ed. Wang Ju-lu (Peking, 1840), 2.14b–15. This passage has been quoted or paraphrased in almost every serious modern history of Chinese art. One can see Tung's identification of the southern style with the amateur style in a slightly earlier passage

in the same work, where he states that *wen-jen chih hua*, literati-painting, began with Wang Wei (*ibid.*, 2.14). The earliest extant appearance of the term *wen-jen hua*, as a synonym first for *shih-ta-fu* (or *shih-fu*) *hua* and later also for *nan hua*, seems to be in the *Hua-p'u* (Treatise on painting) of T'ang Yin (1466–1524), where it is recorded as an expression of Wang Ssu-shan, of the Yüan period; see Ise Senichirō, *Ji Ko Gaishi shi Kei Kō Shina sansuiga shi* (History of Chinese landscape painting from Ku K'ai-chih to Ching Hao) (Kyoto, 1933), 147.

For a discussion of the growing post-Sung correlation between painting style and personal status of the painter, and of Tung Ch'i-ch'ang's friend, Mo Shih-lung, as the original theorist about northern and southern schools and their beginnings, see Yoshizawa Tadashi, 'Nanga to bunjinga' (Southern painting and literati painting), part 1, *Kokka*, 622 (Sept. 1942), 257–8.

The following are among the major pre-Ming painters who were later identified as representative figures in one or the other school: *Northern*—the colourist landscapists Chao Po-chü and his brother Chao Po-su, and the academicians Liu Sung-nien, Li T'ang, Ma Yüan, and Hsia Kuei, all of the Sung dynasty; *Southern* —the Sung painters Li Ch'eng, Fan K'uan, Tung Yüan, and Chü-jan, and the 'four masters' of the Yüan dynasty, Huang Kung-wang, Wu Chen, Ni Tsan, and Wang Meng. See T'eng Ku, 'Kuan-yü yüan-t'i hua ho wen-jen hui chih shih ti k'ao-ch'a' (An examination of the history of 'academic' and 'literati' painting), *Fu-jen hsüeh-chih*, II, No. 2 (Sept. 1930), 68.

32. Taki, 'Shin Keinan *Kudan kinga satsu* ni tsuite' (On the picture-album *Chiu-tuan chin-hua-ts'e*, by Shen Ch'i-nan), *Kokka*, 495 (Feb. 1932), 33.

33. Contag, 'Schriftcharakteristeken', 49.

34. Contag, 'Tung Ch'i-ch'ang', OZ, IX (3–4), 96.

35. Sirèn, *Later Chinese Painting*, I, 182.

36. Yoshizawa, part 3, *Kokka*, 624 (Nov. 1942), 346. *Ching-miao* seems to have become a fairly standard term of qualified praise for academics. A Ch'ing continuation of a Yüan treatise says of Lan Meng, a seventeenth-century painter usually ascribed to the academic Chekiang school (see below), that he was expert in painting landscapes with Sung and Yüan models, and that there were none which were not *ching-miao*; see Hsia Wen-yen, *T'u-hui pao-chien*, ed. Chieh-lu ts'ao t'ang, 7.29.

37. Contag, *Die Beiden Steine* (Braunschweig, 1950), 37.

38. Ise, 'Bunjinga—nanga yori bunjinga e no suii' (Literati

painting—the transition from southern painting to literati painting), *Tōyō bijutsu*, III (Sept. 1929), 7.

39. Shih Yai, 'Sung-li Han-lin t'u-hua yüan chi hua-hsüeh shih shih hsi-nien' (A chronology of notable historical data and works of the Hanlin painting academy of the Sung dynasty), *Chung-kuo wen-hua yen-chiu hui-p'an* (Bulletin of Chinese Studies, Chengtu), III (Sept. 1943), 327.

40. This description holds true even for most of the scholars in the prominent *Lu* (Hsiang-shan)—*Wang* (Yang-ming) tradition, which was more introspective than the examination-sanctioned Chu Hsi tradition, but which was still in the world of conventional cultural standards, whatever the allegations made by orthodox critics of its anti-social implications. What happened to the relatively rare Ming literatus who embraced Ch'an as though he really meant it, with all its aura of apostasy from Confucian morality and rejection of its textual underpinnings, is suggested by Charles Hucker's account of the persecution of Li Chih; see Hucker, 144-5. Obviously, the authoritative exponents of a southern aesthetic in painting met with no such strictures.

41. For the tendency among members of the Academy to make preparatory series of sketches, see Aschwin Lippe, 'The Waterfall', *Bulletin of the Metropolitan Museum of Art*, XII (Oct. 1953), 60.

42. For the disparagement of the concept of fine arts because of its connotation of conscious planning, cf. the late sixteenth century scholars Kao Lien and T'u Lung, quoted in Contag' 'Tung Ch'i-ch'ang's', IX (3-4), 95.

43. Ch'in Chung-wen, *Chung-kuo hui-hua hsüeh shih* (History of Chinese painting) (Peiping, 1934), 150; 'I Fukyū hitsu: sansui zu' (Landscape, by I Fu-chiu), *Kokka*, 174 (Nov. 1904), 108 and plate V.

44. P'an T'ien-shou, *Chung-kuo hui-hua shih* (History of Chinese painting) (Shanghai, 1935), 161-2; Liu Ssu-hsün, *Chung-kuo mei-shu fa-ta shih* (History of the development of Chinese art) (Chungking, 1946), 98. It is true that, especially in the early Ming period, some fine Buddhist figure paintings were executed; but these seem to have derived rather from the early Ming passion for imitating T'ang works than from Buddhist religious commitment.

45. For these as Sung concepts of Su Tung-p'o *et al.*, see, respectively, J. P. Dubosc, 'A New Approach to Chinese Painting', *Oriental Art*, III, No. 2 (1950), 53; Louise Wallace Hackney and Yau Chang-foo, *A Study of Chinese Paintings in the Collection of Ada*

Small Moore (London, New York, and Toronto, 1940), 197; and Alexander Coburn Soper, *Kuo Jo-hsü's 'Experiences in Painting'* (*T'u-Hua Chien-Wen-Chih*) (Washington, 1951), 15.

46. T'ang Chih-ch'i, *Hui shih cheng-yen* (Shanghai, 1935), 1.1.

47. Sirèn, 'An Important Treatise', 155, 161.

48. Lu Ch'ien, *Pa-ku wen hsiao-shih* (Short history of the eight-legged essay) (Shanghai, 1937), 44.

49. Friedrich Hirth, *Native Sources for the History of Chinese Pictorial Art* (New York, 1917), 11; Florence Wheelock Ayscough, *Catalogue of Chinese Paintings Ancient and Modern by Famous Masters* (Shanghai, n.d.), 19.

50. 'Shin Sekiden hitsu "*Zō Go Kan gyō*" emaki kai' (Analysis of Shen Shih-t'ien's scroll-painting, 'A gift to Wu K'uan upon his making a journey'), *Kokka*, 545 (April 1936), 113.

51. Goethe, quoted in Nikolaus Pevsner, *Academies of Art* (Cambridge, 1940), 191.

52. Edward Young, 'Conjectures on Original Composition', *Criticism: the Foundations of Modern Literary Judgment*, ed. Mark Schorer, Josephine Miles, and Gordon McKenzie (New York, 1948), 15.

53. Harold A. Small, ed., *Form and Function, remarks on art by Horatio Greenough* (Berkeley and Los Angeles, 1947), 22.

54. Contag, 'Tung Ch'i-ch'ang's', IX (3–4), 96.

55. Yün Shou-p'ing, 'Ou hsiang kuan hua pa' (*chüan* 11–12, *Ou hsiang kuan chi*), *Pieh hsia chai ts'ung-shu*, ed. Chiang Kuang-hsü (Shanghai, 1923), *ts'e* 16.4.

56. T'eng, 80.

57. Yukio Yashiro, 'Connoisseurship in Chinese Painting', *Journal of the Royal Society of Arts*, LXXXIV, No. 4339 (Jan. 17, 1936), 266.

58. Sheng, *ts'e* 3, 2.3b.

59. Tanaka, 81.

60. Serge Elisséev, 'Sur le paysage à l'encre de Chine du Japon', *Revue des Arts Asiatiques*, 2 (June 1925), 31–2.

61. For this distinction, see Michael Oakeshott, *Experience and Its Modes* (Cambridge, 1933), 21–3.

62. Ananda K. Coomeraswamy, 'The Nature of Buddhist Art', *Figures of Speech or Figures of Thought* (London, 1946), 177. Cf. Croce's distinction between intuitive and intellectual activity, as the distinction between apprehending the individuality of a thing by thinking oneself into it, making its life one's own, and analysing or classifying it from an external point of view: 'Do you wish to

understand the true history of a blade of grass? Try to become a blade of grass; and if you cannot do it, satisfy yourself with analysing its parts. . . .' See Collingwood, *The Idea of History* (Oxford, 1946), 199.

63. H. W. Cassirer, *A Commentary on Kant's 'Critique of Judgment'* (London, 1938), 19; and Christopher Gray, *Cubist Aesthetic Theories* (Baltimore, 1953), 47–9. For the iron law of correlation between ideal and intuition, note also the place of *Ion* (in which art is 'the god speaking through one', hence art cannot be taught) among the dialogues of the greatest idealist, Plato; and for the reverse of the coin, the artist's willing acceptance of the discipline of teachable rules and his denial of the necessity of the intuitive oneness of art and contemplation, note Valéry's warning against the 'devil of the line of least resistance' (i.e. audacious 'anti-academic' refusal of set forms) and his corollary teaching, 'Beautiful lines are matured on the day after inspiration'. See Paul Valéry, *Reflections on the World Today* (London, 1951), 60, 145.

64. The literature of art-criticism ran riot in the Ming era, so that no attempt has since been made to collect it all; see Hirth, 25–6.

65. Contag, 'Das Mallehrbuch für Personen-Malerei des Chieh Tzu Yüan', *T'oung Pao*, XXXIII, No. 1 (1937), 18. The critics' division of painters into three classes, according to talent, went back at least to the T'ang dynasty.

66. *Ibid.*, 20.

67. Elisséev, 32. For descriptions of Ming and Ch'ing recorded vocabularies of abstractions—epitomes of typical and permanent features of natural forms and rules of composition to produce them—see, *inter alia*, Victor Rienaecker, 'Chinese Art (Sixth Article), Painting—I', *Apollo*, XL, No. 236 (Oct. 1944), 81–4; Benjamin March, *Some Technical Terms of Chinese Painting* (Baltimore, 1935) xii–xiii; Fang-chuen Wang, *Chinese Freehand Flower Painting* (Peiping, 1936) 98–9; William Cohn, *Chinese Painting* (London and New York, 1948), 18.

68. Laurence Sickman, in *Great Chinese Painters of the Ming and Ch'ing Dynasties* (catalogue of an exhibition, March 11–April 2, 1949, at Wildenstein Galleries, New York); concurred in by Benjamin Rowland, in *Masterpieces of Chinese Bird and Flower Painting* (catalogue of an exhibition, Oct. 30–Dec. 14, 1951, at the Fogg Art Museum, Cambridge), 4.

69. Arnold, 'The Literary Influence of Academies', *Essays in Criticism* (Boston, 1865), 47–51.

70. Naitō Torajirō, *Shinchō shoga fu* (Treatise on Ch'ing calligraphy and painting) (Osaka, 1917), 3. Text in Chinese.

71. Contag, *Die Beiden Steine*, 10.

72. *Ming-jen shu hua chi* (Collection of calligraphy and painting of famous practitioners) (Shanghai, 1921), IV, plate 2.

73. Sirèn, *The Chinese on the Art of Painting* (Peiping, 1936), 188.

74. Werner Speiser, 'Ba Da Schan Jen', *Sinica*, VIII, No. 2 (March 10, 1933), 49.

75. Sirèn, 'Shih-t'ao, Painter, Poet and Theoretician', *Bulletin of the Museum of Far Eastern Antiquities*, XXI (Stockholm, 1949), 55.

76. Aoki Masaru, 'Sekitō no ga to garon to' (Shih-t'ao's painting and his views on painting), *Shinagaku*, I, No. 8 (April 1921), 583.

77 Yawata Sekitarō, *Shina gajin kenkyū* (Study of Chinese painters) (Tokyo, 1942), 170.

78. Herbert Franke, 'Zur Biographie des Pa-Ta-Shan-Jen', *Asiatica: Festschrift Friedrich Weller* (Leipzig, 1954), 130.

79. *Chung-kuo jen-ming ta tz'u-tien*, quoted in Speiser, 'Ba Da Schan Jen', 46.

80. Yū Yamanoi, 'Meimatsu Shinchō ni okeru keiji jiyō no gaku' (The 'practical affairs' school of the end of the Ming and the beginning of the Ch'ing), *Tōhō gaku ronshū* (Memoirs of the Institute of Eastern Culture) (Tokyo, 1954), 140-1, 149.

81. Bokuyūsō shujin, *Sekitō to Hachidaisenjin* (Shih-t'ao and Pa-ta-shan-jen) (Kanagawa ken, 1952), 3.

82. Aoki, 586. A conventional acceptance of Shih-t'ao's 'no method' principle of unconventionality is indicated, too, in this early seventeenth-century appraisal of Shen Shih-t'ien: 'He was, as Ch'an followers say, "absorbed in play unfettered by rules".' Shen, of course, was entirely in the main stream of the *wen-jen* southern tradition; see Kojiro Tomita and A. Kaiming Chiu, 'An Album of Landscapes and Poems by Shen Chou (1427-1509)', *Bulletin of the Museum of Fine Arts* (Boston), XLVI, No. 265 (Oct. 1948), 60.

83. Sirèn, 'Shih-t'ao', 41.

84. It should be noted that in the Sung period, an age of both Confucian consolidation and Confucianists' patronage of Ch'an ideals, a process called *Ch'an chiao i-chih*, a syncretism of intuition and learning, was observed in Ch'an as sutra-study pushed its way back in; see Heinrich Dumoulin, *The Development of Chinese Zen after the Sixth Patriarch in the Light of Mumonkan* (New York, 1953), 35.

85. Sirèn, *The Chinese on the Art of Painting*, 164. As an example of the literati's disinterest in originality, the same reference to the 'ten thousand volumes' and the 'ten thousand li' may be found in a contemporary treatise by Mo Shih-lung and in the later work, the *Mustard-seed Garden*; see Yoshizawa, 'Nanga to bunjinga' (part 1), *Kokka*, 622 (Sept. 1942), 260, and Petrucci, 4–5.

Sir Herbert Read, shifting the emphasis, misses the strain in Tung Ch'i-ch'ang which makes him such a revealing figure, when he writes: 'But one of the great artists of the Ming epoch, Tung Ch'i-ch'ang, said with perhaps obvious truth that no one was likely to gain such a state of grace, even if he read ten thousand books and ranged over ten thousand leagues; the artist is born, not made.' See Herbert Read, 'Modern Chinese Painting', *A Coat of Many Colours* (London, 1945), 266.

86. Contag, *Die Beiden Steine*, 10.

87. Yün, *ts'e* 16.8–8b.

88. Hackney and Yao, 56.

89. Yoshizawa, 'Nanga to bunjinga' (part 3), *Kokka*, 624 (Nov. 1942), 346.

90. Hsü Ch'in, 'Ming hua lu' (Records of Ming painting), *Ts'ung-shu chi-ch'eng* (Shanghai, 1926), 27.

91. See 'Ran Ei hitsu: *Hisetsu senzen zu kai*' (Analysis of 'Flying snow and a thousand mountains', by Lan Ying), *Kokka*, 477 (Aug. 1930), 228. For the distinction between the Che school (in the Ma Yüan—Hsia Kuei tradition of the monochrome landscape of the Southern Sung academy), Yüan school (particularly figure-painting and decorative colour landscape, 'blue-green', etc., more meticulous than Che), and Wu school (for whom both the preceding schools were academic)—and for an account of their intermingling, see Hu, 150–1, and P'an, 167–70.

92. For Ming and Ch'ing varying assignments of these painters to schools, see Tajima, *Tōyō bijutsu taikan*, X (Tokyo, 1911), 16; Yawata, 68–9; Ichiuji Giryō, *Tōyō bijutsu shi* (History of Far Eastern art) (Tokyo, 1936), 215; Huang Pin-hung, *Ku hua cheng* (Evidence on old painting) (Shanghai, 1931), 30–2; and Speiser, 'T'ang Yin' (Part 2), OZ, XI, Nos. 3–4 (May-Aug. 1935), 109.

93. Yonezawa Yoshiho, 'Kyū Ei hitsu: hakubyō *Tan ran tei* zu' (The *Chuan lan ting*, a picture in the *pai-miao* method, by Ch'iu Ying), *Kokka*, 708 (March 1951), 122; Lin Feng-mien, *I-shu ts'ung-lun* (Essays on art) (Shanghai, 1937), 121; Arthur Waley, 'A Chinese Picture', *The Burlington Magazine*, XXX, No. 1 (Jan. 1917), 10.

94. Unzansei, 'Kyū Ei no gasatsu ni tsuite' (On a picture book by Ch'iu Ying), *Kokka*, 475 (June 1930), 159-60; Kyū Ei Tōjin shii e kai' (Explanation of Ch'iu Ying's paintings on themes from T'ang poetry), *Kokka*, 481 (Dec. 1930), 344-5.

There is a similar album by Shen Shih-t'ien, one of nine paintings, each after an individual early artist; see Taki, 'Shin Keinan *Kudan nishikie satsu* ni tsuite', 35.

95. Sirèn, *Later Chinese Painting*, I, 133-4; Speiser, 'T'ang Yin' (part 1), OZ, XI, 1-2 (Jan.–April 1935), 21. Cf. the note on T'ang by the famous sixteenth-century collector, Wang Shih-chen, which mentions as a matter of course T'ang's derivations (all Wang's notes have an account of derivations at the beginning of his brief biographical sketches). Wang acknowledges a thoroughly eclectic background for T'ang, in which Sung academicians like Li T'ang, Ma Yüan, *et al.*, and Yüan intuitive masters like Huang Kung-wang all figure; see Wang Shih-chen, 'I-yüan chih yen fu lu', *Yen-chou shan jen ssu pu kao*, ed. Shih ching t'ang, n.d., 155, 16b–17.

96. Tajima, *Tōyō bijutsu taikan*, XI, plate 6.

97. See *Kokka*, 481, no. 5 in the illustrated set. Cf. a late Ming account of a Ch'iu Ying painting, which identified the styles (and praised the combinations) of various masters in Ch'iu Ying's stones and mountains, trees, figures, and colouring; see Sirèn, *Later Chinese Painting*, I, 146.

98. 'Sei Moyō hitsu: *Sankyo hōmon* zu kai' (Analysis of 'A visitor to a mountain abode', by Sheng Mao-yeh), *Kokka*, 543 (Feb. 1946), 53. Lan Ying, too, was known to render a background of mountains and mists *à la* Mi Fu (southern), while his pines in the foreground were of the Ma-Hsia, northern type; see 'A Summer Landscape, by Lan Yin (sic)', *Kokka*, 232 (Sept. 1909), 95-6 (in English).

99. Wada Mikio, ed., *Tōyō bijutsu taikan*, XII (Tokyo, 1913), plate 6; Contag, 'Tung Ch'i-ch'ang's' (conclusion), OZ, IX, 5, 181-2. The quotation is from the *Kuo ch'ao hua cheng lu* (1739), by Chang Keng.

100. 'Ō Sekikoku hitsu: semmen sansui zu' (Landscape painted on a fan, by Wang Hui), *Kokka*, 614 (Jan. 1942), 24; 'A Landscape, by Wang Hui', *Kokka*, 250 (March 1911), 283 (in English); 'Ō Sekikoku hitsu: kambaku zu' (Looking at a waterfall, by Wang Hui), *Kokka*, 702 (Sept. 1950), 306.

101. Aimi Shigeichi, *Gumpō seigan* (Tokyo, 1914), II, plate 5; Nakamura Sakutarō and Ojika Bukkai, *Shina ega shi* (History of Chinese painting) (Tokyo, 1923), 163; P'an, 167.

102. Tsou I-kuei, cited in Ch'uan Han-sheng, 'Ch'ing-mo fan-tui Hsi-hua ti yen-lun' (Arguments against westernization in the late Ch'ing period), *Lingnan hsüeh-pao*, V, Nos. 3–4 (Dec. 20, 1936), 128. For *hua-chiang* as a connoisseur's term for mere 'professional qualities', see Gustav Ecke, 'Comments on Calligraphies and Paintings', *Monumenta Nipponica*, III (1938), 569.

103. Wang Shih-chen on T'ang Yin; see Wang Shih-chen, 155.17.

Generally, for the Ming-Ch'ing connoisseurs' cult of brush-work—its sensitivity to nuance, feeling for extra-aesthetic suggestiveness in the painter's strokes, elaborate systems of classification, tendency to proliferate detail (the subject of brushwork) in what might have been truly southern empty space, and gradual change of emphasis from typical motives in an intellectually regulated composition to more individualized motives in free arrangement, more suitable to the range of virtuosity—see, successively, A. Bulling and John Ayers, 'Chinese Art of the Ming Period in the British Museum', *Oriental Art*, III, No. 2 (1950), 79; Contag, *Die Sechs Berühmten Maler der Ch'ing-Dynastie* (Leipzig, 1940), 17; Tomita, 'Brush-strokes in Far Eastern Painting', *Eastern Art*, III (Philadelphia, 1931), 29–31; Waley, *An Introduction to the Study of Chinese Painting* (London, 1923), 247; Fang-chuen Wang, 102; Rienaecker, 'Chinese Art (Seventh Article), Painting—II', *Apollo*, XL, No. 237 (Nov. 1944) 109; Tsou, *ts'e* 3, 2.6; Arthur von Rosthorn, 'Malerei und Kunstkritik in China', *Wiener Beiträge zur Kunst- und Kultur-Geschichte*, IV (1930), 22; George Rowley, 'A Chinese Scroll of the Ming Dynasty: Ming Huang and Yang Kuei-fei Listening to Music', *Worcester Art Museum Annual*, II (1936–7), 70–1; Cohn, 92; John C. Ferguson, *Chinese Painting* (Chicago, 1927), 62; Edouard Chavannes and Raphael Petrucci, *La peinture chinoise au Musée Cernuschi, Avril–Juin 1912* (Ars Asiatica I) (Brussels and Paris, 1914), 49–50; Edgar C. Schenck, 'The Hundred Wild Geese', *Honolulu Academy of Arts Annual Bulletin*, I (1939), 6–10.

104. For details on this prescription of Tung Ch'i-ch'ang *et al.* for the painting of synthetic pictures, see Tung, 2.5–8; Alan Houghton Broderick, *An Outline of Chinese Painting* (London, 1949), 32; Waley, *An Introduction*, 246–50; Contag, 'Schrift-charakteristeken', 48, and *Die Sechs*, 20; Sirèn, *The Chinese on the Art of Painting*, 143, and *Later Chinese Painting*, I, 187; Ferguson, 'Wang Ch'uan', OZ, III, No. 1 (April–June 1914), 58–9.

105. Paul L. Grigaut, 'Art of the Ming Dynasty', *Archaeology*, V, No. 1 (March 1952), 12.

106. As an example of the latter, Waley refers to the transfer of the ideals of literary study to art, in this fashion: a certain river having been mentioned in the *Shih-ching* in connection with autumn, it must always be represented by the painter in an autumn scene. See Waley, *An Introduction*, 246. Sirèn speaks of the Ming taste as demanding an inscription on a painting in a literary style appropriate to the motif and calligraphic style corresponding to the manner in which the picture was painted, i.e. *k'ai-shu* (formal style) calligraphy for *kung-pi* (highly finished, meticulous) painting, and *ts'ao-shu* (cursive style) calligraphy for *hsieh-i* (intuitive) painting; see Sirèn, 'Shih T'ao', 35–6.

107. Kenneth Clark, *Landscape into Art* (London, 1949), 30.

108. C. M. Bowra, *The Creative Experiment* (London, 1949), 2.

109. Speiser, 'Eine Landschaft von Wang Hui in Köln', OZ, XVII, Nos. 1–2 (1941), 170.

110. 'Abe Kojirō zō; Un Nanden hitsu kaki satsu' ('Flowers' by Yün Nan-t'ien in the Abe Kojirō Collection), *Bijutsu kenkyū*, XCII (Aug. 1939), 306.

111. 'Hashimoto Shinjirō zō: Un Nanden hitsu kahin seikyō zu' ('Fruits' by Yün Nan-t'ien in the Hashimoto Shinjirō Collection), *ibid.*, VII (July 1932), 237.

112. Tsou, *ts'e* 3, 1.1.

113. For discussions of this process, see Joseph R. Levenson, *Liang Ch'i-ch'ao and the Mind of Modern China* (Cambridge, 1953), *passim*, esp. 109–28; and below, Chapter VII.

114. For a discussion of nineteenth- and early twentieth-century utilitarian criticism, and proposals for modification, of what had come to appear the aestheticism of the examination-system, see Ssu-yü Teng and John K. Fairbank, *China's Response to the West* (Cambridge, 1954), esp. 139, 145, 178, and 205. For a somewhat earlier suggestion of this mentality, from a time when such opinions were but straws in the wind, see Fang Chao-ying's biography of Kung Tzu-chen (1792–1841), in Arthur W. Hummel, ed., *Eminent Chinese of the Ch'ing Period* (Washington, 1943), I, 432–3: Kung, bitter about his disqualification from the *Han-lin yüan* on grounds of poor calligraphy, became contemptuous of such aesthetic tests for government service and ultimately, charging the Ch'ing regime with decadence, advocated the abolition of the civil service examinations as practised in his day.

As Ralph Powell has pointed out in *The Rise of Chinese Military Power, 1895–1912* (Princeton, 1955), 338, specialization in the newly-founded late-Ch'ing military schools for the training of professional officers riddled the theory of the omnicompetence of Chinese officials.

115. Max Weber, *The Religion of China* (Glencoe, 1951), 248.

116. Chung-li Chang, in *The Chinese Gentry: Studies on Their Role in Nineteenth-Century Chinese Society* (Seattle, 1955), 174–6, has shown that in the first half of the Ch'ing period there was more scope for discussion in the examinations. Classically erudite and formally accomplished exposition, however, was always a *sine qua non*. The eight-legged essay, except for a significantly brief discontinuance in 1663, remained throughout the period the heart of the Ming-Ch'ing examination-system (witness the late-Ch'ing reformist memorials aimed specifically at this feature of the system), and the Ch'ing changes in the eight-legged essay were not in the nature of increasing formalism but of altering details of the forms: viz. (*Tz'u-hai*, I, 325), the number of characters in the essay, which had been fixed at 450 in the Hsün-chih reign (1644–61), was changed to 550 in the next reign and later to 600 and over.

Formalism in the late-Ch'ing period, in so far as it was really more intense than before (and not just an endemic quality, freshly noted), should be seen not as a modern aberration but as an always intrinsic potentiality of the examination-system; cf. Waley, *The Life and Times of Po Chü-i, 772–846 A.D.* (New York, 1949), 28, on the 'judgment form' of T'ang examination essay. The modern critical spirit which brought about the abolition of the examinations in 1905 was in the end a spirit to which the whole system was frankly incomprehensible, not one which discriminated between an allegedly earlier examination emphasis on plausible content and a later, correctible emphasis on stylistic frippery.

117. It is in the light of this modern Chinese development that the Chinese communists have used *pa-ku* as a term of opprobrium, and in the 1940's denounced 'party formalism' within their own ranks as a tissue of eight sins (like the hyper-aesthetic, or useless, addiction to 'lengthy phrases and empty words'), one for each leg of the eight-legged essay; see Albert Borowitz, *Fiction in Communist China* (mimeo.), Centre for International Studies, MIT (Cambridge, 1954), 5.

118. *Tz'u-hai*, I, 325.

INTERLUDE

1. Yüan Chieh (723–72), 'Civilization', in Waley, *Chinese Poems* (London, 1946), 118.

CHAPTER III

1. Ku, II, 7.32.
2. 'Ssu-pien lu chi-yao' (Summary of the *Ssu-pien lu*), *Cheng i t'ang ch'üan-shu*, ed. Chang Pai-hsing, suppl. ed., Tso Tsung-t'ang (1866–87), *ts'e* 109, 1.10b–11.
3. For this link between the development of modern science and the rise of the European merchant class, see Needham, 'Thoughts on the Social Relations of Science and Technology in China', *Centaurus*, III (1953), esp. 45–8.
4. *North China Herald*, April 14, 1866.
5. Hsü Shih-ch'ang, *Ch'ing Ju hsüeh-an* (Ch'ing Confucian scholarship) (Tientsin, 1938), 140.9b–11.
6. Tseng Kuo-fan, 'Jih-chi' (Diary), *Tseng Wen-chang kung ch'üan-chi* (Collected works of Tseng Kuo-fan) (Shanghai, 1917), *ts'e* 44, 1.6b.
7. *Ibid.*, 6b.
8. *Ibid.*, 6.
9. Tseng Chi-tse, *Tseng Hou jih-chi* (Marquis Tseng's diary) (Shanghai, 1881), 6b.
10. Tseng, Kuo-fan, 'Sheng-chih hua-hsiang chi' (Portrait record of philosophical masters), *Tseng Wen-chang kung ch'üan-chi*, *ts'e* 27, 2.3; Hsiao I-shan, *Tseng Kuo-fan* (Chungking, 1944), 30.
11. Chiang Chu-ko, *T'ung-ch'eng wen-p'ai p'ing-shu* (A discussion of the T'ung-ch'eng school of writing) (Shanghai, 1930), 68, 74.
12. Though it was the *li* of 'rites' considered in rather a Sung philosophical light, as 'the natural', in Waley's description (*The Analects of Confucius* [London, 1949], 75) 'what one returns to if he can overcome the personal cravings of his human heart and return to the impersonal state that belongs to the heart of Tao'.
13. Hsiao, 31–3. As Hellmut Wilhelm has pointed out, in 'The Background of Tseng Kuo-fan's Ideology', *Asiatische Studien*, Nos. 3–4 (1949), 95–7, Tseng protested that he revered Sung Confucianism but did not wish the Han school to be eliminated, and that he intended with his *li* conception to integrate society and reconcile former opponents.
14. Hsiao, 37, 46.
15. Wilhelm, 97.
16. Teng and Fairbank, 67.
17. As examples of works executed in the same eclectic spirit

by disciples of Tseng Kuo-fan, see Chu Tz'u-ch'i (1808–82), *Ch'ing-ch'ao Ju tsung* (Confucianism during the Ch'ing dynasty), discussed in Hsü Shih-ch'ang, 171.1b, and Ch'en Li (1810–82), *Tung-shu tu-shu chi* (Record of my reading) (Shanghai, 1898). The latter is particularly close to Tseng's eclecticism, attempting to harmonize the Sung Learning and the Han Learning on the grounds that some members of the Han school had made metaphysical researches like those of the Sung school (though the Han Learning generally emphasized textual criticism), while Chu Hsi, the leader of the highly metaphysical Sung school, was the fountainhead of the Han school's textual criticism; see *chüan* 15.

CHAPTER IV

1. This phrase, from the ancient *Mou-kung* (Art of war), by Sun-tzu, was used by Li Hung-chang in a memorial (1863) urging provision for instruction in foreign languages, and used again by Ma Chien-chung in a memorial (1894) recommending the establishment of a translation bureau; see Jen Shih-hsien, *Shina kyoiku shi* (History of Chinese education), Yamazaki Tatsuo, trans. (Tokyo, 1940), II, 95–6. Wilhelm has remarked (in 'The Problem of Within and Without, a Confucian Attempt in Syncretism', *Journal of the History of Ideas*, XII, No. 1 [Jan. 1951], 50) that everyone in this group of innovators conceived of westernization as a matter of defence.

For a translation of statements by representative Confucian westernizers—Lin Tse-hsü, Hsü Chi-yü, Tseng Kuo-fan, Hsüeh Fu-ch'eng, *et al.*—see Teng and Fairbank, *passim*.

2. Chang Chih-tung, *Ch'üan-hsüeh p'ien*, translated (rather, paraphrased) by Samuel I. Woodbridge under the title, *China's Only Hope* (New York, 1900), 63: 'In order to render China powerful, and at the same time preserve our own institutions, it is absolutely necessary that we should utilize western knowledge. But unless Chinese learning is made the basis of education, and a Chinese direction given to thought, the strong will become anarchists, and the weak, slaves.'

Ibid., 137–8: 'To sum up: Chinese learning is moral, Western learning is practical. Chinese learning concerns itself with moral conduct, Western learning, with the affairs of the world. . . . If the Chinese heart throbs in unison with the heart of the sages, expressing the truth in irreprovable conduct, in filial piety, brotherly love, honesty, integrity, virtue; if government is loyalty and protection, then let government make use of foreign machinery and the railway from morning to night, and nothing untowards will befall the disciples of Confucius.'

For discussions of the use of this rationalization in nineteenth-century China, see Wilhelm, 'The Problem of Within and Without', 48–60, esp. 59–60; and Teng and Fairbank, 50 and 164.

3. Cf. Whitehead's ruthless emphasis on careerism as a major basis of the predominance of the Greek and Roman classics in western education before the modern emergence of new careers for which other training, especially in science, was necessary. See his sympathetic but unsentimental essay, 'The Place of Classics in Education', *The Aims of Education and Other Essays* (New York, 1949), esp. 69.

4. Ch'uan, 134.

5. Lin Tse-hsü and Wei Yüan (1794–1856) respectively, in 1842, quoted in Teng and Fairbank, 28 and 34.

6. *Ibid.,* 53.

7. Fujiwara Sadame, *Kindai Chūgoku shisō* (Modern Chinese thought) (Tokyo, 1948), 95.

8. Chao Feng-t'ien, *Wan-Ch'ing wu-shih nien ching-chi ssu-hsiang shih* (Economic thought during the last fifty years of the Ch'ing period), *Yenching hsüeh-pao*: Monograph 18 (Peiping, 1939), 88–9.

9. Witness the realization of Ch'i-ying, in his negotiations with the British at Nanking in 1842, that something new was on the horizon. Reporting to the emperor conventionally that the barbarians had been curbed, he went on to observe that the ceremonial forms used for dependent tribes would not restrain them—they would not consent to retire and remain as Annam and Liu-ch'iu. See Teng and Fairbank, 39–40.

10. Oakeshott, 98.

11. *Ibid.,* 41.

12. What industrialization, even just a bit of it, could do to traditional Chinese institutions and values there enshrined has been analysed in Marion J. Levy, Jr., *Family Revolution in Modern China* (Cambridge, 1949).

13. R. W. Meyer, *Leibnitz and the Seventeenth-Century Revolution* (Cambridge, 1952), 51.

14. Whitehead, *Modes of Thought,* 26.

15. Aristotle, *Metaphysics,* 1041b.

16. *Ibid.,* 1071b; Maimonides, *Guide of the Perplexed,* tr. M.

Friedlander (New York, n.d.), 178; Aquinas, *Concerning Being and Essence*, tr. George G. Leckie (New York and London, 1937), 7.

17. W. D. Ross, *Aristotle's Prior and Posterior Analytics* (Oxford, 1949), 284, 660; Aquinas, 44. In connection with notes 14–16, cf. the following passage (XVI, i–ii) in the *Chung-yung* (Doctrine of the Mean), a classical text whose importance was greatly emphasized by Chu Hsi (the translation is that of James Legge, *The Chinese Classics* [Oxford, 1893], I, 397): 'The Master said, "How abundantly do spiritual beings display the powers that belong to them! We look for them, but do not see them; we listen to, but do not hear them; yet they enter into (*t'i*) all things, and there is nothing without them!" ' The meaning of the passage is obscure, but one should note the suggestion of contradiction between *t'i* and objects of sense-perception. Used here in a verbal sense, *t'i* is implicitly identifiable with 'that which makes a thing what it generally *is*'.

18. Aquinas, 5.

19. *Lun-yü*, I, xii; Legge, I, 143: 'In practising the rules of propriety, a natural ease is to be prized.'

20. *Chu-tzu ch'üan-shu* (Complete works of Chu Hsi), ed. Li Kuang-ti (1714), 10.37–8. [Hereafter, CTCS.]

21. *Mencius*, III B, ii, 3; Legge, II (1895), 265.

22. CTCS, 20.76b.

23. Elsewhere (*Mencius*, IV A, xxvii, 2), in a passage which Chu Hsi discussed approvingly more than once, Mencius seems to have defined essentials functionally—a *t'i-yung* interpretation without, however, the use of those terms. The translation of the passage is as follows (Legge, II, 313–14): 'Mencius said, "The richest fruit (*shih*) of benevolence (*jen*) is this—the service of one's parents. The richest fruit of righteousness (*i*) is this—the obeying one's elder brothers. The richest fruit of wisdom (*chih*) is this—the knowing those two things, and not departing from them. The richest fruit of propriety (*li*) is this—the ordering and adorning those two things." ' See CTCS, 10.13b and 21.8. It is doubtful whether, at least for Chu Hsi's interpretation, the translation, 'The richest fruit', gives the full functional force of *shih*: it implies here rather the concept of 'bringing into practical being'.

24. CTCS, 10.13b.

25. See above, Chapter III. The parallel to Chu Hsi is striking: cf. CTCS, 13.2b–3, where *wai-mien*, 'outside', identified as the sphere of *yung*, is juxtaposed with *hsin-chung*, 'within the mind', and

it is maintained that the establishment of outer equilibrium is necessarily correlated with the existence of an inner equilibrium. Chu defines functionally the inner quality, *jen*, as that which perfectly regulates the *t'ien-hsia*, the outer world.

Cf. also a passage from a Classic very important to Sung Confucianism, *Ta-hsüeh*, I, iv (Legge, I, 357): 'The ancients who wished to illustrate illustrious virtue (*ming-te*) throughout the kingdom first ordered well their own states (*chih ch'i kuo*). . . .' This, the beginning of a famous circular chain of sorites, seems more comprehensible from the point of view of *t'i-yung* logic than from any other: good government is the necessary external manifestation of illustrious virtue, an essence; *ming-te* is that which is evidenced in *chih-kuo*.

26. Legge, I, 150.

27. CTCS, 12.24.

28. CTCS, 22.37–7b. This particular discussion of *t'i-yung* developed from *Mencius*, VI A, xi, 1 (Legge, II, 414): 'Mencius said, "Benevolence is man's mind, and righteousness is man's path." '

29. J. D. Bernal, 'A Scientist in China', *The New Statesman and Nation*, XLIX, No. 1255 (March 26, 1955), 424.

30. Fung Yu-lan, *Hsin shih lun* (Discussions of new issues) (Changsha, 1940), 50–1.

31. Knight Biggerstaff, 'The T'ung Wen Kuan', *Chinese Social and Political Science Review*, XVIII, No. 3 (Oct. 1934), 321.

32. Jen, 107.

33. Ch'uan, 143, 147–8.

34. Swift, selecting Descartes as the villain, did, as a matter of fact, make an occasional 'English' protest against science as a French and Catholic vogue. But the advancement of science was so obviously a common European pursuit, in a web of international collaboration, that this pretext for anti-scientism could have none of the point of Wo-jen's distinction between China and the West.

35. See above, note 12.

36. Ch'en Teng-yüan, 'Hsi-hsüeh lai Hua shih kuo-jen che wu-tuan t'ai-tu' (Arbitrary Chinese attitudes at the time of the coming of western knowledge to China), *Tung-fang tsa-chih*, XXVII, No. 8 (April 1930), 61.

37. Teng and Fairbank, 145.

CHAPTER V

1. I have given a general account of the sources, content, and implications of the *chin-wen* reformist doctrine in *Liang Ch'i-ch'ao and the Mind of Modern China*, esp. 34–51.

2. In the nineteenth century, Protestant missionaries were much more active than Catholic missionaries in the field of secular western education; see Kenneth Scott Latourette, *A History of Christian Missions in China* (New York, 1929), 478.

3. The collaboration of missionaries with reformers is well known—e.g. the Welsh missionary, Timothy Richard, after reading one of K'ang Yu-wei's memorials on the subject of modernization, wrote him a letter which expressed his surprise that K'ang had arrived at Richard's conclusions, remarked that their aims seemed to be the same, and suggested consultations. A meeting of K'ang and Richard took place in Peking, and K'ang's disciple, Liang Ch'i-ch'ao, became Richard's Chinese secretary soon after. See Ch'en Kung-lu, *Chung-kuo chin-tai shih* (History of modern China) (Shanghai, 1935), 439–40.

Reformers and official westernizers met on the common ground of *tzu-ch'iang*, 'self-strengthening'. This phrase, which appears in texts of official recommendations for westernization at least as early as 1863, in Li Hung-chang's memorial recommending the study of foreign languages, was a favourite phrase of the reformers, whose principal organizations, active in Peking and Shanghai in 1895–6, were called the *Ch'iang-hsüeh hui* (Society for the study of strengthening). For this aspect of Li's memorial, see Shu Hsin-ch'eng, *Chin-tai Chung-kuo chiao-yü ssu-hsiang shih* (History of modern Chinese educational thought) (Shanghai, 1929), 25–6.

4. Wu Shih-ch'ang, *Chung-kuo wen-hua yü hsien-tai-hua wen-t'i* (Chinese culture and the question of modernization) (Shanghai, 1948), 55–6.

5. For a summary of the *Ta-t'ung shu*, K'ang's most explicit effort to outline his programme for action and to make Confucius its patron, see Itano Chōhachi, 'Kō Yūi no Daido Shisō' (K'ang Yu-wei's idea of the 'Great Harmony'), *Kindai Chūgoku kenkyū* (Modern Chinese researches), ed. Niida Noboru (Tokyo, 1948), 165–204.

6. Sanetō Keishu, *Shin Chūgoku no Jukyō hihan* (A critique of modern Chinese Confucianism) (Tokyo, 1948), 55, 59.

7. Tanouchi Takatsugi, *Shina kyoikugaku shi* (History of educational theory in China) (Tokyo, 1942), 520.

8. T'an Ssu-t'ung 'Jen hsüeh' (Study of benevolence), *T'an Ssu-t'ung ch'üan-chi* (Collected works of T'an Ssu-t'ung) (Peking, 1954), 69.

9. *Ibid.*, 55.

10. Liang, 'Nan-hai K'ang hsien-sheng chuan' (Biography of K'ang Yu-wei), YPSHC: WC, III, 6.67.

11. For this identification of Luther with freedom of thought, see Liang, 'Lun hsüeh-shu chih shih-li tso-yu shih-chieh' (On the power of learning to control the world), YPSHC: WC, III, 6.111, and elsewhere. Liang wrote of Luther in this fashion after he abandoned the *chin-wen* school's practice of invoking the Classics to justify innovation.

12. A description and analysis of the iconoclasm which succeeded *chin-wen* Confucianism in Liang's writings during the first decade of the twentieth century appears in Levenson, 92–101.

CHAPTER VI

1. See Ch'i Ssu-ho, 'Professor Hung on the Ch'un-ch'iu', *Yenching Journal of Social Studies*, I, No. 1 (June 1938), 49–71, esp. 55–6.

2. See Liang, 'Ch'ing-tai hsüeh-shu kai-lun' (A summary of Ch'ing scholarship), YPSHC: CC, IX, 34.63, where he says that in his thirtieth year he ceased discussion of the 'false classics'.

3. Wei Ying-ch'i, *Chung-kuo shih-hsüeh shih* (History of Chinese historiography) (Shanghai, 1941), 243.

4. E.g. Sun Yat-sen's manifesto at Nanking on Jan. 5, 1912, after he had been named by revolutionaries the first president of the Chinese Republic: '. . . Hitherto irremediable suppression of the individual qualities and the natural aspirations of the people having arrested the intellectual, moral, and material development of China, the aid of revolution was invoked to extirpate the primary cause. . . . Dominated by ignorance and selfishness, the Manchus closed the land to the outer world and plunged the Chinese into a state of benighted mentality calculated to operate inversely to their natural talents. . . .' See Benoy Kumar Sarkar, *The Sociology of Races, Cultures, and Human Progress* (Calcutta, 1939), 177–8.

5. Chan Wing-tsit, *Religious Trends in Modern China* (New York,

1953), 9; Kuo Chan-po, *Chin wu-shih nien Chung-kuo ssu-hsiang shih* (History of Chinese thought in the last fifty years) (Shanghai, 1926), 64–5.

6. Henri Van Boven, *Histoire de la littérature chinoise moderne* (Peiping, 1946), 11.

7. Roswell S. Britton, *The Chinese Periodical Press, 1800–1912* (Shanghai, 1933), 122; Ko Kung-chen, *Chung-kuo pao hsüeh shih* (History of Chinese journalism) (Shanghai, 1927), 140.

8. S. Tretiakov, ed., *A Chinese Testament, the Autobiography of Tan Shih-hua* (New York, 1934), 83.

9. Motoda Shigeyuki, *Ching-hsüeh shih-lun* (On the history of classical scholarship), trans. Chiang Chieh-an (Shanghai, 1934), 365.

10. On this point, see Ch'i, 50–1.

11. Derk Bodde, 'Harmony and Conflict in Chinese Philosophy', *Studies in Chinese Thought*, ed. Arthur J. Wright (Chicago, 1953), 34.

12. Ojima Sukema, 'Rokuhen seru Ryō no gakusetsu (Six stages in the development of Liao P'ing's theories), *Shinagaku*, II, No. 9 (May 1922), 714.

13. Chang Ping-lin, 'Kuo-ku lun-heng' (Discussion of national origins), 2.73b, *Chang-shih ts'ung-shu* (Che-chiang t'u-shu kuan, 1917–19).

14. Wu Ching-hsien, 'Chang T'ai-yen chih min-ts'u chü-i shih-hsüeh' (Chang Ping-lin's nationalist historiography), *Tung-fang tsa-chih*, XLIV, No. 4 (April 1948), 40.

15. Chang Ping-lin, 2.67b.

16. The first words of the *Wen-shih t'ung-i* (General principles of literature and history) of Chang Hsüeh-ch'eng. The same sentiment was expressed and elaborated upon by Chang Hsüeh-ch'eng in many texts, both formal treatises and personal letters. See David Shepherd Nivison, *The Literary and Historical Thought of Chang Hsüeh-ch'eng (1738–1801): a Study of His Life and Writing, with Translations of Six Essays from the 'Wen-shih t'ung-i'*, unpublished Ph.D. thesis, Harvard University (May 1953), 67, 114, 127–30, 190; and Nivison, 'The Problem of "Knowledge" and "Action" in Chinese Thought since Wang Yang-ming', in Wright, 127.

17. Liang, 'Chung-kuo li-shih yen-chiu fa' (Methods of research in Chinese history), YPSHC: CC, XVI, 73.9.

18. Su Hsün, 'Shih-lun shang' (First discourse [of three] on history), *Chia yu chi*, Ssu-pu pei-yao, ed. (Shanghai, n.d.), 8.1b.

19. Nivison, *The Literary and Historical Thought of Chang Hsüeh-ch'eng*, 130.

20. Nivison, *ibid.*, 202, points out Hu Shih's error in representing Chang as a modern critic before his time, seeing the Classics as 'historical material'.

21. Chou Yü-tung, *Ching chin-ku-wen hsüeh* (Study of the *chin-wen, ku-wen* classics issue) (Shanghai, 1926), 32.

22. Wu Ching-hsien, 40–1.

23. Tjan Tjoe Som, *Po Hu T'ung: the Comprehensive Discussions in the White Tiger Hall* (Leiden, 1949), I, 119. The greater part of Ku's researches have been published in *Ku shih pien* (Symposium on ancient history) (Peking and Shanghai, 1926–41), vols. I–VII.

24. See *The Autobiography of a Chinese Historian: Being the Preface to a Symposium on Ancient Chinese History (Ku Shih Pien)*, trans. Arthur W. Hummel (Leiden, 1931), esp. 40–7.

25. Ch'i Ssu-ho, 'Wei Yüan yü wan-Ch'ing hsüeh-fu' (Wei Yüan and late-Ch'ing scholarship), *Yenching hsüeh-pao*, XXXIX (Dec. 1950), 222.

26. Cf. Ku's ultimate reservations about the otherwise highly regarded textual critic, Ts'ui Shu (1740–1816). Ts'ui Shu had done excellent work in the exposure of forgeries, particularly in his discovery of chronological strata of deposits of legend in early literature. Yet, said Ku, Ts'ui Shu probed for forgeries only to establish the really orthodox materials of the ancient sages. He only criticized post-*Chan-kuo* texts for falsifying pre-*Chan-kuo* facts; he did not look at pre-*Chan-kuo* texts (i.e. the Classics) to test their own authenticity. 'He was only a *Ju-che* (Confucianist) making his discriminations in ancient history, not a historian doing so.' And— 'The distinction between "Classics" (*ching-shu*) and "tales" (*ch'uan-chi*) is only one of time.' See Wei, 244.

CHAPTER VII

1. Not, of course, its ultimate cause. I am speaking here in terms of logical sequence, not of social consequence.

2. Fujiwara, 136.

3. At the very beginning of Manchu rule in China there were edicts warning the Manchu princes and highest nobles against adopting Chinese costume and language, lest the Manchus lose their identity and their dynasty collapse; see Schuyler Cammann, *China's Dragon Robes* (New York, 1952), 20.

4. Ichiko Chūzō, 'Giwaken no seikaku' (The characteristics of the *I-ho ch'üan*), in Niida, 252. For a picture of a Boxer banner bearing the slogan, 'Fu Ch'ing Mieh Yang', see Chien Po-tsan *et al.*, ed., *I-ho t'uan* (The Boxer movement) (Shanghai, 1953), I, frontispiece.

5. Chang Ping-lin, for example, edited a compilation of works by the anti-Manchu scholar, Wang Fu-shih (1619–92). Wang did, indeed, denounce the Manchus fiercely, but his emphasis was more cultural than political, anti-barbarian rather than anti-Manchu *per se*. Note the tone of these extracts from his *Ch'un-ch'iu chia shuo* (1646), wherein it is implied (allegorically) that the Manchus are not just foreign nationals but unregenerate aliens to Chinese, civilized culture:

'Any strife with the barbarians the Middle Kingdom should not call a war. . . . For to annihilate them is not cruel, to deceive them is not unfaithful, to occupy their territory and confiscate their property is not unjust. . . .'
'To annihilate them and thereby safeguard our people is called benevolent, to deceive them and thereby do to them what they must dislike is called faithful, to occupy their territory and thereby transform their customs by virtue of our letters and morals as well as to confiscate their property and thereby increase the provisions of our own people is called righteous.'

See *Ch'uan-shan i-shu* (Remaining works of Wang Fu-chih) (Shanghai, 1933), *ts'e* 29, 3.16b–17.
In the text, Wang specifically distinguishes between strife among the various states of the Empire (hence, civilized states) and strife between a Chinese state and barbarians. Thus, there is a cultural, not a political test as to whether strife is pursued under rules of honour or ruthlessly.

6. Onogawa Hidemi, 'Shō Heirin no minzoku shisō' (The nationalism of Chang Ping-lin), part 2, *Tōyōshi kenkyū* (Journal of Oriental Researches), XIV, No. 3 (Nov. 1955), 46; Wu Ching-hsien, 39.

7. For documented accounts of social-Darwinism in early Chinese nationalism, see Levenson, 115–21, and Onogawa, 'Shimmatsu no shisō to shinkaron' (Late Ch'ing political thought and the theory of evolution), *Tōhō gakuhō* (Journal of Oriental Studies), XXI (March 1952), 1–36.

8. Huang Tsung-hsi, 'Ming-i tai-fang lu', *Hsiao-shih shan-fang*

ts'ung-shu, ed. Ku Hsiang (1874), *ts'e* 5, 1b–2b. A translation of part of this passage appears in Teng and Fairbank, 18.

9. Huang, 4.

10. Ku, I, 1.13.

11. *Ibid.*, I, 13.41.

12. *Ibid.*, I, 13.42.

13. *Ibid.*, I, 7.27.

14. *Mencius*, VII, V, xiii; see Legge, II, 483: 'There are instances of individuals without benevolence who have got possession of a (single) state, but there has been no instance of the throne's being got by someone without benevolence.'

15. Ku, I, 12.9.

16. *Ibid.*, I, 2.41.

17. Liang, 'Hsin-min shuo' (Discourses on the new people), YPSHC: CC, III, 4.20.

18. Ts'ai Shang-ssu, *Chung-kuo ch'uan-t'ung ssu-hsiang tsung p'i-p'an* (General criticism of traditional Chinese thought) (Shanghai, 1949), 13–14. Cf. Emile Durkheim, *Sociology and Philosophy* (London, 1953), 59: 'Society . . . is above all a composition of ideas, beliefs and sentiments of all sorts which realize themselves through individuals. Foremost of these ideas is the moral ideal which is its principal *raison d'être*. To love one's society is to love this ideal, and one loves it so that one would rather see society disappear as a material entity than renounce the ideal which it embodies.'

19. But not meaningless just because it does not apply in actual individual instances. Cf. Ernst Cassirer, 'Einstein's Theory of Relativity Considered from the Epistemological Standpoint', supplement to *Substance and Function* (Chicago, 1923), 419: 'The philosopher . . . is ever again brought to the fact that there are ultimate ideal determinations without which the concrete cannot be considered and made intelligible.'

20. Nakayama Kujirō, 'Gendai Shina no Kōjikyō mondai ni tsuite' (On the question of Confucianism in contemporary China), *Tōa ronsō*, II (Tokyo, 1940), 4.

21. Henri Bernard-Maitre, *Sagesse chinoise et philosophie chrétienne* (Paris, 1935), 260.

22. M. H. Abrams, *The Mirror and the Lamp: Romantic Theory and the Critical Tradition* (New York, 1953), 219. For an excellent discussion of Chiang K'ai-shek's nationalistic Confucianism as a romantic deviation from both nationalist anti-traditionalism and the rational and universal qualities of Confucianism as

traditionally conceived, see Mary Wright, 'From Revolution to Restoration: the Transformation of Kuomintang Ideology', *Far Eastern Quarterly*, XIV, No. 4 (Aug. 1955), 515–32, esp. 520–1 and 525.

23. Van Boven, 147.

24. Liang, 'Ta Chung-hua fa-k'an-tz'u' (Foreword to *Ta Chung-hua*), YPSHC: WC, XII, 33.83–4.

CHAPTER VIII

1. Hsiao Kung-ch'uan, *Chung-kuo cheng-shih ssu-hsiang shih* (History of Chinese political thought) (Shanghai, 1946), II, 424.

2. T. K. Chuan, 'Philosophy Chronicle', *T'ien Hsia Monthly*, IV, No. 3 (March 1936), 291.

3. Ts'ai Shang-ssu, *Ts'ai Yüan-p'ei hsüeh-shu ssu-hsiang ch'üan-chi* (An account of the scholarship and thought of Ts'ai Yüan-p'ei) (Shanghai, 1951), 267–8.

4. Robert K. Sakai, 'Ts'ai Yüan-p'ei as a Synthesizer of Western and Chinese Thought', *Papers on China* (mimeo.), III (Harvard University, May 1949), 180.

5. Ts'ai, *Ts'ai*, 104.

6. Sakai, 182–3.

7. Tai Chin-hsieo, *The Life and Work of Ts'ai Yüan-p'ei*, unpublished Ph.D. thesis, Harvard University (1952), 42.

8. Ts'ai, *Ts'ai*, 133–4.

9. For Zao Wou-ki, see 'La peinture chinoise contemporaine', catalogue of an exhibition at the Musée Cernuschi (Paris, 1946); Neste Jacometti, 'Zao Wou-ki', *Art Documents*, VII (1951), 3; and *Lecture par Henri Michaux de huit lithographies de Zao Wou-ki* (Paris, 1951).

10. Feng Yu-lan, 'Chinese Philosophy and Its Possible Contribution to a Universal Philosophy', *East and West*, I, No. 4 (Jan. 1951), 215.

11. Yeh Ch'ing, *Tsen-yang yen-chiu 'San Min Chü-i'* (How study the 'Three People's Principles'?) (Taipei, 1951), 70–7.

12. Kuo, 61. According to Ts'ai Yüan-p'ei (quoted in Onogawa, 'Shimmatsu no shisō to shinkaron', 8), Yen Fu, who had translated Huxley's *Evolution and Ethics* in 1896, had had an eight-character personal motto in those earlier days: 'Revere the people and rebel against the prince; revere the present and rebel against the past.'

13. Ya-tung t'u-shu-kuan (publ.), *K'o-hsüeh yü jen-sheng-kuan* (Science and the philosophy of life—a symposium), 2 vols. (Shanghai, 1923), and Yang Ming-chai, *P'ing Chung Hsi wen-hua kuan* (A critique of views on Chinese and western civilizations) (Peking, 1924), probably provide the best introduction to the vast post-war literature in the anti-materialist, anti-'western progress' vein.

CHAPTER IX

1. Jacques Maritain, *Religion et culture* (Paris, 1930), 56.
2. *L'art chrétien chinois*, special number of *Dossiers de la commission synodale*, V, No. 5 (Peiping, May 1932), 411.
3. Bernard-Maitre, 113.
4. *Ibid.*, 121.
5. A China Missionary, 'First Thoughts on the Debacle of Christian Missions in China', *African Affairs*, LI, No. 202 (Jan. 1952), 33.
6. Liang, 'Pao-chiao fei so-i tsun K'ung lun' (To preserve the Confucian doctrine is not the way to honour Confucius), YPSHC: WC, IV, 9.53.
7. Léon Wieger, *Le flot montant (Chine moderne*, II) (Hsien-hsien, 1921), 9–11. *Hsin ch'ing-nien* and *Hsin ch'ao* were periodicals first appearing in 1915 and 1919, respectively. The *Hsin-ch'ao* society which sponsored the periodical of that name was founded in December 1918.
8. Benjamin I. Schwartz, *Chinese Communism and the Rise of Mao* (Cambridge, 1951), 17–18; Wieger, 10.
9. Fukuda Masazō, 'Shakai bunka hen (kyoiku)' (Section on society and culture—education), *Gendai Shina kōza* (Lectures on modern China), ed. Hideshima Tatsuo (Shanghai, 1939), VI, 4.
10. Hsü Mou-yung, *Wen i ssu-ch'ao hsiao-shih* (Short history of the literary and artistic thought-tide) (Changchun, 1949—author's preface, 1936), 100.
11. Chiang, 91–3.
12. Aoki Masaru, 'Go Teki wo chūshin ni uzumaite iru bungaku katsumei' (A literary revolution in China with Hu Shih as its central figure), part 2, *Shinagaku*, I, No. 2 (Oct. 1920), 124–5.
13. William Ayers, 'The Society for Literary Studies, 1921–1930', *Papers on China*, VIII (Feb. 1953), 51–3.
14. Cf. Lu Hsün, 'The Diary of a Madman', *Ah Q and Others*, tr. Wang Chi-chen (New York, 1941), 205–19, a condemnation,

in the form of tragic irony, of the classical tradition as a scourge of society. The tradition's claims to a rarefied philosophical value are denounced as pretence, as a camouflage for vicious social control.

15. Mannheim, 99. See also pp. 136–7: 'The sympathetic grasp of the nature of historic growth which Burke achieved would never have been possible had not certain strata felt that their social position was threatened and that their world might perish.'

16. Chou Ling, *La peinture chinoise contemporaine de style traditionel* (Paris, 1949), 9–10.

17. Ch'in, 188.

18. Lu Feng-tzu, 'Chung-kuo hua t'e-yu ti chi-shu' (Technical principles peculiar to Chinese painting), *Chin-ling hsüeh-pao* (Nanking Journal), II, No. 1 (May 1932), 163.

19. Judith Burling and Arthur Hart, 'Contemporary Chinese Painting', *Magazine of Art*, XLII, No. 6 (Oct. 1949), 218.

20. Edward Sapir, 'Culture, Genuine and Spurious', *Selected Writings of Edward Sapir in Language, Culture, and Personality*, ed. David G. Mandelbaum (Berkeley and Los Angeles, 1949), 321.

21. The definition of eclecticism in Theodore Meyer Greene, *The Arts and the Art of Criticism* (Princeton, 1947), 383, applies: 'Eclecticism in the bad sense may be defined as the arbitrary juxtaposition of antipathetic stylistic factors or, alternatively, as the use in a single work of art of unassimilated aspects of sharply divergent styles.'

22. Kao Weng, 'The Art of Painting Is Not Lifeless', *An Exhibition of Paintings by Kao Weng and Chang K'un-i*, Metropolitan Museum of Art (New York, 1944). Cf. the Lingnan group, founded in 1919, which attempted to create a new style by portrayal of modern subject matter (ships, aeroplanes, bridges, etc.) in traditional technique; see Michael Sullivan, 'The Traditional Trend in Contemporary Chinese Art', *Oriental Art*, II, No. 3 (Winter 1949–50), 108, and Jen Yu-wen, 'Art Chronicle', *T'ien Hsia Monthly*, VI, No. 2 (Feb. 1938), 145.

23. Burling and Hart, 218. (Wu's gambit leaves him open, of course, to a rather effective counter-ploy—a recommendation of painting the nude.)

24. Whitehead, *Symbolism, Its Meaning and Effect* (New York, 1927), 88.

25. Martin Buber, *Moses* (Oxford and London, 1946), 18. Cf. T. S. Eliot, *What Is A Classic?* (London, 1945), 15: 'The persistence of literary creativeness in any people, accordingly, consists

in the maintenance of an unconscious balance between tradition in the larger sense—the collected personality, so to speak, realized in the literature of the past—and the originality of the living generation.' Cf. also D. H. Lawrence's acute distinction, in 'John Galsworthy', *Selected Essays* (Harmondsworth, 1950), 222: 'They keep up convention, but they cannot carry on a tradition. There is a tremendous difference between the two things. To carry on a tradition, you must add something to the tradition . . .'; and the architect, Walter Gropius, in 'Tradition and the Center', *Harvard Alumni Bulletin*, LIII, No. 2 (Oct. 14, 1950), 69: 'Whenever man imagined he had found "eternal beauty" he fell back into imitation and stagnation. True tradition is the result of constant growth. Its quality must be dynamic, not static, to serve as an inexhaustible stimulus to man.'

26. Sapir, 321.

27. Eliot, 15.

CHAPTER X

1. Robert Payne, *China Awake* (New York, 1947), 378.

2. Schwartz, 'Marx and Lenin in China', *Far Eastern Survey*, XVIII, No. 15 (July 27, 1949), 178.

3. Liu Shao-chi, *On the Party* (Peking, 1950), 31.

4. *Ibid.*, 29.

5. *A Guide to New China*, 1953 (Peking, 1953), 112.

6. See *Postage Stamps of the People's Republic of China, 1949–1954* (Supplement to *China Reconstructs*, IV (April 1955), 31–2, for an account of the stamps devoted to the second quartet of giants; the first had not been publicized in this effective way.

7. Chou Yang, 'The People's New Literature', *The People's New Literature* (Peking, 1950), 105.

8. *Ibid.*, 105–6.

9. *Ibid.*, 115–16.

10. *Ibid.*, 116–17.

11. *Folk Arts of New China* (Peking, 1954), 18.

12. Chou Yang, 103.

13. Chou En-lai, 'The People's Liberation War and Problems in Literature and Art', *The People's New Literature*, 32–4.

14. Communist interest in the T'ai-p'ing Rebellion has been enormous. There has been a great output of communist literature on the subject, particularly in 1950, the centenary year. A cursory study of modern Chinese intellectual history, but one which gives

the quintessence of communist opinion, describes the T'ai-p'ing Rebellion as *k'ung-hsiang* (fantasy) socialism; see Fei Min, *Chungkuo chin-tai ssu-hsiang fa-chan chien-shih* (Brief history of the development of modern Chinese thought) (Shanghai, 1949), 12. For another reference to the sound instincts but historical limitations of these forerunners, see 'Soochow Remembers the Taipings', *China Reconstructs*, I (Jan.–Feb. 1953), 49–51.

15. Hsü Mou-yung, 98–9.

16. Chung Chi-ming, *Hsiang min-chien wen i hsüeh-shu* (Studies towards a people's literature and art) (Shanghai, 1950), 2.

17. Kwei Chen, 'Po Chu-i: People's Poet', *China Reconstructs*, IV (July–Aug. 1953), 31.

18. Feng Hsüeh-feng, 'Lu Hsun, His Life and Thought', *Chinese Literature*, 2 (Spring 1952)—reprinted in *Current Background*, 217 (Oct. 30, 1952) (American Consulate General, Hong Kong), 7.

19. Chung, 18–19.

20. Mao Tse-tung, 'Stalin—Friend of the Chinese People', *People's China*, I, No. 1 (Jan. 1, 1950), 4.

21. *Postage Stamps of the People's Republic of China, 1949–1954*, 29–31.

22. See *The New York Times*, Nov. 14, 1954 (Hong Kong dateline), for an account of a government-sponsored movement to promote Chinese herb medicine, acupuncture, etc., and to integrate what is called 'the old national legacy' with modern medical techniques.

23. Kuo Mo-Jo, 'Culture chinoise et occident', *Democratie nouvelle*, V, No. 2 (Feb. 1951), 69.

24. Kuo Mo-jo, 'The United Front in Literature and Art', *People's China*, I, 1 (Jan. 1, 1950), 29.

25. Ch'ien Tuan-sheng, 'Study [*hsüeh-hsi*] for the Purpose of Self Reform and Better Service to the Fatherland', *Jen-min jih-pao* (Peking, Nov. 6, 1951), Chao Kuo-chün, trans. (Harvard University, 1952: mimeo.), 4.

26. Chou Yang, 104–5. Note that western-trained Chinese doctors who oppose 'the motherland's medical legacy' (i.e. a 'popular' tradition) are said to have been 'poisoned by bourgeois ideology'; see *The New York Times, loc. cit.*

27. Li Ch'ang-chih, *Chung-kuo hua-lun t'i-hsi chi ch'i p'i-p'ing* (Chinese systems of aesthetics and a criticism of them) (Chungking, 1944), 9–13.

28. Wen Chao-t'ung, *Hsin Chung-kuo ti hsin mei-shu* (The new fine arts of the new China) (Shanghai, 1950), 1–3.

29. Mao, *Problems of Art and Literature* (New York, 1950), 32.

30. Wen, 1.

31. *Ibid.*, 11–12.

32. *Ibid.*, 2.

33. Cf. the description of an exhibition of proletarian paintings in Peking, 1949, in Bodde, *Peking Diary* (New York, 1950), 182.

34. Yeh Chien-yu, 'On the Classical Tradition in Chinese Painting', *People's China*, VII (1954), 15, 17. Cf. Chou Yang, *China's New Literature and Art* (Peking, 1954), 38, making the convenient identification of the national heritage with the 'popular', not the 'feudal' past: 'The main lesson to be drawn from our national heritage is its spirit of realism.' Some years earlier, Mao Tun (the naturalistic writer, always close to the communists) had characterized as 'national form' the portrayal of the life of all classes in all its reality and completeness; see Amitendranath Tagore, 'Wartime Literature of China—Its Trends and Tendencies', *The Visva-Bharati Quarterly*, XVI, No. 2 (Aug.–Oct. 1950), 128.

35. Chang Jen-hsia, 'Flower-and-Bird Painting', *China Reconstructs*, III (May–June 1953), 51.

36. For this emphasis, *ibid.*, 51–2.

37. *Postage Stamps of the People's Republic of China, 1949–1954*, 15–16, 27.

38. C. P. Fitzgerald, 'The Renaissance Movement in China', *Meanjin*, IX, No. 2 (Winter 1950), 107.

39. Ai Chung-hsin, 'Hsü Pei-hung—an Outstanding Painter', *People's China*, III (1954), 36.

40. Ch'en Yuan, 'Chinese Culture in Wartime', *Journal of the Royal Society of Arts*, XCIV, No. 4728 (Oct. 11, 1946), 681–2.

41. *Folk Arts of New China*, 45. Cf. Lu Chi on music: 'China's new songs of the masses are, on the one hand, a negation of Chinese feudal music and music of the people of the city, and, on the other hand, a negation of the music of European and American capitalism.' Quoted in Clarence Moy, 'Communist China's Use of the Yang-ko', *Papers on China*, VI (March 1952), 123.

CONCLUSION

1. Needham, *Science and Civilization in China*, I, 4.

2. Kobayashi Taichiro, 'Hokusai and Degas', *Contemporary Japan*, XV, Nos. 9–12 (Sept.–Dec. 1946), 359–68.

3. Nagassé Takashiro, *Le paysage dans l'art de Hokuçai* (Paris, 1937), 13-15, 19, 180.

4. Nien Hsi-yao, superintendent (1726-36) of the imperial porcelain factory, quoted in Soame Jenyns, *Later Chinese Porcelain* (New York, n.d.), 44. For the transmission of European rules of perspective to China in the seventeenth century and their employment, by imperial order, in the preparation of two famous sets of engravings, one on agricultural and the other on military and domestic themes, see Paul Pelliot, *Les influences européennes sur l'art chinois au XVIIe et au XVIIIe siècle* (Paris, 1948), 7-8; Pelliot, 'Les "Conquêtes de l'empereur de la Chine" ', *T'oung pao*, XX (1921), 266-7; and Jean Monval, 'Les conquêtes de la Chine: une commande de l'empereur de Chine en France au XVIIIe siècle', *La revue de l'art ancien et moderne*, II (1905), 150. For Chinese appreciation of the eighteenth-century missionary artist, Castiglione (Lang Shih-ning), who combined western technique with predominantly Chinese conventions, see Pelliot, 'Les "Conquêtes" ', 186-9.

5. This point has been made in another connection in Edwin G. Pulleyblank, *Chinese History and World History* (Cambridge, 1955), 9.

6. See Teng and Fairbank, 12, where a late Ming writer on Ricci is quoted as follows: '. . . I am very much delighted with his ideas, which are close to Confucianism but more earnest in exhorting society not to resemble the Buddhists, who always like to use obscure, incoherent words to fool and frighten the populace. . . .'

7. See Teng and Fairbank, 34, for Wei Yüan's apologetic reference (1842) to K'ang-hsi's use of Dutch ships to reduce Formosa, Jesuit-cast cannon to suppress the rebellion of Wu San-kuei, and European appointments to the Imperial Board of Astronomy; and *ibid.*, 83, for Tso Tsung-t'ang's similar reference (1866), in his argument for steamships, to these seventeenth-century cannon.

8. Ku, II, 29.10.

9. We are speaking here of change in peripheral values, not of anything central like the substitution of Christianity for Confucianism, which simply could not generally happen without general social change.

10. This similarity is noted in Bodde, 'Harmony and Conflict in Chinese Philosophy', 72.

11. For an analysis of the conflict, especially in the Six Dynasties period, between the gentry's social commitment to Confucian

society and intellectual attraction to the Buddhist church, and a suggestion of the issue of this conflict in a Buddhist-influenced Confucianism and a revived imperial bureaucratic state, see Arthur F. Wright, 'Fu I and the Rejection of Buddhism', *Journal of the History of Ideas*, XII, No. 1 (Jan. 1951), 31–47.

12. *Mencius*, III A, iv, 6; Legge, II, 249–50: 'Hence, there is the saying, "Some labour with their minds, and some labour with their strength. Those who labour with their minds govern others; those who labour with their strength are governed by others. Those who are governed by others support them; those who govern others are supported by them." This is a principle universally recognized.'

Bibliography

A. CHINESE AND JAPANESE

'Abe Kojirō zō: Un Nanden hitsu kaki satsu' ('Flowers' by Yün Nan-t'ien in the Abe Kojirō Collection), *Bijutsu kenkyū*, XCII (Aug. 1939), pp. 306–7.

Aimi Shigeichi, *Gumpō seigan* (Tokyo, 1914).

Aoki Masaru, 'Go Teki wo chūshin ni uzumaite iru bungaku katsumei' (A literary revolution in China with Hu Shih as its central figure), *Shinagaku*, I, No. 1 (Sept. 1920), 11–26; No. 2 (Oct. 1920), 112–30; No. 3 (Nov. 1920), 199–219.

   'Sekitō no ga to garon to' (Shih-t'ao's painting and his views on painting), *Shinagaku*, I, No. 8 (April 1921), pp. 575–92.

Bokuyūsō shujin, *Sekitō to Hachidaisenjin* (Shih-t'ao and Pa-ta shan-jen) (Kanagawa ken, 1952).

Chang Ping-lin, 'Kuo-ku lun-heng' (Discussion of national origins), *Chang-shih ts'ung-shu* (Che-chiang t'u-shu kuan, 1917–19).

Chao Feng-t'ien, *Wan-Ch'ing wu-shih nien ching-chi ssu-hsiang shih* (Economic thought during the last fifty years of the Ch'ing period), *Yenching hsüeh-pao*: Monograph 18 (Peiping, 1939).

Ch'en Kung-lu, *Chung-kuo chin-tai shih* (History of Modern China) (Shanghai, 1935).

Ch'en Li, *Tung-shu tu-shu chi* (Record of my reading) (Shanghai, 1898).

Ch'en Teng-yüan, 'Hsi-hsüeh lai Hua shih kuo-jen che wu-tuan t'ai-tu' (Arbitrary Chinese attitudes at the time of the coming of western knowledge of China), *Tung-fang tsa-chih*, XXVII, No. 8 (April 1930), pp. 61–76.

Ch'i Ssu-ho, 'Wei Yüan yü wan—Ch'ing hsüeh-fu' (Wei Yüan and late-Ch'ing scholarship), *Yenching hsüeh-pao*, XXXIV (Dec. 1950), pp. 177–226.

Chiang Shu-ko, *T'ung-ch'eng wen-p'ai p'ing shu* (A discussion of the T'ung-ch'eng school of writing) (Shanghai, 1930).

Chien Po-tsan *et al.*, ed., *I-ho t'uan* (The Boxer movement) (Shanghai, 1953).

Ch'ien Mu, *Chung-kuo chin san-pai nien hsüeh-shu shih* (History of Chinese scholarship in the last three hundred years) (Chungking, 1945).

BIBLIOGRAPHY

Ch'ing Chung-wen, *Chung-kuo hui-hua hsüeh shih* (History of Chinese painting) (Peiping, 1934).

Chou Yü-tung, *Ching chin-ku-wen hsüeh* (Study of the *chin-wen*, *ku-wen* classics issue) (Shanghai, 1926).

Ch'üan Han-sheng, 'Ch'ing-mo fan-tui Hsi-hua ti yen-lun' (Arguments against westernization in the late Ch'ing period), *Lingnan hsüeh-pao*, V, Nos. 3–4 (Dec. 20, 1936), pp. 122–66.

Chung Chi-ming, *Hsiang min-chien wen i hsüeh-shu* (Studies towards a people's literature and art) (Shanghai, 1950).

Fei Min, *Chung-kuo chin-tai ssu-hsiang fa-chan chien-shih* (Brief history of the development of modern Chinese thought) (Shanghai, 1949).

Fujiwara Sadame, *Kindai Chūgoku shisō* (Modern Chinese thought) (Tokyo, 1948).

Fukuda Masazō, 'Shakai bunka hen (kyoiku)' (Section on society and culture—education), *Gendai Shina kōza* (Lectures on modern China), ed. Hideshima Tatsuo (Shanghai, 1939), VI, pp. 1–40.

Fung Yu-lan, *Hsin shih lun* (Discussions of new issues) (Changsha, 1940).

'Hashimoto Shinjirō zō: Un Nanden hitsu kahin seikyō zu' ('Fruits' by Yün Nan-t'ien in the Hashimoto Shinjirō Collection), *Bijutsu kenkyū*, VII (July 1932), p. 237.

Hou Wai-lu, *Chin-tai Chung-kuo ssu-hsiang hsüeh-shuo shih* (Intellectual history of modern China) (Shanghai, 1947).

Hsia Wen-yen, *T'u-hui pao-chien*, ed. Chieh-lu ts'ao t'ang.

Hsiao I-shan, *Ch'ing-tai t'ung-shih* (General history of the Ch'ing period) (Shanghai, 1927).

Tseng Kuo-fan (Chungking, 1944).

Hsiao Kung-ch'uan, *Chung-kuo cheng-shih ssu-hsiang shih* (History of Chinese political thought) (Shanghai, 1946).

Hsü Ch'in, 'Ming hua lu' (Records of Ming painting), *Ts'ung-shu chi-ch'eng* (Shanghai, 1926).

Hsü Mou-yung, *Wen i ssu-ch'ao hsiao-shih* (Short history of the literary and artistic thought-tide) (Changchun, 1949).

Hsü Shih-ch'ang, *Ch'ing Ju hsüeh-an* (Ch'ing Confucian Scholarship) (Tientsin, 1938).

Hu Man, *Chung-kuo mei-shu shih* (History of Chinese art) (Shanghai, 1950).

Huang Pin-hung, *Ku hua cheng* (Evidence on old painting) (Shanghai, 1931).

Huang Tsung-hsi, 'Ming-i tai-fang lu', *Hsiao-shih shan-fang ts'ung-shu*, ed. Ku Hsiang (1874).

'I Fukyū hitsu: sansui zu' (Landscape, by I Fu-chiu), *Kokka*, 174 (Nov. 1904), p. 108 and plate V.

Ichiko Chūzō, 'Giwaken no seikaku' (The characteristics of the *I-ho ch'üan*), *Kindai Chūgoku kenkyū* (Modern Chinese researches), ed. Niida Noboru (Tokyo, 1948), pp. 245–67.

Ichiuji Giryō, *Tōyō bijutsu shi* (History of Far Eastern art) (Tokyo, 1936).

BIBLIOGRAPHY

Ise Senichirō, 'Bunjinga—nanga yori bunjinga e no suii' (Literati painting—the transition from southern painting to literati painting),
Tōyō bijutsu, III (Sept. 1929), pp. 2–12.

Ji Ko Gaishi shi Kei Kō Shina sansuiga shi (History of Chinese
landscape painting from Ku K'ai-chih to Ching Hao) (Kyoto,
1933).

Itano Chōhachi, 'Kō Yūi no Daido Shisō' (K'ang Yu-wei's idea of the
'Great Harmony'), *Kindai Chūgoku kenkyū* (Modern Chinese researches), ed. Niida Noboru (Tokyo, 1948), pp. 165–204.

Jen Shih-hsien, *Shina kyoiku shi* (History of Chinese education), Yamazaki
Tatsuo, tr. (Tokyo, 1940).

Ko Kung-chen, *Chung-kuo pao-hsüeh shih* (History of Chinese journalism)
(Shanghai, 1927).

Ku-kung shu-hua chi (Palace Museum collection of painting and calligraphy) (Peiping, 1930).

Ku Yen-wu, *Jih-chih lu* (Shanghai, 1933).

Kuo Chan-po, *Chin wu-shih nien Chung-kuo ssu-hsiang shih* (History of
Chinese thought in the last fifty years) (Shanghai, 1926).

'Kyū Ei Tōjin shii e kai' (Explanation of Ch'iu Ying's paintings on
themes from T'ang poetry), *Kokka*, 481 (Dec. 1930), pp. 344–6.

Li Ch'ang-chih, *Chung-kuo hua-lun t'i-hsi chi ch'i p'i-p'ing* (Chinese systems
of aesthetics and a criticism of them) (Chungking, 1944).

Liang Ch'i-ch'ao, 'Ch'ing-tai hsüeh-shu kai-lun' (A summary of Ch'ing
scholarship), *Yin-ping-shih ho-chi* (Shanghai, 1936), *chuan-chi*, IX.

'Chung-kuo chin san-pai nien hsüeh-shu shih' (History of Chinese
scholarship in the last three hundred years), *Yin-ping-shih ho-chi,
chuan-chi*, XVII.

'Chung-kuo li-shih yen-chin fa' (Methods of research in Chinese history), *Yin-ping-shih ho-chi, chuan-chi*, XVI.

'Hsin-min shuo' (Discourses on the new people), *Yin-ping-shih ho-chi*,
III.

'Lun hsüeh-shu chih shih-li tso-yu shih-chien' (On the power of
learning to control the world), *Yin-ping-shih ho-chi, wen-chi*, III.

'Nan-hai K'ang hsien-sheng chuan' (Biography of K'ang Yu-wei),
Yin-ping-shih ho-chi, wen-chi, III.

'Pao-chiao fei so-i tsun K'ung lun' (To preserve the Confucian doctrine is not the way to honour Confucius), *Yin-ping-ho-chi, wen-chi*,
IV.

'Ta Chung-hua fa k'an-tz'u' (Foreword to *Ta Chung-hua*), *Yin-ping-
shih ho-chi, wen-chi*, XII.

'Tai Tung-yüan sheng-jih ni-pai nien chi-nien hui yüan-ch'i' (The
origins of the conference to commemorate the two hundredth
anniversary of the birth of Tai Tung-yüan), *Yin-ping-shih ho-chi,
wen-chi*, XIV.

'Yen-Li hsüeh-p'ai yü hsien-tai chiao-yü ssu-ch'ao' (The Yen-Li school
and the contemporary educational thought-tide) *Yin-ping-shih
ho-chi, wen-chi*, XIV.

Lin Feng-mien, *I-shu ts'ung-lun* (Essays on art) (Shanghai, 1937).

Liu Ssu-hsün, *Chung-kuo mei-shu fa-ta shih* (History of the development of Chinese art) (Chungking, 1946).

Lu Ch'ien, *Pa-ku wen hsiao-shih* (Short history of the eight-legged essay) (Shanghai, 1937).

Lu Feng-tzu, 'Chung-kuo hua t'e-yu ti chi-shu' (Technical principles peculiar to Chinese painting), *Chin-ling hsüeh-pao* (Nanking Journal), II, No. 1 (May 1932), pp. 161–4.

Ming-jen shu hua chi (Collection of calligraphy and painting of famous practitioners) (Shanghai, 1921).

Motoda Shigeyuki, *Ching-hsüeh shih-lun* (On the history of classical scholarship), tr. Chiang Chieh-an (Shanghai, 1934).

Naitō Konan, 'Tō Kishō Sai Bunki ezō' (Tung Ch'i-ch'ang's portrait of Ts-ai Wen-chi), *Tōyō bijutsu* (Far Eastern Art), I (April 1929), pp. 64–5.

Naitō Torajirō, *Shinchō shoga fu* (Treatise on Ch'ing calligraphy and painting) (Osaka, 1917).

Nakamura Sakutarō and Ojika Bukkai, *Shina ega shi* (History of Chinese painting) (Tokyo, 1923).

Nakayama Kujirō, 'Gendai Shina no Kōjikyō mondai ni tsuite' (On the question of Confucianism in contemporary China), *Tōa ronsō* II (Tokyo, 1940), pp. 1–11.

'Ō Sekikoku hitsu: kambaku zu' (Looking at a waterfall, by Wang Hui), *Kokka*, 702 (Sept. 1950), pp. 305–6.

'Ō Sekikoku hitsu: semmen sansui zu' (Landscape painted on a fan, by Wang Hui), *Kokka*, 614 (Jan. 1942), p. 24.

Ojima Sukema, 'Rokuhen seru Ryō Hei no gakusetsu' (Six stages in the development of Liao P'ing's theories), *Shinagaku*, II, No. 9 (May 1922), pp. 707–14.

Onogawa Hidemi, 'Shimmatsu no shisō to shinkaron' (Late Ch'ing political thought and the theory of evolution), *Tōhō gakuhō* (Journal of Oriental Studies), XXI (March 1952), pp. 1–36.

'Shō Heirin no minzoku shisō' (The nationalism of Chang Ping-lin), *Tōyōshi kenkyū* (Journal of Oriental Researches), XIII, No. 3 (Aug. 1954), pp. 39–58; XIV, No. 3 (Nov. 1955), pp. 45–58.

P'an T'ien-shuo. *Chung-kuo hui-hua shih* (History of Chinese painting) (Shanghai, 1935).

'Ran Ei hitsu: *Hisetsu senzen* zu kai' (Analysis of 'Flying snow and a thousand mountains', by Lan Ying), *Kokka*, 477 (Aug. 1930), p. 228.

Sanetō Keishū, *Shin Chūgoku no Jukyō hihan* (A critique of modern Chinese Confucianism) (Tokyo, 1948.)

'Sei Moyō hitsu: *Sankyo hōmon* zu kai' (Analysis of 'A visitor to a mountain abode', by Shang Mao-yeh), *Kokka*, 543 (Feb. 1946), p. 53.

Sheng Tsung-ch'ien, 'Chieh-chou hsüeh hua pien', *Hua-lun ts'ung-k'an* (Collection of treatises on painting), ed. Yü Hai-yen (Peiping, 1937).

Shih Yai, 'Sung-li Han-lin t'u-hua yüan chi hua-hsüeh shih shih hsi-nien' (A chronology of notable historical data and works of the Hanlin painting academy of the Sung dynasty), *Chung-kuo wen-hua yen-chiu hui-p'an* (Bulletin of Chinese Studies, Chengtu), III (Sept. 1943), pp. 327–60.

'Shin Sekiden hitsu 'Zō Go Kan gyō emaki kai' (Analysis of Shen Shih-t'ien's scroll-painting, 'A gift to Wu K'uan upon his making a journey'), *Kokka*, 545 (April 1936), pp. 113–14.

Shu Hsin-ch'eng, *Chin-tai Chung-kuo chiao-yü ssu-hsiang shih* (History of modern Chinese educational thought) (Shanghai, 1929).

'Ssu-pien lu chi-yao' (Summary of the *Ssu-pien lu*), *Cheng i t'ang ch'üan-shu*, ed. Chang Pai-hsing, suppl. ed., Tso Tsung-t'ang (1866–87).

Su Hsün, 'Shih-lun shang' (First discourse on history), *Chia yu chi*, Ssu-pu pi-yao ed. (Shanghai, n.d.).

Suzuki, Torao, 'Kobun hihō no zenku' (The development of the forms of *pa-ku wen*) *Shinagaku*, IV, No. 1 (July 1926), pp. 27–46.

Tai Chen, 'Meng-tzu tzu-i su-cheng', *An-hui ts'ung-shu*, 6th Ser. (Shanghai, 1936).

'Tung-yüan wen-chi', *An-hui ts'ung-shu*, 6th Ser. (Shanghai, 1936).

Tajima Shiichi, ed., *Tōyō bijutsu taikan* (General view of Far Eastern Art), X (Tokyo, 1911); XI (Tokyo, 1912).

Taki Seiichi, 'Shina e no ni dai chōryū' (The two main currents of Chinese painting), *Kokka*, 438 (Jan. 1929), pp. 3–8.

Taki Seiichirō, 'Shin Keinan *Kudan nishikie satsu* ni tsuite' (On the picture album *Chin-tuan chin-hua-ts'e*, by Shen Ch'i-nan), *Kokka*, 495 (Feb. 1932), pp. 33–40.

T'an P'i-mu, *Ch'ing-tai ssu-hsiang shih-kang* (Historical outline of Ch'ing thought) (Shanghai, 1940).

T'an Ssu-t'ung, 'Jen-hsüeh' (Study of Benevolence), *T'an Ssu-t'ung ch'üan-chi* (Collected works of T'an Ssu-t'ung) (Peking, 1954).

Tanaka Toyozō, *Tōyō bijutsu dansō* (Discussions on Far Eastern Art) (Tokyo, 1949).

T'ang Chih-ch'i, *Hui shih cheng-yen* (Shanghai, 1935).

Tanouchi Takatsugi, *Shina kyoikugaku shi* (History of educational theory in China) (Tokyo, 1942).

Tempō Imazeki, 'Shin Seikiden jiseki' (Biographical note on Shen Shih-t'ien), *Kokka*, 457 (Dec. 1928), pp. 349–54; 458 (Jan. 1929), 15–20.

T'eng Ku, 'Kuan-yü yüan-t'i hua ho wen-jen hua chih shih ti k'ao-ch'a' (An examination of the history of 'academic' and 'literati' painting), *Fu-jen hsüeh-chih*, II, No. 2 (Sept. 1930), pp. 65–86.

Ts'ai Shang-ssu, *Chung-kuo ch'uan-t'ung ssu-hsiang tsung p'i-p'an* (General criticism of traditional Chinese thought) (Shanghai, 1949).

Ts'ai Yüan-p'ei hsüeh-shu ssu-hsiang ch'uan-chi (An account of the scholarship and thought of Ts'ai Yüan-p'ei) (Shanghai, 1951).

Tseng Chi-tse, *Tseng Hou jih-chi* (Marquis Tseng's diary) (Shanghai, 1881).

Tseng Kuo-fan, 'Jih-chi' (Diary), *Tseng Wen-chang kung ch'üan-chi* (Collected works of Tseng Kuo-fan), (Shanghai, 1917).

'Sheng-chih hua-hsiang chi' (Portrait record of philosophical masters), *Tseng Wen-chang kung ch'üan-chi.*

Tsou I-kuei, 'Hsiao-shan hua-p'u', *Ssu t'ung ku chai lun hua chi k'o*, ed. Chang Hsiang-ho (Peking, 1909).

Tung Ch'i-ch'ang, *Hua Ch'an shih sui-pi*, ed. Wang Ju-lu (Peking, 1840). *Tz'u-hai* (Shanghai, 1936).

Unzansei, 'Kyū Ei no gasatsu ni tsuite' (On a picture book by Ch'iu Ying), *Kokka*, 475 (June 1930), pp. 159–67.

Wada Mikio, ed., *Tōyō bijutsu taikan* (General view of Far Eastern Art), XII (Tokyo, 1913).

Wang Fu-chih, 'Ch'un-ch'iu chia shuo', *Ch'uan-shan i-shu* (Remaining works of Wang Fu-chih) (Shanghai, 1933).

Wang Shih-chen, 'I-yüan chih yen fu lu', *Yen-chou shan jen ssu pu kao*, ed. Shih ching t'ang.

Wei Ying-ch'i, *Chung-kuo shih-hsüeh shih* (History of Chinese historiography) (Shanghai, 1941).

Wen Chao-t'ung, *Hsin Chung-kuo ti hsin mei-shu* (The new fine arts of the new China) (Shanghai, 1950).

Wu Ching-hsien, 'Chang T'ai-yen chih min-ts'u chü-i shih-hsüeh' (Chang Ping-lin's nationalist historiography), *Tung-fang tsa-chih* XLIV, No. 4 (April 1948), pp. 38–42.

Wu Shih-ch'ang, *Chung-kuo wen-hua yü hsien-tai-hua wen-t'i* (Chinese culture and the question of modernization) (Shanghai, 1948).

Ya-tung t'u-shu-kuan, publ., *K'o hsüeh yü jen-sheng-kuan* (Science and the philosophy of life—a symposium) (Shanghai, 1923).

Yang Ming-chai, *P'ing Chung Hsi wen-hua kuan* (A critique of views on Chinese and western civilizations) (Peking, 1924).

Yawata Sekitarō, *Shina gajin kenkyū* (Study of Chinese painters) (Tokyo, 1942).

Yeh Ch'ing, *Tsen-yang yen-chin 'San Min Chü-i'* (How study the 'Three People's Principles'?) (Taipei, 1951).

Yen Yüan, 'Ts'un hsüeh pien', *Chi-fu ts'ung-shu* (1879).

Yonezawa Yoshiho, 'Kyū Ei hitsui hakubyō *Tan ran tei* zu' (The *Chuan lan ting*, a picture in the *pai-miao* method, by Ch'iu Ying), *Kokka*, 708 (March 1951), pp. 121–5.

Yoshizawa Tadashi, 'Nanga to bunjinga' (Southern painting and literati painting), *Kokka*, 622 (Sept. 1942), pp. 257–62; 624 (Nov. 1942), pp. 345–50; 625 (Dec. 1942), pp. 376–81; 626 (Jan. 1943), 27–32.

Yū Yamanoi, 'Meimatsu Shinchō ni okeru keiji jiyō no gaku' (The 'Practical affairs' school of the end of the Ming and the beginning of the Ch'ing), *Tōhō gaku ronshū* (Memoirs of the Institute of Eastern Culture) (Tokyo, 1954), pp. 136–50.

Yün Shou-p'ing, '*Ou hsiang kuan hua pa* (*chüan* 11–12, *Ou hsiang kuan chi*), *Pieh hsia chai ts'ung-shu*, ed. Chiang Kuang-hsü (Shanghai, 1923).

BIBLIOGRAPHY

B. WESTERN

A China Missionary, 'First Thoughts on the Debacle of Christian Missions in China', *African Affairs*, LI, No. 202 (Jan. 1952), pp. 33–41.

A Guide to New China, 1953 (Peking, 1953).

'A Landscape, by Wang Hui', *Kokka*, 250 (March 1911), pp. 283–4.

'A Summer Landscape, by Lan Yin (sic)', *Kokka*, 232 (Sept. 1909), pp. 95–6.

Aaron, R. I., *The Theory of Universals* (Oxford, 1952).

Abrams, M. H., *The Mirror and the Lamp: Romantic Theory and the Critical Tradition* (New York, 1953).

Ai Chung-hsin, 'Hsü Pei-hung—an Outstanding Painter', *People's China*, III (1954), pp. 36–40.

Annan, Noel Gilroy, *Leslie Stephen: His Thought and Character in Relation to His Time* (Cambridge, 1952).

Aquinas, Thomas, *Concerning Being and Essence*, tr. George G. Leckie (New York and London, 1937).

Aristotle, *Metaphysics*.

Arnold, Matthew, *Culture and Anarchy* (London, 1920).

Essays in Criticism (Boston, 1865).

Ayers, William, 'The Society for Literary Studies, 1921–1930', *Papers on China* (mimeo.), VIII (Harvard University, Feb. 1953), pp. 34–79.

Ayscough, Florence Wheelock, *Catalogue of Chinese Paintings Ancient and Modern by Famous Masters* (Shanghai, n.d.).

Balázs, Etienne, 'Les aspects significatifs de la société chinoise', *Asiatische Studien*, VI (1952), pp. 77–87.

Baldwin, James, *Notes of a Native Son* (Boston, 1955).

Bernal, J. D., 'A Scientist in China', *The New Statesman and Nation*, XLIX, No. 1255 (March 26, 1955), pp. 424–6.

Bernard-Maitre, Henri, *Sagesse chinoise et philosophie chrétienne* (Paris, 1935).

Biggerstaff, Knight, 'The T'ung Wen Kuan', *Chinese Social and Political Science Review*, XVIII, No. 3 (Oct. 1934), pp. 307–40.

Boas, Franz, *The Mind of Primitive Man* (New York, 1938).

Bodde, Derk, 'Harmony and Conflict in Chinese Philosophy', *Studies in Chinese Thought*, ed. Arthur F. Wright (Chicago, 1953), pp. 19–80.

Peking Diary (New York, 1950).

Borowitz, Albert, *Fiction in Communist China*, mimeo., Centre for International Studies, MIT (Cambridge, 1954).

Bowra, C. M., *The Creative Experiment* (London, 1949).

Bradley, Kenneth, 'Personal Portrait: Sir Andrew Cohen', *London Calling*, No. 745 (Feb. 11, 1954), p. 13.

Britton, Roswell S., *The Chinese Periodical Press, 1800–1912* (Shanghai, 1933).

Broderick, Alan Houghton, *An Outline of Chinese Painting* (London, 1949).

BIBLIOGRAPHY

Bronowski, J., *William Blake, 1757–1827* (Harmondsworth, 1954).

Buber, Martin, *Moses* (Oxford and London, 1946).

Bulling, A. and Ayers, John, 'Chinese Art of the Ming Period in the British Museum', *Oriental Art*, III, No. 2 (1950), pp. 79–81.

Burling, Judith and Hart, Arthur, 'Contemporary Chinese Painting', *Magazine of Art*, XLII, No. 6 (Oct. 1949), pp. 218–20.

Cammann, Schuyler, *China's Dragon Robes* (New York, 1952).

Cassirer, Ernst, *Substance and Function* (Chicago, 1923).

The Myth of the State (New Haven, 1946).

The Problem of Knowledge (New Haven, 1950).

Cassirer, H. W., *A Commentary on Kant's 'Critique of Judgment'* (London, 1938).

Chan, Albert, *The Decline and Fall of the Ming Dynasty, a Study of the Internal Factors*, MS. (Harvard University, 1953).

Chan Wing-tsit, *Religious Trends in Modern China* (New York, 1953).

Chang Chung-li, *The Chinese Gentry: Studies on Their Role in Nineteenth Century Chinese Society* (Seattle, 1955).

Chang Jen-hsia, 'Flower-and-Bird Painting', *China Reconstructs*, III (May–June 1953), pp. 50–2.

Chavannes, Edouard and Petrucci, Raphael, *La peinture chinoise au Musée Cernuschi, Avril–Juin 1912* (Ars Asiatica, I) (Brussels and Paris, 1914).

Ch'en Yuan, 'Chinese Culture in Wartime', *Journal of the Royal Society of Arts*, XCIV, No. 4728 (Oct. 11, 1946), pp. 674–83.

Ch'i Ssu-ho, 'Professor Hung on the Ch'un-ch'iu', *Yenching Journal of Social Studies*, I, No. 1 (June 1938), pp. 49–71.

Ch'ien Tuan-sheng, 'Study [*hsüeh-hsi*] for the Purpose of Self Reform and Better Service to the Fatherland', *Jen-min jih-pao* (Peking, Nov. 6, 1951), Chao Kuo-chün, tr. (Harvard University, 1952, mimeo.).

Chou En-lai, 'The People's Liberation War and Problems in Literature and Art', *The People's New Literature* (Peking, 1950), pp. 13–40.

Chou Ling, *La peinture chinoise contemporaine de style traditionel* (Paris, 1949).

Chou Yang, *China's New Literature and Art* (Peking, 1954).

'The People's New Literature', *The People's New Literature* (Peking, 1950), pp. 89–131.

Chuan, T. K., 'Philosophy Chronicle', *T'ien Hsia Monthly*, IV, No. 3 (March 1936), pp. 287–93.

Clark, Kenneth, *Landscape into Art* (London, 1949).

Cohn, William, *Chinese Painting* (London and New York, 1948).

Collingwood, R. G., *An Autobiography* (Harmondsworth, 1944).

An Essay in Philosophical Method (Oxford, 1933).

The Idea of History (Oxford, 1946).

Contag, Victoria, 'Das Mallehrbuch für Personen-Malerei des Chieh Tzu Yüan', *T'oung Pao*, XXXIII, No. 1 (1937), 15–90.

Die Beiden Steine (Braunschweig, 1950).

Contag, Victoria, *Die Sechs Berühmten Maler der Ch'ing-Dynastie* (Leipzig, 1940).

'Schriftcharakteristeken in der Malerei, dargestellt an Bildern Wang Meng's und Anderer Maler der Südschule', *Ostasiatische Zeitschrift*, XVII, No. 1–2 (1941), 46–61.

'Tung Chi-ch'ang's *Hua Ch'an Shih Sui Pi* und das *Hua Shuo* des Mo Shih-lung', *Ostasiatische Zeitschrift*, IX, Nos. 3–4 (May–Aug., 1933), pp. 83–97; No. 5 (Oct. 1933), pp. 174–87.

Coomeraswamy, Ananda K., *Figures of Speech or Figures of Thought* (London, 1946).

Copland, Aaron, *Music and Imagination* (Cambridge, 1952).

Crombie, A. C., *Augustine to Galileo* (London, 1952).

Dubosc, J. P., 'A New Approach to Chinese Painting', *Oriental Art*, III, No. 2 (1950), pp. 50–7.

Dumoulin, Heinrich, *The Development of Chinese Zen after the Sixth Patriarch in the Light of Mumonkan* (New York, 1953).

Duncan, C. S., 'The Scientist as a Comic Type', *Modern Philology*, XIV, No. 5 (Sept. 1916), pp. 89–99.

Durkheim, Emile, *Sociology and Philosophy* (London, 1953).

Ecke, Gustav, 'Comments on Calligraphies and Paintings', *Monumenta Nipponica*, III (1938), pp. 565–78.

Einstein, Albert, 'Autobiographical Notes', *Albert Einstein: Philosopher-Scientist*, ed. Paul Arthur Schilpp (Evanston, 1949), pp. 1–95.

Eliot, T. S., *What Is A Classic?* (London, 1945).

Elisséev, Serge, 'Sur le paysage à l'encre de Chine du Japon', *Revue des Arts Asiatiques*, 2 (June 1925), pp. 30–8.

Evans, B. Ifor, *Literature and Science* (London, 1954).

Fei Hsiao-tung, *China's Gentry: Essays in Rural-Urban Relations* (Chicago, 1953).

Feng Hsüeh, 'Lu Hsun, His Life and Thought', Chinese Literature, 2 (Spring 1952)—reprinted in *Current Background*, 217 (Oct. 30, 1952) (American Consulate General, Hong Kong), pp. 1–14.

Feng Yu-lan, 'Chinese Philosophy and Its Possible Contribution to a Universal Philosophy', *East and West*, I, No. 4 (Jan. 1951), pp. 212–17.

Ferguson, John C., *Chinese Painting* (Chicago, 1927).

'Wang Ch'uan', *Ostasiatische Zeitschrift*, III, No. 1 (April–June 1914), pp. 51–60.

Fitzgerald, C. P., 'The Renaissance Movement in China', *Meanjin*, IX, No. 2 (Winter 1950), pp. 98–108.

Folk Arts of New China (Peking, 1954).

Forbes, Duncan, 'James Mill and India', *The Cambridge Journal* V, No. 1 (Oct. 1951), pp. 19–33.

Franke, Herbert, 'Zur Biographie des Pa-Ta-Shan-Jen', *Asiatica: Festschrift Friedrich Weller* (Leipzig, 1954), pp. 119–30.

Freeman, Mansfield, 'Yen Hsi Chai, a Seventeenth Century Philosopher', *Journal of the North China Branch of the Royal Asiatic Society*, LVII (1926), pp. 70–91.

BIBLIOGRAPHY

Giles, Herbert A., *An Introduction to the History of Chinese Pictorial Art* (London, 1918).

Glatzer, Nahum, ed., *Franz Rosenzweig, His Life and Thought* (Philadelphia, 1953).

Gray, Christopher, *Cubist Aesthetic Theories* (Baltimore, 1953).

Great Chinese Painters of the Ming and Ch'ing Dynasties (Wildenstein Galleries, New York, 1949).

Greene, Theodore Meyer, *The Arts and the Art of Criticism* (Princeton, 1947).

Grigaut, Paul L., 'Art of the Ming Dynasty', *Archaeology*, V, No. 1 (March 1952), pp. 11–13.

Gropius, Walter, 'Tradition and the Center', *Harvard Alumni Bulletin*, LIII, No. 2 (Oct. 14, 1950), pp. 68–71.

Hackney, Louis Wallace and Yau Chang-foo, *A Study of Chinese Paintings in the Collection of Ada Small Moore* (London, New York, and Toronto, 1940).

Hazard, Paul, *European Thought in the Eighteenth Century, from Montesquieu to Lessing* (New Haven, 1954).

Henderson, Lawrence J., *The Order of Nature* (Cambridge, 1917).

Hippolyte, Jean, *Introduction à l'étude de la philosophie de l'histoire de Hégel* (Paris, 1948).

Hirth, Friedrich, *Native Sources for the History of Chinese Pictorial Art* (New York, 1917).

Houghton, Walter, E., Jr., 'The English Virtuoso in the Seventeenth Century', *Journal of the History of Ideas*, III, No. 1 (Jan. 1942), 51–73; No. 2 (April 1942), 190–219.

Huang Siu-chi, *Lu Hsiang-shan, a Twelfth-Century Chinese Idealist Philosopher* (New Haven, 1944).

Hucker, Charles O., 'The "Eastern Forest" Movement of the Late Ming Period', *Thought and Institutions in China*, ed. John K. Fairbank (Chicago, 1956).

Hummel, Arthur W., ed., *Eminent Chinese of the Ch'ing Period* (Washington, 1943 and 1944).

tr., *The Autobiography of a Chinese Historian: Being the Preface to a Symposium on Ancient Chinese History (Ku Shih Pien)* (Leiden, 1931).

Jacometti, Neste, 'Zao Wou-ki', *Art Documents*, VII (1951), p. 3.

Jaeger, Werner, *Paideia: the Ideals of Greek Culture* (New York, 1943).

Jen Yu-wen, 'Art Chronicle', *T'ien Asia Monthly*, VI, No. 2 (Feb. 1938), pp. 144–47.

Jenyns, Soame, *Later Chinese Porcelain* (New York, n.d.).

Kao Weng, 'The Art of Painting Is not Lifeless', *An Exhibition of Paintings by Kao Weng and Chang K'un-i*, Metropolitan Museum of Art (New York, 1944).

Kobayashi Taichiro, 'Hokusai and Degas', *Contemporary Japan*, XV, Nos. 9–12 (Sept.–Dec. 1946), pp. 359–68.

Kuo Mo Jo, 'Culture chinoise et occident', *Démocratie nouvelle*, V, No. 2 (Feb. 1951), pp. 68–70.

BIBLIOGRAPHY

Kuo Mo Jo, 'The United Front in Literature and Art', *People's China*, I (Jan. 1, 1950), pp. 11–12, 29–30.

Kwei Chen, 'Po Chu-i: People's Poet', *China Reconstructs*, IV (July–Aug. 1953), pp. 31–5.

'La peinture chinoise contemporaine', Musée Cernuschi (Paris, 1946).

Langer, Susanne K., *Philosophy in a New Key* (New York, 1948).

L'art chrétien chinois, special number of *Dossiers de la commission synodale*, V, No. 5 (Peiping, May 1932).

Latourette, Kenneth Scott, *A History of Christian Missions in China* (New York, 1929).

Lawrence, D. H., *Selected Essays* (Harmondsworth, 1950).

Lecture par Henri Michaux de huit lithographies de Zao Wou-ki (Paris, 1951).

Lehrs, Ernst, *Man or Matter* (London, 1951).

Legge, James, tr., 'Chung-yung' (Doctrine of the Mean), *The Chinese Classics*, I (Oxford, 1893).

— tr., 'Lun-yü' (Confucian Analects), *The Chinese Classics*, I.

— tr., 'Mencius', *The Chinese Classics*, II (Oxford, 1895).

— tr., 'Ta-hsüeh' (The Great Learning), *The Chinese Classics*, I.

Levenson, Joseph R., *Liang Ch'i-ch'ao and the Mind of Modern China* (Cambridge, 1953).

Levy, Marion J., Jr., *Family Revolution in Modern China* (Cambridge, 1949).

Lewis, W. Arthur, *The Theory of Economic Growth* (London, 1955).

Lippe, Aschwin, 'The Waterfall', *Bulletin of the Metropolitan Museum of Art*, XII (Oct. 1953), pp. 60–7.

Liu Shao-chi, *On the Party* (Peking, 1950).

'Lotus Flowers, by Liu (sic) Chih', *Kokka*, 315 (Aug. 1916), p. 38.

Lu Hsün, *Ah Q and Others*, tr. Wang Chi-chen (New York, 1941).

Luthy, Herbert, 'Montaigne, or the Art of Being Truthful', *Encounter*, I, No. 2 (Nov. 1953), pp. 33–44.

Maimonides, Moses, *Guide of the Perplexed*, tr. M. Friedlander (New York, n.d.).

Mannheim, Karl, *Essays on Sociology and Social Psychology* (New York, 1953).

Mao Tse-tung, *Problems of Art and Literature* (New York, 1950).

— 'Stalin—Friend of the Chinese People', *People's China*, I, No. 1 (Jan. 1, 1950), p. 4.

March, Benjamin, *Some Technical Terms of Chinese Painting* (Baltimore, 1935).

Maritain, Jacques, *Religion et culture* (Paris, 1930).

Martin, Kingsley, 'Rangoon Reflections', *The New Statesman and Nation*, XLV, No. 1142 (Jan. 24, 1953), pp. 84–5.

Masterpieces of Chinese Bird and Flower Painting (Fogg Art Museum, Cambridge, 1951).

McKeon, Richard, 'Conflicts of Values in a Community of Cultures', *The Journal of Philosophy*, XLVII, No. 8 (April 13, 1950), pp. 197–210.

Meyer, R. W., *Leibnitz and the Seventeenth-Century Revolution* (Cambridge, 1952).

Mills, C. Wright, *White Collar: the American Middle Classes* (New York, 1951).

Monval, Jean, 'Les conquêtes de la Chine; une commande de l'empereur de Chine en France au XVIIIe siècle', *La revue de l'art ancien et moderne*, II (1905), pp. 147–60.

Moy, Clarence, 'Communist China's Use of the Yang-ko', *Papers on China* (mimeo.), VI (Harvard University, March 1952), pp. 112–48.

Nagassé Takashiro, *Le paysage dans l'art de Hokuçai* (Paris, 1937).

Needham, Joseph, *Science and Civilization in China*, I (Cambridge, 1954).

'Thoughts on the Social Relations of Science and Technology in China', *Centaurus*, III (1953), pp. 40–8.

Nef, John U., 'The Genesis of Industrialism and of Modern Science, 1560–1640', *Essays in Honor of Conyers Read*, ed. Norton Downs (Chicago, 1953), pp. 200–69.

New York Times.

Nivison, David Shepherd, *The Literary and Historical Thought of Chang Hsüeh-ch'eng (1738–1801): a Study of His Life and Writing, with Translations of Six Essays from the 'Wen-shih t'ung-i'*, MS. (Harvard University, 1953).

'The Problem of "Knowledge" and "Action" in Chinese Thought since Wang Yang-ming', *Studies in Chinese Thought*, ed. Arthur F. Wright (Chicago, 1953), pp. 112–45.

North China Herald, Shanghai.

Oakeshott, Michael, *Experience and Its Modes* (Cambridge, 1933).

Payne, Robert, *China Awake* (New York, 1947).

Pelliot, Paul, 'Les "Conquêtes de l'empereur de la Chine" ', *T'oung pao*, XX (1921), pp. 183–274.

Les influences européennes sur l'art chinois au XVIIe et au XVIIIe siècle (Paris, 1948).

Petrucci, Raphael, tr., *Encyclopédie de la peinture chinoise* (Paris, 1918).

Pevsner, Nikolaus, *Academies of Art* (Cambridge, 1940).

Plato, *Ion.*

Postage Stamps of the People's Republic of China, 1949–1954 (Supplement to *China Reconstructs*), IV (April 1955).

Powell, Ralph, *The Rise of Chinese Military Power, 1895–1912* (Princeton, 1955).

Pulleyblank, Edwin G., *Chinese History and World History* (Cambridge, 1955).

Read, Herbert, *A Coat of Many Colours* (London, 1945).

Rienaecker, Victor, 'Chinese Art (Sixth Article), Painting—I', *Apollo*, XL, No. 236 (Oct. 1944), pp. 81–4.

'Chinese Art (Seventh Article), Painting—II', *Apollo*, XL, No. 237 (Nov. 1944), pp. 108–13.

Ross, W. D., *Aristotle's Prior and Posterior Analytics* (Oxford, 1949).

BIBLIOGRAPHY

Rowley, George, 'A Chinese Scroll of the Ming Dynasty: Ming Huang and Yang Kuei-fei Listening to Music', *Worcester Art Museum Annual*, II (1936–37), pp. 63–79.

Sakai, Robert K., 'Ts'ai Yüan-p'ei as a Synthesizer of Western and Chinese Thought', *Papers on China* (mimeo.), III (Harvard University, May 1949), pp. 170–92.

Sandor, Paul, *Histoire de la dialectique* (Paris, 1947).

Sapir, Edward, 'Culture, Genuine and Spurious', *Selected Writings of Edward Sapir, in Language, Culture, and Personality*, ed. David G. Mandelbaum (Berkeley and Los Angeles, 1949), pp. 308–31.

Sarkar, Benoy Kumar, *The Sociology of Races, Cultures, and Human Progress* (Calcutta, 1939).

Sarton, George, *Introduction to the History of Science* (Washington, 1931).

Schenck, Edgar C., 'The Hundred Wild Geese', *Honolulu Academy of Arts Annual Bulletin*, I (1939), pp. 3–14.

Schücking, Levin L., *The Sociology of Literary Taste* (New York, 1944).

Schwartz, Benjamin I., *Chinese Communism and the Rise of Mao* (Cambridge, 1951).

'Marx and Lenin in China', *Far Eastern Survey*, XVIII, No. 15 (July 27, 1949), pp. 174–8.

Sirèn, Osvald, *A History of Later Chinese Painting* (London, 1938).

'An Important Treatise on Painting from the Beginning of the Eighteenth Century', *T'oung pao*, XXXIV, No. 3 (1938), pp. 153–164.

Early Chinese Paintings from the A. W. Bahr Collection (London, 1938).

'Shih-t'ao, Painter, Poet, and Theoretician', *Bulletin of the Museum of Far Eastern Antiquities*, XXI (Stockholm, 1949), pp. 31–62.

The Chinese on the Art of Painting (Peiping, 1936).

Small, Harold A., ed., *Form and Function, remarks on art by Horatio Greenough* (Berkeley and Los Angeles, 1947).

'Soochow Remembers the Taipings', *China Reconstructs*, I (Jan.–Feb. 1953), pp. 49–51.

Soper, Alexander Coburn, *Kuo Jo-hsü's 'Experiences in Painting'* (*T'u-Hua Chien-Wen-Chih*) (Washington, 1951).

Speiser, Werner, 'Ba Dan Schan Jen', *Sinica*, VIII, No. 2 (March 10, 1933), pp. 46–9.

'Eine Landschaft von Wang Hui in Köln', *Ostasiatische Zeitschrift*, XVII, Nos. 1–2 (1941), pp. 169–72.

'T'ang Yin', *Ostasiatische Zeitschrift*, XI, Nos. 1–2 (Jan.–April 1935), pp. 1–21; Nos. 3–4 (May–Aug. 1935), pp. 96–117.

Spengler, Oswald, *The Decline of the West* (New York, 1934).

Starkman, Miriam Kosh, *Swift's Satire on Learning in 'A Tale of a Tub'* (Princeton, 1950).

Sullivan, Michael, 'The Traditional Trend in Contemporary Chinese Art', *Oriental Art*, II, No. 3 (Winter 1949–50), pp. 105–10.

Swift, Jonathan, *An Account of a Battel between the Antient and Modern Books in St. James' Library*.

Gulliver's Travels.

BIBLIOGRAPHY

Tagore, Amitendranath, 'Wartime Literature of China—Its Trends and Tendencies', *The Visva-Bharati Quarterly*, XVI, No. 2 (Aug.–Oct. 1950), pp. 120–9.

Tai Chin-hsieo, *The Life and Work of Ts'ai Yüan-p'ei*, MS. (Harvard University, 1952).

Teng Ssu-yü and Fairbank, John K., *China's Response to the West* (Cambridge, 1954).

Thorlby, Anthony, 'The Poetry of *Four Quartets*', *The Cambridge Journal*, V, No. 5 (Feb. 1952), pp. 280–99.

Tjan Tjoe Som, *Po Hu T'ung: the Comprehensive Discussions in the White Tiger Hall* (Leiden, 1949).

Tomita Kojiro, 'Brush-strokes in Far Eastern Painting', *Eastern Art*, III (Philadelphia, 1931), pp. 29–37.

—— and Chiu, A. Kaiming, 'An Album of Landscapes and Poems by Shen Chou (1427–1509)', *Bulletin of the Museum of Fine Arts* (Boston), XLVI, No. 265 (Oct. 1948), pp. 55–64.

Tretiakov, S., ed., *A Chinese Testament, the Autobiography of T'an Shih-hua* (New York, 1934).

Valéry, Paul, *Reflections on the World Today* (London, 1951).

Van Boven, Henri, *Histoire de la littérature chinoise moderne* (Peiping, 1946).

von Rosthorn, Arthur, 'Malerei und Kunstkritik in China', *Wiener Beigräge zur Kunst- und Kultur-Geschichte*, IV, (1930), pp. 9–26.

Waley, Arthur, 'A Chinese Picture', *The Burlington Magazine*, XXX, No. 1 (Jan. 1917), pp. 3–10.

—— *An Introduction to the Study of Chinese Painting* (London, 1923).

—— *Chinese Poems* (London, 1946).

—— *The Analects of Confucius* (London, 1949).

—— *The Life and Times of Po Chü-i, 772–846 A.D.* (New York, 1949).

Wang Fang-chuen, *Chinese Freehand Flower Painting* (Peiping, 1936).

Weber, Max, *The Religion of China* (Glencoe, 1951).

Wenley, A. G., 'A Note on the So-called Sung Academy of Painting', *Harvard Journal of Asiatic Studies*, VI, No. 2 (June 1941), pp. 269–72.

Whitehead, Alfred North, *Adventures of Ideas* (New York, 1933).

—— *Modes of Thought* (New York, 1938).

—— *Process and Reality* (New York, 1929).

—— *Science and the Modern World* (New York, 1937).

—— *Symbolism, Its Meaning and Effect* (New York, 1927).

—— *The Aims of Education and other Essays* (New York, 1949).

Wieger, Leon, *Le flot montant* (*Chine moderne*, II) (Hsien-hsien, 1921).

Wiley, Margaret L., *The Subtle Knot, Creative Scepticism in Seventeenth-Century England* (Cambridge, 1952).

Wilhelm, Hellmut, 'The Background of Tseng Kuo-fan's Ideology', *Asiatische Studien*, Nos. 3–4 (1949), pp. 90–100.

—— 'The Problem of Within and Without, a Confucian Attempt in Syncretism', *Journal of the History of Ideas*, XII, No. 1 (Jan. 1951), pp. 48–60.

BIBLIOGRAPHY

Willey, Basil, *The Seventeenth Century Background* (London, 1950).

Woodbridge, Samuel I., *China's Only Hope* (New York, 1900).

Wright, Arthur F., 'Fu I and the Rejection of Buddhism', *Journal of the History of Ideas*, XII, No. 1 (Jan. 1951), pp. 31–47.

Wright, Mary, 'From Revolution to Restoration: the Transformation of Kuomintang Ideology', *Far Eastern Quarterly*, XIV, No. 4 (Aug. 1955), pp. 515–32.

Yashiro Yukio, 'Connoisseurship in Chinese Painting', *Journal of the Royal Society of Arts*, LXXXIV, No. 4339 (Jan. 17, 1936), pp. 262–72.

Yeh Chien-yu, 'On the Classical Tradition in Chinese Painting', *People's China*, VII (1954), pp. 15–17.

Young, Edward, 'Conjectures on Original Composition', *Criticism: the Foundations of Modern Literary Judgment*, ed. Mark Schorer, Josephine Miles, and Gordon McKenzie (New York, 1948), pp. 12–30.

Index

INDEX

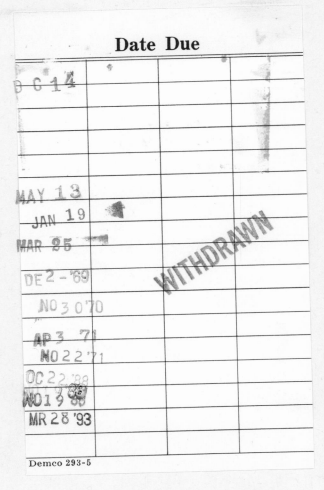